FOXOCRACY

ALSO BY TOBIN SMITH

ChangeWave Investing
(New York Times Bestseller)

ChangeWave Investing 2.0

Billion Dollar Green: Profit from the ECO Revolution

FOXOCRACY

INSIDE THE NETWORK'S PLAYBOOK OF TRIBAL WARFARE

TOBIN SMITH

DIVERSION
BOOKS

For more information, email info@diversionbooks.com

Diversion Books
A division of Diversion Publishing Corp.
443 Park Avenue South, suite 1004
New York, NY 10016
www.diversionbooks.com

Book design by Neuwirth & Associates

First Diversion Books edition October 2019
Hardcover ISBN: 978-1-63576-661-5
eBook ISBN: 978-1-63576-662-2

Printed in The United States of America

1 3 5 7 9 10 8 6 4 2

Library of Congress cataloging-in-publication data is available on file.

For Brenda, Leslie, Marjorie,
and John Sydney McCain II.

FOXOCRACY

CONTENTS

NOTE TO READERS

I held off publishing this book out of respect for my dear friend Brenda Buttner, who was also host of my weekly weekend Fox News opinion program *Bulls & Bears*. Brenda passed away in early 2016 after a long and courageous fight against cancer.

Frankly, with all the firsthand observations, secrets, and stories I accumulated as a fourteen-year insider within Fox's Sixth Avenue New York headquarters, I was also more than a little afraid of Roger Ailes, until his passing in May of 2017.

Ultimately, when I discovered how what we were doing affected the millions of folks who fell down the Foxhole, I became ashamed of what I had helped Fox News accomplish. I am hopeful that more former Fox News opinion-program producers and contributors will add their stories to the record. Already, brave reporters like my old friend and longtime FNC reporter Adam Housley, Col. Ralph Peters, and recently Carl Cameron have quit Fox News in protest.

For the good of our country and its democracy, I hope more come forward.

MY IMPORTANT MESSAGE
FOR SELF-IDENTIFIED CONSERVATIVE
OR "DEPLORABLE" READERS

Now listen up—if you are a self-identified conservative or a proud card-carrying Republican or simply a proud Deplorable—take a deep breath—it's going to be ok, and you are going to learn to love my book (ok, you will learn to *tolerate* it).

First let's be truthful with each other: If you self-identify as a "proud Republican," "proud conservative Evangelical," or "proud Deplorable," I am going to assume a loved one or friend suggested you read my book. They very well may have *bought* this book for you, shoved it in your hands, and said "Dad/Mom/Brother/Sister/Aunt/Uncle, you *need to read this book.*"

Or maybe as a committed conservative, you may have watched me on Fox News from 2000 to 2013, and maybe you're just darn curious about what I have to offer that has never been written before by anyone about Fox News.

So listen, friend—this is important. If someone you love *suggested* you read this book, I must warn you that you will *reflexively* find these lessons and insights of mine into Fox News tribal warfare strategies and tactics to be "fake news."

To this, all I can say to *you* is "buck up, buttercup—you aren't a snowflake, are you?" I can assure you that these disclosures I am sharing are *not* fake news or made up—they are very, very real because as a paid Fox News contributor, part-time guest host, and full-time after work drinking buddy to the Foxeratti staff, I *lived* each and every one of these experiences and lessons.

INTRODUCTION

FNC's Rigged Opinion-Segment-Scam:
Confessions of a Fox News Hit Man

America's sense of reality is dictated by what it is trying to avoid.
—JAMES BALDWIN

∎

Illusion is the first of all pleasures.
—VOLTAIRE

To begin to tell the story of how a little right-wing "niche" cable channel became the most politically powerful force in America (and the free world), let's first disperse with the label "cable news channel." In the grand scheme of things, the traditional concept of a conservative cable news channel is now mostly irrelevant.

Let me give you a little play-by-play on the recent Mueller Report to illustrate my point. As we all now know all too well these days, creating and controlling the first twenty-four-hour narrative of any national political story is now decidedly in the hands of a certain right-wing $3 billion a year for-profit public company. But the real yet almost unimaginable power of Fox News is how it operates as an entire media and non-secular ecosystem that I have come to describe as the American Foxocracy.

Why? Because with Fox News's now one hundred million-plus monthly audience reach for its emotionally overpowering content, the contest to be the first to own the Mueller story was never in doubt. More importantly, by the time Robert Mueller's report on Russian interference landed on Attorney General Barr's desk, the battle to spin it had already been won.

My point here is that narrative spin contest was not "won" within the confines of what many people still see as a cable news channel.

It is very true that in today's digital device ecosphere, the battle to own the dominant twenty-four-hour news cycle narrative is professional life and death for digital media publishers. Whatever media complex gets the most views, clicks, likes, shares, and streams wins the day (and the enormous ad dollars). For Fox News and its phalanx of White House insiders, Trumpism sycophants, and highly paid spin-doctor contributors like me all spinning the same mutually agreed upon fifth-grade language catchphrase twenty million times—"No collusion, no obstruction, complete exoneration."—the game to own the political narrative was over after just a few hours.

In reality, it was over before the attorney general started to speak.

Why? Because with the twenty times larger audience reach on Facebook and YouTube than the other competitors fighting to win the narrative, there was only going to be one clear winner: Fox News. What almost all the media still misses is the crucial lynchpin, the enormous political and cultural power I've dubbed the Foxocracy. With the introduction in 2008 of what we now call "digital surveillance capitalism," aka Facebook, YouTube, and Twitter social media platforms, the audience reach and daily audience engagement time of FNC's white tribal identity content exploded thirty times bigger than FNC's primordial three million prime-time cable-only audience pre-2008.

Fox News provides its content consumers with what they absolutely value more than almost life itself: the most emotionally engaging and satisfying content on the planet—with the exception of kitty and puppy videos—for free.

Social media platforms know what clicks/shares/comments best because every second of every day they digitally surveil their audience to measure and identify the most emotionally engaging content on their digital platform. According to the social media traffic and engagement ratings/metrics, the "most engageable content on social media" is Fox News's material. They have algorithmically targeted the white folks aged fifty years and older who have shown themselves to be the most emotionally vulnerable and likely to engage with what I call Fox's white tribal activation content.

And guess what? Starting in 2012, fifty-plus-year-old social media users became the largest and most active segment of Facebook's 240 million American users.

Coincidence?

Hardly.

The network's favorable interpretation of the Mueller Report—that it exonerated the president—furiously vacuumed up reactions, comments, and shares on social media that exceeded the night's cable ratings by incredible magnitudes. In fact, Fox News's main Facebook page nearly doubled CNN's in total engagements the day the Report dropped according to the analytics firm CrowdTangle. The *New York Times* and the *Washington Post* each mustered just one-sixth the number of Facebook interactions. MSNBC, Fox News's liberal foil, drew just one-tenth.

Like I told ya—when it comes to the raw power of spinning and propagating any national political narrative in America, today there is no more lethal force in the free world than the American Foxocracy. It's not a race, it's a digital slaughter.

And what no one until now has reported in-depth is the extensive and heartbreaking collateral damage to American families, our democracy, and the way our voting citizen sees and votes regarding America's future.

How did this all really happen? How did a tiny niche cable channel become the most powerful voter persuasion weapon known to the free world? How did a large part of America become the American Foxocracy?

Read on.

You may think you already understand Fox News's opinion programming; that it is nothing more than highly choreographed and rigged WWE-like performance art carefully designed to deliver a confirmation bias rich 24/7 tribal-validation feedback loop to its core tribal partisan base/addicts. But I am going to help you *really* understand by opening the Fox News opinion-program producer's kimono and exposing the fixed-outcome strategy, tactics, and production process that I participated in during most of my fourteen years at Fox News.

Yes, like pro wrestling, Fox News has season-long narratives that require the good-guy hero protagonists ("the baby faces") to always win and the bad-guy antagonists ("the heels") to lose. The difference is the WWE audience knows the matches are rigged; in wrestling, the fans' suspension of disbelief is called *kayfabe*. (The concept of kayfabe offers a fascinating insight into the psychology of the Fox News addict as well, which I'll get deeper into later in the book.)

And just like a WWE wrestling match, FNC producers create and fix the outcome of their white tribal identity segments from back to front. They start by defining the viewers' accepted tribal partisan ideology. Then they script and choreograph the order of the talking head opinion sequence to reach the ultimate conclusion. And just like a WWE or reality show producer, Fox News producers and hosts are trained to script and choreograph a carefully orchestrated set of what TV producers and executives like to call "moments."

If you were listening inside a Fox News production studio or editing room, or you heard what I heard in my ear from a producer before a show I hosted, you always heard directions like "make it a moment" or "make it land." This instruction refers to any of the important moments in the segment's story line—an individual sentence, a sudden realization, or the split-second look before it looks like a physical fight might break out.

But invariably at Fox News the term "moment" means the same thing: make sure you hit the audience's most powerful emotional triggers in a very precise sequence—and then squeeze out every possible ounce of drama or outrage possible before the conservative hit man drops the liberal opponent like an anvil to end the segment in a righteous victory for the Foxocracy.

After you're done reading, when you see a Fox News opinion program, you will understand and recognize this scripted eight-point emotional moment journey from fear to victory in a different light. You will understand the careful choreography and addictive flow and rhythm of white tribal identity porn:

1. The viewer sees and/or hears the "Fox News Alert" or cold-open tribal heresy or threat (even though the opinion show is not a news program at all). The amygdala (your brain's danger and risk assessment system) subconsciously decides that this is a fight-or-flight event and provides the viewer an adrenaline, cortisol, and epinephrine boost.

2. The Fox host then purposely scares the crap out of or pisses off the viewer with sound-on-tape B-roll (known as a "SOT" in TV lingo) of a liberal politician/celebrity/talking head impugning, insulting, or mocking the viewer's right-wing tribal belief system/orthodoxy.

3. The viewer naturally enters active tribal mode, with the tribal brain kicking in. The viewer's risk-assessing amygdala silently shouts, "Say it again, and I'll punch you out!"

4. The tribal enemy (aka libtard) stands his/her ground, repeating the pronouncement and tribal heresy with more authority.

5. The right-wing host and paid contributor heroes step in, coming to the defense of the right-wing tribe, rhetorically punching the tribal enemy in the nose for the viewer.

6. *Boom!* The fight-or-flight adrenaline rush the viewer got from the opening tribal threat is replaced with a nice big dose of the brain chemical dopamine.

7. The dopamine sets the viewer into anticipation of another tribal victory.

8. With the thrill of victory triggered by the validation of tribal orthodoxy and feelings of continued safety, the viewer's brain now releases the good stuff—serotonin, the opiate-like chemical.

Repeat, repeat, and repeat. Imagine what happens to a sixty-eight-year-old viewer going through this highly choreographed fear-to-victory roller coaster thousands and thousands of times. It reminds me of that old Bill Withers song, "If it feels this good being used, you can keep using me until you use me up!"

ONE OF A THOUSAND EXAMPLES OF THE BALL GAME AND THE POV SHUFFLE

To orchestrate and guarantee the right-wing partisan viewer's happy dance, everything started with CEO Roger Ailes's talking points Memo. Consider the memo the producer's emotional trigger targets of the day. Here's an example: Since my show, *Bulls & Bears*, was, in theory, a business-and-markets show, we had a recurring theme of "hidden inflation" that was "destroying household budgets" and of "the real unemployment rates were fake" and being manipulated by the Obama administration. This conspiracy perpetrated a lie on the American people blah blah blah. (Not coincidentally, this was a favorite Trump conspiracy talking point as well.)

Bear in mind, I ran (and still run) an economic and equities research shop that used government data and our proprietary economic data to successfully forecast recessions and bear stock markets (which we knock-on-wood have done since 1994).

I follow the stats from the Bureau of Labor and from the Consumer Price Index (CPI) very carefully. My firm (like virtually every other analyst or firm except for right-wing partisans) also uses inflation data without food or energy prices, for one reason: Food and energy prices swing wildly based on weather and commodity feed-related costs. My point here is that if you forecast inflation based on those non-economy-related variables, you make lousy trend forecasts and suffer from "garbage-in, garbage-out" syndrome.

But at Fox News our favorite inflammatory angle was attacking the Consumer Price Index inflation rate because it excluded food and energy prices. Roger deemed that the CPI was an underhanded manipulation because of course households bought food and used energy every week. At least once a month after 2009, *Bulls & Bears* would have a segment about the "fake inflation numbers."

So every friggin' month, I would get this call or sit-down from my segment producer Jen: "Toby, I need you to take the point on the 'fake inflation numbers.' First I need you not to say your same old shit of 'no one gauges the real inflation rates by blah blah blah.' Our audience shops at the market, and when bread prices or vegetables or beef prices are higher this week than last week, that is what inflation is to them. When the price of gasoline is higher this week than last week, that is inflation to them, so I need you to play ball with me on this one; we have no one else from our right-wing guests or contributors who will make this case!"

I would say, "Gee, I wonder why? Why is this so important?" even though I knew by this time she had no control over the segment selections because they all came from the second floor and Roger's daily Talking Points Memo.

"Jesus, Toby, just give me what I need. We have an hour to go to the taping. Here are the talking points I need you to make for me!" I knew she was under a microscope to make sure we held and built our audience from the previous show. And, again, at this point I knew our show was like a right-wing ideological confirmation bias Pez dispenser—there were no objective facts; only the subjective beliefs and feelings of our audience mattered.

The liberal crash dummy prop the segment producer booked to be sacrificed on the right-wing economic altar would open the segment with something like, "Look—no one sophisticated in economics measures US inflation rates including the monthly price swings in gasoline/oil or commodities. What matters to the stock market is the inflation trend, and that trend is blah blah."

Then, for the last shot at the liberal heretic, the host would say, "Okay, Toby, what say you?" and I would hit the liberal with my carefully constructed, scripted, and rehearsed rhetorical kill shot. The performance was to mix sarcasm and snark for the enemy liberal with a smile to support the mindset of the viewer at home. By this time, I had mastered the machine gun + machete liberal disembowelment strike and could do it in my sleep.

For this segment, the kill shot that most importantly the producer *did not share* with the poor liberal victim-of-the-day went like this:

"Well first, thanks for calling our viewers at home unsophisticated. I'm sure they appreciate that. Second, here is what I know and, more importantly, what our viewers know: Forget the CPI numbers. They have so many seasonal smoothing computations, they have not been correct for years." (Now I'm gathering steam.) "But more important, our viewers, unlike you, go to the grocery store and don't have their dinner out at Le Cirque or delivered; they fill up their own vehicles with gas and don't just step into a town car like you do. What they see are prices going up and their income going down under Obamanomics. They see rents going up. They see medical costs in a never ending upward spiral."

I'm just getting warmed up and the tribal right-wingers from Small Town USA are already getting their lovely dopamine hits as they anticipate the final death blow against their hated liberal big-city blowhard.

"They also see the big banks and insurance companies bailed out. They see Fannie Mae and Freddie Mac bailed out on hundreds of billions of dollars in upside-down mortgages while they are losing jobs and losing their homes. It takes a lot for you to sit here and tell our viewers they are unsophisticated boobs. They look plenty sophisticated from where I sit!"

The host would say, "And that's the last word. Coming up: Why are home prices going up in DC and down everywhere else? We'll report; you decide!"

BOOM, shakalaka! Drop the mike.

The liberal pundit didn't know what had hit her because no one had given her that POV (point of view comments from the panel members are traditionally shared by the segment producer with all the panel members left and right) from me before the show—which made the scam work like buttah for most of my fourteen years and especially after our show went 100 percent tribal porn programming after the 2008 election.

The protocol for political talk TV is to share the POVs of the segment so people arrive with different points to make. I hardly ever used my stated POV because the producer almost always gave me the script she wanted performed—that is why some of the crew came to call me "The Hitman." And the token liberal would not complain (much) about being blindsided because all they really care about is face time on Fox News defending their tribal belief system and building their tribal identity brand.

At home, the right-wing tribal partisan viewer cheered, "Yeah, baby! Way to go, Toby; screw that know-it-all liberal socialist!" and as we went to break, I heard in my ear from the segment producer, "Way to go, Tobe. Udaman!"

At Del Frisco's after the show, I would get the real story from the Gen-X aged producer: "Dude, that inflation shizzle was dope. You get it now. Every segment has a beginning, middle, and end—but it's the end that keeps the viewer coming back to the next segment. I don't choose the segments; I produce what I'm told to produce most of the time. You made me look good tonight; thanks!"

That segment happened a thousand times in my experience at Fox News. It was like the movie *Groundhog Day*—always the same.

THE PRODUCER'S MEMO: THIS IS WHAT THE POV SHUFFLE LOOKS LIKE ON PAPER

Below is an actual email from the producer of this fixed debate ball game that we right-wingers got but the left-wingers most certainly did not. This particular "rundown" in TV speak is from right after the 2009 financial meltdown, but it could have been from any week. Understand that this is representative evidence of how the Fox News producers would stack the deck against the liberal pundit before the show ever started.

And don't forget that, as always, the "left-winger" guest was a no-name non-threatening "DemoPublican" already way out of his/her league on the issue in the first place; in fourteen years I never participated in an "opinion debate" segment that in any way was produced to be fair or in any way balanced.

At Fox News, the rule was and still is that the liberal panelists were always two strikes down before they got to the plate. That was just one part of the Fox News audience grift strategy—there's a lot more to come, trust me.

A BLOCK: PRES OBAMA DECLARING THE MASSIVE FINANCIAL OVERHAUL MEANS NO MORE TAXPAYER-FUNDED BANK BAILOUTS

New financial reform law, new promise. The president saying today, "Because of this law, the American people will never again be asked to foot the bill for Wall Street's mistakes. There will be no more taxpayer-funded bailouts. Period."

The same day, a new report out saying taxpayers could be on the hook for another $700B because of Fannie and Freddie. So is the president right . . . is this the end of taxpayer funded bailouts?

((Focus on how taxpayer funded bailouts are NOT over. This is NOT a Freddie, Fannie or housing debate—don't go there!))

Please come with other examples that prove the president's promise wrong.

Taxpayer Tab for Fannie, Freddie, Other Housing Bulges by $700 Billion
http://www.moneynews.com/Headline/Taxpayer-Tab-Fannie-Freddie-700-Billion/2010/07/21/id/365249

U.S. bailout watchdogs slam Obama housing programs
http://www.reuters.com/article/idUSN2116858520100721

Next after Obama signing of financial reform bill: Fannie Mae, Freddie Mac
http://www.csmonitor.com/Commentary/the-monitors-view/2010/0721/Next-after-Obama-signing-of-financial-reform-bill-Fannie-Mae-Freddie-Mac

About 40 percent leave federal mortgage aid program
http://www.usatoday.com/money/economy/housing/2010-07-20-mortgage-aid_N.htm

B BLOCK: HOUSE SPEAKER PELOSI SAYS PAYING FOR JOBLESS BENEFITS WOULD BLUNT JOB CREATION

On Tuesday House Speaker Nancy Pelosi said: "People who get unemployment insurance need it, they spend the money immediately, injects demand into economy and creates jobs. That stimulus effect is completely blunted if you therefore say 'we're going to have to pay for it.'"

((Please keep your focus on how or why the "stimulus effect" is blunted if unemployment benefits are paid for.))

With Unemployment Extension Set to Pass, Republicans Do the Unthinkable and Stall
http://www.associatedcontent.com/article/5608860/with_unemployment_extension_set_to.html

Unemployment Extension In Agonizing Endgame Slog: When Will The Checks Go Out?
http://www.huffingtonpost.com/2010/07/21/unemployment-extension-endgame_n_654859.html

CBO: Unemployment benefits might, or might not, stimulate economy
http://www.americanthinker.com/blog/2010/07/cbo_unemployment_benefits_migh.html

C BLOCK: 75% OF YOUNG AMERICANS THINK THEY WON'T SEE ONE PENNY FROM SOCIAL SECURITY

New poll out this week saying three-fourths of those aged between 18 to 34 don't expect to get a Social Security check when they retire.

Is this actually great news for America? Focus on how Social Security is going broke because of Obama's runaway spending

Poll: Faith in Social Security system tanking

http://www.usatoday.com/news/washington/2010-07-20-1Asocialsecurity 20_ ST_N.htm

The Kids Who Could Save Social Security

http://www.huffingtonpost.com/eric-schurenberg/the-kids-who-could-save-s_b_654082.html

D BLOCK: PREDICTIONS

If you need any ideas shoot me an email or give me a call.

THE GAME-SHOW FIXING OF THE 1950S VS. FOX NEWS OPINION-PROGRAM FIXING

The motive behind fixing a Fox News opinion program is no different than the motive behind fixing game shows in the 1950s (busted in 1959) or WWE wrestling matches after that (busted in 1994): to keep the audience emotionally engaged. The most popular game shows in the '50s were the ones with winners who won multiple games. Game shows of the late 1950s were always produced with live audiences, and when a champion became a multi-show winner, the audience would not leave! Winners of *The $64,000 Question* became cult heroes. (Remember Dr. Joyce Brothers?)

The fixed game show scam then was that the big winners were shown the answers before the show or the questions were tailored for the big winner based on questions he had been asked before the show.

Roger Ailes started his TV production career a little after the '50s game show scandals, but he never forgot the lesson: TV viewers love the feeling of watching their hero win. It's well known in the TV industry that Ailes admitted he fixed the "debates" he produced for Richard Nixon in 1972—Roger was indeed the originator and master of the fixed outcome TV debate program.

Key Point: When that hero on your screen is not just someone off the street but a man or woman the viewer knows and has trusted for years as a tribal blood brother, the viewer-pundit connection is visceral and ten times stronger. The Fox News analyst or contributor who delivers tribal victory for years becomes a hero to the FNC addict. That's why Fox News has so many hosts and talking heads that have been in their positions for years and years: The more the viewer trusts them and the better their Q (likeability) scores, the more valuable they are to the rigged-outcome opinion segments.

It's why I still have people walk up in airports and heavy GOP zip codes and say, "Hey Toby—miss you kicking lame liberal butt on Fox News" after being gone for five years. It's also why the segment producers gave me advanced talking points before the show that others did not get—why risk the viewer's hero *not* winning when you can ensure a "noble death" for the tribal enemy in our blood-and-circus gladiatorial-like events. If you remember, Roman emperors fixed their "contests" so the heroes won, too.

DRAMATIC EFFECT COUNTS TOO

If you are the host's go-to hit man, it's much more dramatic and visually compelling to rhetorically kill the libtard enemy face-to-face in-studio than from a satellite location. Most of our liberal guests were in New York City for the taping for that reason, although the really feeble ones could do their "hits" from DC or other Fox News locations because they were so easy to take down that no one needed to face off eyeball-to-eyeball.

After a few years, I had the Fox News fixed outcome production scam figured out, so I played along and performed my role exactly the way Roger had designed the process produced by the opinion-programming production team. I became the most dependable hit man, and though other contributors were let go in the 2008–2010 recession, I kept getting new one-year contracts.

Why? Because the producer and host could count on me to rhetorically dispatch and dismiss the liberal prop/crash dummy nine-out-of-ten times. That is what they call at Fox News "great TV, brother!"

FOX NEWS FINALLY DID AWAY WITH THE "FAIR AND BALANCED" LIE, BUT NOT THE OPINION-DEBATE SCAM

I can only assume that after Roger Ailes was fired by Fox News in 2016 for various sexual harassment and assault issues, the Murdoch family finally concluded that selling the false promise Roger made a hundred times a day—that Fox News was the only fair and balanced news on television—was not only ironic and farcical but legally fraudulent as well.

In 2016, Fox News stopped making the "fair and balanced" claim. But I can tell you from watching recently, Fox News in no way ended the rigged "opinion" programming scam. Now that Fox News is operating as de facto Trump TV, the charade is simply more visible.

WHO IS TOBIN SMITH?

Even assuming you've read this book's flap copy and maybe the About the Author page, unless you are a longtime Fox News junkie or investment newsletter junkie, you may be asking yourself "Who is Tobin Smith? Why does he think he knows so much about Fox News that others don't?"

Great questions—you do need to know and understand a few important things about me. First, my political and cultural biases are simple: registered Independent, former Republican, part-time media and cultural critic (at StopTheFoxocracy.com), and full-time investment newsletter publisher and editor-in-chief at www.transformityresearch.com.

But most importantly, I was at Fox News on the air many times every week for fourteen years. And I got enough face time with Roger Ailes—the head of Fox News—and his lieutenants at the headquarters in New York City to learn every aspect of his programming philosophy and tribal warfare playbook.

If you know and understand Roger Ailes's psyche, you'll understand Fox News. So let's you and I start on that quest now.

From my conversations with him and those who worked for him, I am able to decode and share the key parts of his massive imprint on our "cable news network" masquerade and tribal warfare tactics for you.

Ailes was (and still is today even after his death) the proxy persona that FNC producers write to and direct for. If you could push his instinctual emotional hot buttons and get his white tribal partisan reflexes reflexing, producers knew they could hit the Fox News audience's emotional hot buttons and emotional reflexes.

At an office event early in my career I cornered Roger and asked, "So Roger, just who is our target audience? Describe them to me please—give me a mental picture of the viewer at home."

Roger responded, "Look at me—I am the audience. White, fat, balding, age fifty-five-to-dead. I'm a red state Midwest conservative guy sitting at home in his favorite chair with a remote control surgically attached to his hand."

"What does the viewer most want from me?" I asked.

"Well after the producers and host scares the shit out of them, he wants to see you tear those smug condescending know-it-all East Coast liberals to pieces . . . limb by limb . . . until he jumps up out of his La-Z-Boy, high fives the TV, and screams 'Way to go Toby . . . you KILLED that libtard!'"

"Why do you and they hate liberals so much?" I asked.

"Wait," Ailes said, "are you a liberal, Tobin?"

"Nope—card-carrying Republican (I lied). But I don't viscerally hate liberals—I just find that so many of them are just so poorly educated about how capitalism works and how the laws of economics work—I try to help them understand them better—that's why I am here."

"Well Toby—here's why guys like me fucking hate liberals. For one thing—liberals hate America—they all hate capitalism—and they think anyone waving an American flag on the Fourth of July is a gap-toothed, slack-jawed hillbilly.

"They also think they are all better than you and guys like me. To them I'm a small towner hick from the sticks. Of course, they all went to a better college than me too. They are so smug and so much smarter and richer than me. They never miss a chance to rub my face in something stupid I said or did twenty or thirty years ago.

"For chrissakes, they already own all the important newspapers, all TV, all the movie studios, important colleges, and all the rest of the entertainment industries—but that is not enough—they always want more! They want me and guys like me to shut the fuck up and let the Masters of the Universe run the world.

"Why do I hate liberals? This is why: If I was on the ground outside bleeding on Sixth Avenue, they would walk over and snap my neck with their Gucci loafers and not blink.

"Well guess what—payback is a mofo ain't it!"

So there ya go—he was a few cocktails in. I wish we could have talked all night—but I got the main point; for the short, fat, sickly Roger Ailes (he had hemophilia for decades), Fox News's Liberal Death Star plan wasn't business; it was personal. It was payback for every liberal who had underestimated him and every insult and disrespect he endured as a right-winger in left-wing industries.

What I learned early on about our fearless leader (and later our core audience) was that his hatred of liberals was not just an act where we produced televised and digital tribal warfare—our audience was also bitter. To use a sports analogy, think of the bitter hatred between fans of the Los Angeles Dodgers and San Francisco Giants. Both teams were exports out of New York City to California—and they were rivals. But when Giants pitcher Juan Marichal turned around in the batting box and smashed his bat into the head of our beloved catcher John Roseboro on August 22, 1965 (not that I remember the date . . .) Dodger-fan hatred of the Giants became personal and bitter.

My point: I can tell you this firsthand—for thousands of Fox News viewers whom I have met in person or on social media, Fox News is very personal for them too. Their hatred of liberalism and liberals and cultural PC-ism is bitter and visceral, too. They too have metastasized and bone-marrow-level hurt feelings from the disrespect and condescension they feel they get from every corner of liberal America.

Conversely, to them Fox News is like a campfire where they can safely huddle around and feel pride about themselves and their close pals. To use one of the combat metaphors that many viewers are so fond of, Fox News is a digital foxhole where they feel safe while they watch their tribal heroes bring the fight to "those people" who constantly disrespect their Retro America culture and orthodoxy and want to confiscate their guns and disrespect their God. The foxhole camaraderie with their Fox News hosts feels real to them—even though to the hosts it's just an act (ok, maybe not Hannity—that dude believes his own bullshit, for sure).

Here's another thing I learned from my early and frequent appearances

THE FIVE KEY EMOTIONAL PILLARS

The emotional exploitation pillars of the Fox News tribal warfare playbook are:

1. Existential white tribal fear

2. Bitter hatred and feelings of disrespect

3. Blasphemous outrage

4. Visceral bitter resentment

5. Victimhood and blame of "elites" and "others"

on *Fox & Friends* in the morning: the show (and most of FNC opinion programming) was just Roger's unleashed ID being televised. Whatever pissed off Roger the most that morning and could most likely be manufactured to manipulate the five key emotional pillars of Fox News's right-wing traumatic tribal emotion amplification spiral is what made it to air.

Most people don't know there was a secret daily memo from Roger and SVP John Moody (who was an even bigger Attila the Hun right-wing zealot than Ailes!) to the production staff. I learned about the "The Memo" early on in my career and developed sources through the years to forward me copies to a safe email address.

This memo was the actual emotional targeting strategy for the day. Seeing and reading Fox News's primary targeting and narrative daily playbook taught me how the Fox News tribal warfare playbook worked in real life. It's how I became a reliable Fox News hit man—the guy who the producer and host could count on to plunge the rhetorical sword and make the final kill shot through the heart of our token liberal prop of the day. I became the guy who the producer needed in order to elicit the at-home audience member's high-five for another libtard ass-kicking.

Anyway, the reason Roger Ailes was so good at his previous job—creating right-wing attack ads and electing right-wing presidents—was that his ID was the mirror image of his audience's ID. Until Fox News had its own audience emotional engagement surveillance machine (FoxNews.com), Fox News's programming strategy was:

1. Take the daily Roger's ID memo.

2. And manufacture or amplify whatever piece of the right-wing tribal identity activation and amplification spiral Roger thought had the most red meat on the bone that day.

3. And then, evoke and stoke the most powerful mental chain reaction possible in the minds of our audience based on what currently pissed off Roger the most.

Not many Fox News contributors got the time I did with Roger Ailes and senior management. I was stationed at the New York headquarters. And I was the first inside person to come clean on the Fox News tribal activation, distortion, and amplification. Many others know this playbook—but they still work at Fox (or now at MSNBC or CNN), other streaming tribal TV services, or they hope to get hired by right-wing Sinclair Broadcasting as they create their new version of tribalized Retro America TV.

I performed in over two thousand thoroughly rigged Fox News opinion segments. My contract was renewed for fourteen years until it all ended in 2013 during a dispute over my newsletter business. I got very high Q ratings, and I was asked by producers to guest host more than fifty episodes of various Planet Fox live opinion shows. By the time I was guest hosting shows in 2009, I knew the Fox News tribal warfare playbook better than most of the hosts I sat in for.

And understand this: since 1980, I have made my living understanding, monetizing, and profiting from mankind's most innate emotions—but primarily fear. I started on Wall Street helping stockbrokers use fear to sell investment products. Later on, before and during my Fox News career, I worked for one of the largest investment newsletter publishers, Phillips Publishing, writing and distributing investment research and newsletters. There, I helped produce powerful printed direct-marketing brochures. Our grift was that they looked like magazines, so we called them magalogs, and people opened them up because they thought they were getting a free magazine. Today those magalogs are called "advertorials," but that's just putting lipstick on the "Gee it looks like I got a free four-color magazine—I should open this!" pig. In short, I know the power of fear and emotional grifting. Given my fourteen years exploiting right-wing tribal fear, and twenty-five years creating fear-based advertising content, I humbly surmise there are few people who know more about fomenting and monetizing tribal and existential fear than I do.

But I do know this: Rupert Murdoch, Roger Ailes, and TV televangelists have monetized more fear than me in my career by a million times.

Fear, fear, fear, fear!

All consumers of political or cultural media should know that when you declare yourself a "proud conservative" or now a "proud Deplorable," you have told me (and more importantly you just told Fox News producers) *exactly* how to grift you. Did you know that? When you press your remote control to Fox News, it's like you just sent up a flare that reads "I'm yours." Your arrival at my doorstep tells me all I need to know to use the FNC white tribal warfare playbook to suck hours and hours of your life into my programming.

Let me get this straight. You *do* know about the "hidden" emotional manipulation and addiction elements embedded in social media—but you didn't know that Fox News tribal identity and validation opinion shows are nothing more than a televised grift done at a previously unimaginable scale?

Fox News has without question leapt into the pantheon of the Media Grifters Hall of Fame. We dislodged the former king of emotional grifting—WWE wrestling—as the most profitable professional grift. But the difference between Fox News and WWE pro wrestling fans is that WWE fans know they are being emotionally grifted.

Fox News started the $10 billion a year tribal identity porn industry in America and others followed. Today's America features a huge commercial digital media industry that monetizes cultural and political fear and hatred by staging gladiatorial cage matches featuring well-dressed proxies of Metro vs. Retro America as cathartic and ego-gratifying entertainment products.

How has the mental and physical collateral damage from the mass consumption of billions of cumulative hours of Fox News's emotional weapons of mass cultural/political destruction been so hidden in plain sight?

Because the damage of culturally and/or politically tribalized and desocialized Foxhole dads, moms, sisters, and brothers is atomized—it happens one family at a time. It's like that Nigerian Prince email scam where a person gets an email from a "Nigerian Prince" who desperately needs to get money out of Nigeria, and if you will just send him your bank account number, he will send you $2.5 million.

When someone falls for that grift and becomes a walking, talking Foxhole—no one talks about it! That is the beauty of that grift—it was kept quiet for decades by the people that were grifted because they were embarrassed to admit they got taken!

What many now identify as "Fox News brain" or a walking, ranting Foxhole happened under the cloak of that darkness, too, because no one took the time (until pollster Frank Luntz) to actually measure how deep the disease of tribalized partisan identity had become in America (spoiler alert: the answer is eighty-plus million).

Today the Fox News talk show segments really just work one overall macro narrative grift: "Retro American culture and religion (and guns—always guns) are under a massive existential siege by hordes of Metro American liberals and immigrants. If we don't go to tribal war against those viperous left-wing socialists and immigrants of color who constantly disrespect you/your culture/our God, you are going to lose what is left of your crumbling grip on economic and white cultural power. That, and it's all the elites' fault—the elites think you are their servants."

The conservative talk radio wing of the American Foxocracy has been forced to go even darker. The transcripts I get from the tribal warfare mongers on talk radio today are talking all day and night about how real tribal civil warfare is coming—not just digital battles—*real* tribal civil warfare that is coming soon.

Rolling Stone's award-winning cultural journalist Matt Taibbi writes in his analysis of American political news media in his book *Hate, Inc:* "The news today is a reality show where you're part of the cast: (Retro) America vs. (Metro) America, on every channel. The trick here is getting audiences to think they're punching up, when they're actually punching sideways, at other media consumers just like themselves, who just happen to be in a different silo. Hate (and fear) is a great blinding mechanism. Once you've been in the business long enough, you become immersed in its nuances. If you can get people to accept a sequence of simple, powerful ideas, they're yours forever."

Yes, you most certainly can, Matt. What's so wrong with tens of millions of sixty-five-plus-year-old white Americans binge-watching thousands and thousands of hours of this much emotional toxic waste sold as a "news channel?" What's wrong with verbally demonizing or "punching" your tribal enemy in the nose? Is that a sign of a healthy society? No, it is not, according to the many mental and physical health experts I consulted for this book. Do populist grifter demagogic rabble rousers like Donald Trump and his Make America 1980 Again grift rise in healthy countries?

No, they don't.

More importantly—who set the table for Donald Trump to grift sixty-five million Americans into thinking he could magically turn 2016 into 1982?

The conditioning started with conservative radio of course—but the emotional impact of seeing your political and/or cultural enemies' faces and eyes is an order of magnitude more powerful than merely listening to Rush Limbaugh or Glenn Beck rant and rave while you are driving home or cooking in the kitchen.

This book will show you how the Fox News playbook helped make them so powerful. It looks at how FNC figured out how to use viewers' own brain chemistry to addict them to the scams—and to always keep them watching. And it will show you how you can use that knowledge to start fighting back and learn the antidote to Fox News addiction.

You don't have to become or stay a Foxhole—and I can prove it.

CHAPTER 1

How Did the Fox News Tribal Identity Porn Playbook Become So Powerful?

The Fox Hate Channel's white tribal partisan identity playbook for the Foxhole spiral is not new. But its power to manipulate American right-wingers got supercharged by very powerful regulatory and information technology disruption combined with a hundred years of practice and the presidential election of 2008.

Understand this—the white tribal identity media panic and fear spiral grift has been around for 125 years—it just took a set of massively transformational and disruptive inventions and regulatory shifts to turn it into emotional plutonium.

But before I tell that story, let's keep score here on all the benefits that have come to millions of Foxhole addicts watching nuclear powered Fox News white tribal identity porn every day of their rapidly ending lives:

1. An uncountable number of divorces.

2. Tens of millions of important and emotionally nurturing friendships and family relationships poisoned.

3. An epidemic of tribalized white political and cultural intensity disorder.

4. A growing number of senior-aged Americans suffering from chronic and deadly isolation following the loss of nurturing family relationships and friendships poisoned by their constant hyper-partisan zealotry.

Public health data states that the top reason for elder estrangement is "pushing away family and friends." For many, isolation leads to a chronic loneliness that (according to the latest research) brings them up to a 60 percent higher risk of premature death.

America is in the middle of a "silver tsunami." FNC's target audience in America (white people over sixty-five) adds sixteen thousand new targets every day until 2030. Fox News and Planet Fox anticipate more than sixty million new emotionally vulnerable and isolated targets in America for their predatory and seductive brand of white tribal identity porn—what I call the "Foxhole spiral." If you add in the UK and Australia, Planet Fox is perfectly positioned to ride the silver tsunami of aging Baby Boomers around the English-speaking world.

Planet Fox must be so proud that their little right-wing propaganda channel turned into the most emotionally destructive white tribal identity media factory since—well, you know—1930s Germany.

To communicate a big complex story well, it really helps to find the right analogies. I used the Nigerian Prince scam to illustrate how the damage from digital and viral scams stays hidden because of the shame and embarrassment of falling for that ridiculous scam.

So now to introduce how and why the Fox News tribal identity activation and amplification playbook works so powerfully well, why it is so insanely profitable, and why I came to refer to it as a weapon of mass emotional destruction, I present . . . the nuclear powered Hot Pot pressure cooker.

Don't laugh—stay with me. The Foxhole panic spiral phenomenon I am detailing has been around for ages—but when it got digitized on the front end and combined with social media's emotional targeting on the back end, it became an emotionally and psychologically radioactive cloud like Chernobyl that never ends. First off, if you don't know what a Hot Pot is, it's a cool digitally controlled pressure cooker. My favorite stew that takes me hours to cook in the oven takes about twenty-five minutes in my Hot Pot. It's magic—I have two of them.

In the performance art that is Fox News opinion programming, we performed our emotionally destructive alchemy like any grifter would:

- We first hook your attention with visual images we knew would automatically trigger the emotionally corrosive but powerful feelings of political or cultural fear, hatred, outrage, personal resentment, and deep-seated feelings of social or economic grievance.

- And then, we choreograph the grand finale of the segment so your political/cultural team wins yet another righteous victory and sweet tribal revenge so that you get that cathartic rush of positive emotions and ego stimulation (plus a big dose of feel-good neurochemicals) when your tribal fears are relieved and replaced with the self-esteem/ego building that comes from your team being proven righteously superior again.

IDENTITY PORN

Fox News tribal identity addiction falls into the category that addiction professionals call a "process addiction." Neuroscience has proven that when anyone with a process addiction partakes in his/her binge behavior of choice—whether that behavior is eating, using the internet, gambling, consuming sexual pornography, or watching Fox News's partisan opinion programming—the reaction in the brain is the same.

Research psychologists such as Dr. Peggy Drexler tell us that resentment is "really the feeling of indignation in reaction to a real or perceived slight, a sense of insult or inadequacy caused by the actions, comments, or simple existence of someone or something else." Said more simply, you experience resentment when you feel that you're not getting your fair share while someone else is getting more than their fair share. And boy oh boy, does cultural and political tribal resentment trigger feelings of hate, anger, and outrage—the addictive trifecta of tribal partisan pornography.

Dr. Drexler also points out that resentments actually have a benefit for tribal-outrage addicts. A 2017 study published in the Journal of Experimental Psychology, with more than 2,300 subjects from around the world, found that short-term resentment actually helps to boost self-esteem by allowing us to blame others for our problems.

Does that sound familiar?

But in the aggregate, resentment is highly toxic. A 2011 clinical review of the emotional and physiological effects of anger and resentment on the body showed that chronic bitterness can slow metabolism, immune-system function, and organ function.

Some psychologists even believe that if left unchecked, resentment can turn into a condition known as posttraumatic embitterment disorder, which manifests as anxiety, depression, and fits of rage.

Key Point: Watching a lot of TV to pass your free time may become addicting, but watching hard news is just habit; there is no "addicting process" to become addicted to. Breaking news may be thrilling, but it's way too intermittent and unscheduled to be addictive.

The Fox News addictive-programming process uses addictive anger and resentment to:

- Understand the elderly white conservative viewer's pre-tribal mindset, which is a compilation of their resentments, indignations, cultural values, religious values, political values, racial perspectives, regional outlooks, and worldviews.

- Scare or outrage the crap out of viewers by boring down on a recently exposed tribal nerve like a psychic dentist with a drill, presenting a heresy or an innately scary image of non-white/non-Christian foreigners, immigrants, or terrorists doing horrible things.

- Produce each seven-minute rigged outcome opinion-debate segment around the carefully selected partisan heresy such that the "fair and balanced" debate is massively rigged for the conservative pundit(s) on the program to . . .

- Deliver the climactic and righteous rhetorical victory for the partisan right-wing viewer to trigger the jolt of dopamine and serotonin that the addict anticipated and knew was coming.

It costs Fox News about $2 billion a year to create their digital crop of toxic white tribal identity porn. It is planted, fertilized, and then amplified in the old white audience's brains. To monetize this emotional toxic stew, all the partisan media company has to do is:

- activate one or more primal emotions, and more importantly,

- amplify one or more soul crushing negative visceral narratives for a few minutes and then end the segment with a soul feeding and neurochemical rush that comes from yet another tribal victory or glimmer of hope in order to sell ads to advertisers and content usage licenses to pay TV distributors.

Repeat, repeat, repeat. It's a great business—especially if you create the emotional plutonium (the white tribal identity activation and amplification content) and you own part of the nuclear-powered tribal radicalization machine (in FNC's case the Fox News cable and online digital distribution platform).

But understand: white tribal identity mongering became an unbelievable business when the world's digital surveillance platforms like Facebook, Instagram, Twitter, and YouTube began in 2008 to redistribute and retarget Fox News's white tribal identity content—for free. The power and intensity of the white tribal identity intensity spiral on these emotional manipulation social media platforms is now astonishing.

Why? It's the digital Hot Pot. When social media's hyper-targeting is combined with Fox News's emotionally powerful white tribal identity porn content, these social media platforms create a killer digital Hot Pot tribal identity amplifying monster.

Here is why I use the Hot Pot metaphor. In the old pre-internet days, it used to take decades to create a wild-eyed foam-at-the-mouth hyperpartisan—you know—that crazy uncle who sees a conspiracy behind everything and won't shut up about it. Today that radicalization process takes only a few years—or even months. The reason is the emotional manipulation power of social media's emotion vulnerability assessment and content targeting algorithms.

Their algorithms redistribute and remonetize Fox News tribal identity porn by identifying the most powerful Fox News white tribal identity content and then placing it in the newsfeed of the most emotionally vulnerable users they have identified via likes/clicks/shares on the Facebook or YouTube or Twitter app.

In Facebook and Google/YouTube's case, they know exactly which segment of Fox News white tribal identity porn is engaging best in real time across two hundred forty million Americans. This hyper-targeting is one of the intended consequences of this so-called surveillance capitalism industry. But this emotional predation on social media platforms produced consequences that their twenty-something-aged founders never thought about while they were coding their algorithms (can you say "Russian trolls" or "social media addiction?"). And they perform this emotional predation with zero cost for the content and zero liability for any of the unintended consequences—even when a white supremacist radicalized by online hate groups commits mass murder livestreamed on his Facebook page for the entire world to see.

Just like digital Planet Fox, the intent of social media is to activate your engagement time with images or videos that they know you are most vulnerable to engage with. They know this because you showed them exactly what kind of visual content you are most emotionally engaged and vulnerable to: Every click and like and share is just another data point hoovered up into their engagement assessment and targeting machine.

How do they all get away with this?

NEW TECHNOLOGY AND REGULATIONS DRIVE NEWS MEDIA GRIFTS

Yes, dear friend, in addition to the very intended consequences of the Reagan White House's decision to end TV's thirty-five-year political content regulatory framework in 1986 (the FCC's Fairness Doctrine, which we will get to)—the small Section 230 of the ironically named 1996 "Communications Decency Act" (CDA) created the most emotionally powerful and destructive white tribal identity spiral since 1930s Germany. Yes, I dare say it—it's an indisputable fact. Thank God digital social media platforms were not available to Nazi propaganda head Joseph Goebbels (pronounced Gerbels, soft G).

Fox News's founders had no idea what social media was or would become. Murdoch bought MySpace, but it had no emotional engagement surveillance engine. But when the CDA stipulated that web platforms cannot be held liable for the content they host and algorithmically retarget and weaponize—one of the unintended consequences was the creation of the 100 percent digital Fox moral panic spiral. There would be no Foxhole spiral without the audience multiplier effect of emotionally weaponized social media. Even if the content social media redistributes is patently deceptive and dupes one hundred million people every month with carefully orchestrated white tribal partisan propaganda—zero liability!

A book publisher and author can be sued for libel if they knowingly make a false claim about someone or some company—they can be sued for "irreparable harm and emotional damages." But if that irreparable harm and very real emotional damage came from social media distribution, no dice—Facebook is allowed to monetize as much fear and hate porn as they possibly can—so they do.

The white tribal panic spiral is an amazing business model—and understanding amazing business models is how I have made my primary living for decades. First off, like I said, there's no content cost for social media platforms to access, activate, and amplify their partisan audience's emotions. But a white tribal identity cable network like Fox News gets paid $1 to $2 a month per cable subscriber by the cable or satellite TV distributor!

I nicknamed Fox News's fixed-outcome opinion segment format the Foxhole spiral for a reason: The Foxhole spiral is a very powerful psychological technique that I first learned about when I started hosting live Fox shows for the network. I'll get into the entire tribal warfare playbook in a bit—but first you must understand this: When these white tribal identity segments got posted to social media and streamed to over one hundred million viewers a month—and achieved more than 1.2 billion engagements a year—the original FNC tribal activation and amplification playbook spiraled out of control. It really was like a pressure-cooking Hot Pot had been created on every digital screen: Just dump in the partisan rage, insults, fears, and resentment and eventually out pops another tribalized hyperpartisan brain braised in a toxic emotional stew at very high pressure for three-plus hours a day. Like one of my favorite cultural and political commentators Peggy Noonan writes:

> It is just such an air of extremeness on the field now, and it reflects a larger sense of societal alienation. We have the fierce teamism of the lonely, who find fellowship in their online fighting group and will say anything for its approval. There are the angry who find relief in politics because they can funnel their rage there, into that external thing, instead of examining closer and more uncomfortable causes. There are the people who cannot consider God and religion and have to put that energy somewhere . . . America isn't making fewer of the lonely, angry and unaffiliated, it's making more every day.

In its present form and stage, the whole Foxhole tribal amplification spiral is clearly an emotionally predatory business. The American Foxocracy is a $10 billion a year business model based solely on the fact that evolution failed to prepare our reptilian caveman brain to binge watch white tribal identity porn that activates and monetizes white tribal fear and hatred—and the $140 billion emotion surveillance and hyper-targeting social media industry then retargets and remonetizes that fear and hate to an audience thirty times bigger than Fox's cable audience.

That it literally has changed the outcome of American presidential elections and destroyed millions of family and friend relationships should no longer be surprising—because the whole activating and amplifying white tribal identity grift was the big idea of Fox News from the beginning.

The reason why America is becoming more lonely, angry, and unaffiliated every day is because the business model of activating and converting fearful white Americans into hyper-partisan tribalized zealots is now a $10 billion industry.

As the *New York Times* reports in its Planet Fox report, this is the same grift that has toppled two democratic governments in the UK and Australia and clearly destabilized the American form of bipartisan adversarial democracy.

In fact, to me, after researching the psychological damage of the Foxhole spiral and how it spun out of control, Fox News 3.0 (the conversion to Trump TV in 2016) feels analogous to a nuclear power plant accident. When Fox News's emotionally powerful and psychologically toxic content became a 24/7 Donald Trump infomercial and went from reaching a few hundred thousand people per day in 2000 to engaging one hundred million people per month in 2019 via social media distribution and redistribution, it was like a massive tribal identity activation and partisan identity amplification bomb exploded within the psyche of America. Making more tribally activated and angry Americans is the explicit business model of Planet Fox. After twenty-five years of practice, Fox News's radioactive right-wing partisan brain dust is now being absorbed into the emotional brains of one hundred million people per month for the sole purpose of monetizing the attention of their angry, lonely, and disaffected victims with ads and content licensing fees.

What did we think was going to happen to millions of Americans who consume white tribal activation and amplification fear/hate/blame and resentment pornography daily—that we were going to have *fewer* lonely, angry, and tribally activated Americans? Look—free online sex porn is now reported to have tens of millions of addicts worldwide and addiction recovery centers everywhere—and nobody watches three-plus hours a day of that stuff.

If we had an emotional Geiger counter implanted in every digital device and TV in America, we would get readings that would indicate "unhealthy levels of emotional radiation and damage" in tens of millions of Americans. It's already happened in Australia and the UK where other parts of the Murdoch white tribal identity porn empire are thriving.

That level of emotional mayhem and social dysfunction is stunning. But that is not all: In America in 2019 we have millions of Fox News viewers who are without question psychologically addicted to the regular jolts of powerful pleasure neurochemicals that they get in the rigged Fox News "opinion-debate" programming.

Are you still skeptical that Fox News rigs its "fair and balanced" opinion debate programming? Well I performed in two thousand of those segments over fourteen years—here is exactly how it really works.

First, the cold open (i.e., the prerecorded opening) hooks the viewer/streamer's attention and then builds interest with an image and narrative that is basically this: Your world looks like it's either ending or at least gravely threatened by whatever tribal monster is underneath your bed and getting the highest engagement as measured by the Planet Fox digital surveillance and two-minute ratings of the cable network. The viewer now wants to get revenge for the latest left-wing apostasy or cultural desecration.

Then after that existential fight-or-flight bomb is thrown, miraculously, those negative emotions are replaced with the sweet revenge of a tribal victory—or at least hope that a tribal victory is close. That tribal victory feels glorious—and it activates your brain's feel-good chemistry set.

It's the swing and range of emotions from impending threat of doom and then a real glimmer of hope that is the Foxhole spiral which hooks the viewers' attention, gains their interest, creates desire for a tribal victory, and activates the involuntary reflex of self-esteem-building chemicals with a righteous tribal victory.

Every seven or eight minutes you are made fearful and then made surer of the righteousness of your white conservative team, and it feels great to see and hear evidence that makes your team the winner and superior to your tribal enemy. As social scientist Crispin Sartwell shares in his recent *Wall Street Journal* article, detesting your political enemies is an immensely satisfying feeling. Why? Sartwell writes, "Because the compensatory pleasures of hatred—in particular its enhancement of self-esteem—are underrated. Hatred is self-congratulatory. It involves expressing superiority to its objects, and patting yourself on the back for not being them. When you declare your opponents to be obviously evil and stupid, you are congratulating not only yourself but the people who agree with you for being intelligent and good."

For the chronically lonely, it feels great to be on the digital battlefield with your tribal blood brothers; the Foxhole camaraderie is invigorating.

And by tribal extension, it feels even greater to win when, in your real life outside the digital Foxocracy bubble, things aren't so great. When there is not much winning in real life, many people come to Fox News to feed their lost sense of pride and accomplishment by watching their tribe winning onscreen. No one knows better than Fox News that tribal hatred enhances the viewers' self-esteem. Tribal hatred *is* self-congratulatory—and the more proof the viewers see and hear of how "stupid and retarded" their tribal enemy is, the more self-congratulatory it feels to be proud members of the righteous tribe.

If you watch Fox News and you don't understand that the opinion-debate segments are rigged (with a few exceptions) and the left-wing antagonists are nothing more than props in a carefully produced and choreographed performance, your motivated reasoning—let's call it your right-wing tribally motivated cognition—is very strong. (By the time you finish this book you will know the exact formula for rigged outcome opinion segments.)

What is *motivated cognition*? It's super important to this story. It is one of our innate and involuntary human reflexes. It's when we become so "tribalized" or hyper-partisan about anything that we only cognitively engage with tribally approved content. More importantly, our brains also are hardwired to not cognitively process content that does not square with accepted tribal ideology and orthodoxy. Understand this if you are someone who watches thousands of hours of Tribal TV: motivated cognition is the primary psychological ingredient that powers the Fox News white tribal partisan grift.

Cognitive psychologists tell us motivated cognition is the act of innately deciding what you want to believe and then using your cognitive reasoning power to build a case in your mind that proves your belief.

Why do we do this?

Cognitive science teaches us via social experiments that humans primarily use our unique ability to reason in order to figure out how best to ingratiate and integrate ourselves into our chosen tribe. Turns out our ability to band together and work together for shared goals (like kill those pesky Vikings who kept invading my native Scottish home in the old days) was a primary weapon of survival.

But we might as well call this cognitive phenomenon "motivated ignorance."

In 2019 not much has changed in our brains from our caveman ancestors. We still primarily use our brain to keep in good standing with our selected tribe—not so much for protection now but to *feel* the warm emotions of belonging to a like-minded tribe. We also want to avoid the pain of cognitive dissonance (the extreme discomfort felt when those who hold core beliefs are presented with evidence that disproves those beliefs). For the tribalized Fox News viewer or proud Deplorable, new contrary evidence simply cannot be processed or accepted—it does not pass through your cognitive dissonance force field.

This drive to feel a part of a tribe and our need for a "shared non-dissonant reality" is especially virulent when it comes to shared values/hatreds/scores to settle with *other* tribes—that is, partisan politics.

Key Point: Cognitive and social science is pretty clear; our innate need for a shared tribal reality is not only the main source of dysfunction in politics; it's also the psychological key to $3 billion of Fox News's revenues.

It is our innate "fundamental need for a shared reality with other people" that cognitive and social scientists research and describe all too often that overshadows incentives to weigh evidence or to be objective when it comes to political discussions. These experts also point to an even more basic incentive for not processing information dissonant to the tribal belief system; it takes a lot more energy. Our brains already consume twenty-plus percent of our daily energy—evolution taught us to use our noggins for more important things like finding a mate and defending our family members.

This dark truth: Our innate "need for shared reality" and the powerful associated cognitive dissonance that supports it lies at the heart of all partisan politics, "alternative facts," and the drive to discount otherwise objective facts as "fake news."

In fact, our brains are hardwired to automatically have an easier time remembering information that fits our worldviews. We're much quicker to recognize information that confirms what we already know (confirmation bias), which makes us blind to facts that discount it. We have an innate drive to avoid painful cognitive dissonance and an inner need for confirmation bias that seeks to reinforce previously held beliefs and opinions.

After all, one partisan's cognitively dissonant TV program is another partisan's twenty-four-hour confirmation bias tribal spa, right?

All Fox News and the Foxhole spiral has to do to accomplish its magic is move you into the tribal partisan camp—and then Fox News owns not only your brain stem; they own your psyche.

IT'S NOT JUST THE FEEL-GOOD NEUROCHEMICAL RUSH THAT'S ADDICTING

What I found most interesting in researching this book is many chronically lonely and emotionally isolated viewers are also addicted to their imagined sense of human connection and the perceived camaraderie they get from "fighting the good fight" against the "Libocracy" with their fellow hyper-partisan comrades-in-arms.

I have a chapter coming on the addictive power of emotional bonding and connection. But before the internet, right-wing partisans could not reach out and share the tribal victories and begrudge the tribal heresies inflicted on them by the left-wing "others" with so many people.

Many of these Foxhole addicts feel they are actively and not just vicariously participating in a culture war by watching their partisan blood brothers and sisters on Fox News and Foxnews.com fighting the righteous and heroic fight on their TV screen or digital device against the hated liberals/libtards/socialists who they viscerally feel:

- Attack and threaten their virtue.

- Disrespect their culture.

- Are trying to take away their way of making a living.

- Disparage their inerrant Evangelical Bible.

- Insult their immortal savior Jesus Christ.

- And, of course, are manically driven to confiscate the guns that they own, in part, as an insurance policy against the coming civil war they are told a hundred times each week by conservative media is coming to America "soon."

In short, millions of people have developed "Fox News brain," and it feels like no one in America really gives a shit. Compare this with the definition of video gaming disorder from the World Health Organization—which says the serious problem of "video gaming disorder" is a "pattern of behavior characterized by:

- impaired control over gaming time (check).

- increasing priority to gaming over other activities (check).

- continuation or escalation of gaming despite the occurrence of negative social and personal consequences (double check).

You know—"negative consequences" like estrangement from your kids and friends. Divorce. Self-induced higher levels of chronic loneliness. Higher risk of premature death.

RETRO AND METRO AMERICA AND THE GREAT DIVIDE

The Great Divide is a reframing of the blue state/red state concept born after the 2000 election. The Great Divide acknowledges that in America today, there exists such a deep and wide economic, cultural, racial, religious, and political gap that the "United States of America" is, for all intents and purpose, effectively two nations. According to *The Great Divide: Retro vs. Metro America* by John Sperling and Suzanne Wiggans Helburn, "Retro America, the one culturally, traditionally and economically rooted in the past, and Metro America, the one culturally heterogeneous, culturally modern and economically focused on the future." These two Americas are divided along racial, ethnic, religious, cultural, political, and geographic lines as well as economics. The great battle, going on in America, they write, is not Left versus Right; rather, it's Metro versus Retro America.

Within the two Americas—Metro and Retro America—as Peggy Noonan makes clear we have an epidemic fever of emotional toxicity, and most victims don't even know it until it's too late. No one seems to understand how and why they need to slow down and detoxify these Foxhole fever victims to a healthy level where they can reengage with their estranged family and friends.

Don't believe me? Am I exaggerating the epidemic of emotional mayhem? The American Psychological Association's recent Stress in America™ poll shows the US at its highest stress level ever. Nearly two-thirds of Americans (63 percent) say the future of the nation is a very or somewhat significant source of stress, slightly more than perennial stressors like money (62 percent) and work (61 percent). More than half of Americans (59 percent) said they consider this the lowest point in US history that they can remember—including those who lived through World War II and Vietnam, the Cuban Missile Crisis, and the September 11 terrorist attacks.

When asked to think about the nation in 2019, nearly six in ten adults (59 percent) report that the current social and political divisiveness causes them stress. A majority of adults from both political parties say the future of the nation is a major source of stress, though the number is significantly higher for Democrats (73 percent) than for Republicans (56 percent) and Independents (59 percent).

"We're seeing significant stress transcending party lines," said Arthur C. Evans Jr., PhD, APA's chief executive officer. "The uncertainty and unpredictability tied to the future of our nation is affecting the health and well-being of many Americans in a way that feels unique to this period in recent history."

My message to you is this—I do care, and I do know how to detoxify many of these eighty million people. But clearly much of this stress comes from the emotional power of Fox News's huge digital mind share in Retro and parts of Metro America in 2019.

To detoxify is a simple and necessary two-step process. First, people with this Foxhole fever need to be educated and aware of:

- How they are stalked by emotional media predators.

- How this emotional predation works and what are the mental and physical health risks that come from over-marinating in hours per day of emotionally toxic white identity fear/hate/blame/resentment porn.

This book and my site www.FoxNewsRehab.com will do the trick in most cases. We also plan on holding workshops where the most toxically addicted Fox News viewers live.

But this book and our detoxification workshops are not nearly enough.

If the toxic Foxhole fever epidemic was a diagnosed clinical mental condition, it would statistically only be exceeded by the clinical diagnosis of chronic loneliness and depression in America and the 60 percent higher risk of premature death that comes with it. And the biggest cause of chronic loneliness, as reported by UC San Francisco public health research on loneliness, comes from "pushing people away" from their lives.

What is the number one way old people "push people away" from their lives? When a person becomes that brainwashed ranting-and-raving hyperpartisan political culture warrior who no one can stand to be around any longer.

Look—the original audience engagement thesis when I was working inside Fox News between 2000 and 2013 was "what if we took the most emotionally powerful right-wing partisan issues of the day presented on right-wing talk radio and amplified their emotional impact by using Roger Ailes's proven emotional manipulation format he pioneered for televised attack ads?"

No one had ever done that before. And because people watching TV got to see the facial cues of their beloved TV host/partisan blood brother protagonists and the faces and ethnicity of their hated libtard antagonists in fully scripted and rigged outcome "opinion debate" segments, the emotional impact was ten times more powerful than radio.

Of course we have had radio and TV partisan attack ads in America for decades—every two years. Fox News co-founder and tribal identity porn guru Roger Ailes's former TV attack ad shop would create, test, and roll out TV attack ads to carpet bomb their right-wing client's opponent. That opponent could be another conservative in a primary race, but most likely their target was a liberal in a congressional, Senate, or presidential race. They used weaponized TV and radio ads during the campaign—but saved the most emotionally powerful TV ads for a saturation bombing run in the last few weeks of any campaign.

The objective was always the same:

1. Find a fear- and hate-inducing negative theme that resonates with voters.

2. Make it ten times more emotionally powerful via Ailes's television propaganda arts and techniques.

3. Then via TV ads, saturation bomb the opponent in the eyes of voters to make the voter hate the opponent more than they hate or dislike your client.

The brilliance was that Ailes's shop knew they could not in most cases make anyone love their candidate (because of the opponent's saturation bombing from the left). But all they had to do was make their voting audience hate or fear their candidate less.

The brilliance of the technique on TV was made more powerful by the fact that with Fox, this propaganda was being brought to you under the identity mantle of a "news channel." Under the pretense of being a news channel, Roger Ailes, his producers, and I created a new form of televised psychological warfare that Americans had never seen: The Fox News seven to eight minute white tribal emotion activation and amplification attack ad disguised as a "political or cultural debate" segment where we duped the viewer into thinking they were watching "the news." We made Republican Party propaganda infomercials disguised as talk show segments.

The masquerade worked. The older, 94 percent white audience thought they were watching "the news" (and still do). The reason was the decades of conditioning they had from watching the previous form of televised news programming from the three political news networks—ABC, CBS, and NBC. The brain is an amazing piece of equipment, but it has limitations and shortcuts. One shortcut is called "plasticity." This is where the brain sets up contextual shortcuts or "frame circuits" to understand what it is seeing or doing. Fox News channel was a "news channel," and therefore to your sixty-plus-year-old brain it *was* news.

The other reason was CER—conditioned emotional response. Think of those white rat experiments in a cage with two water bottles—one pure and one laced with cocaine. After a while the rats exclusively drink the cocaine water—who knew?

Or Pavlov's dog. Classical conditioning (also known as Pavlovian conditioning) is learning through association and was discovered by Pavlov, a Russian physiologist. In simple terms, two stimuli are linked together to produce a new learned response in a person or animal. Classical conditioning is why most non-news opinion programming opens with a red banner and the host saying "Fox News Alert" blah blah blah. The faux alert banner and "This is a Fox News Alert" claptrap are pure Pavlovian conditional response tactics.

When I say Fox News's experiment in clandestine emotional predation and manipulation "jumped the rails" and morphed into an emotional plague, it's because two things happened to this powerful white tribal identity content that they never thought would happen or ever dreamed would happen:

One is emotionally vulnerable senior aged cable viewers (the current median age of Fox News viewers is sixty-eight) who already on average watched 7.2 hours of television per day started binge-watching Fox News seven to eight minute white tribal attack ads disguised as a "political or cultural debate" for 3-5 hours *every* day.

Neither the producers nor I ever considered what would happen to a person's state-of-mind and general behavior if an older person marinated their brain in thousands of hours per year of the most emotionally powerful televised attack ads and GOP propaganda instead of just a few random minutes of attack ads during election seasons.

And then the biggest unexpected and emotionally powerful event of all:

What would happen if a new technology called "social media" took their already emotionally powerful hyperpartisan attack ads and diced the most emotionally engaging ones (which they knew to target from their emotional surveillance data) into three-minute digital grenades that would saturate bomb one hundred million people every month via social media streaming?

We all understand that tribal behavior and instinct is in our DNA— it's an indelible part of human nature. But evolution especially sensitized humans to danger most of all. Yet in our modern lives, our tribal nature has remained basically dormant since (1) most of us no longer live in actual tribes and (2) our sense of personal safety—the most powerful and important part of being human—is not dependent on joining and staying in a literal tribe.

What happened with millions of conservative viewers is FNC's white tribal identity porn, when combined with 24/7 emotional engagement based social media retargeting, exploded the hyper-partisan activation rate for millions of previously "agree-to-disagree" Americans who cooked their minds for thousands of hours inside the world's first digital white tribal identity radicalization factory—and like Peggy Noonan described so well, the explosion in tribalized right-wing Americans changed America.

THE WORLD CHANGED FOR FOX NEWS IN THE TWENTY-FIRST CENTURY

When Fox News started in 1995, there was not much emotionally activating or animating stuff going on. Yes, Bill Clinton was POTUS, but the economy was humming, the Internet Age had started, and FNC never got more than 100,000 viewers. There was no TV streaming. There was no social media like today.

But Fox News version 1.0 caught a break—the Monica Lewinsky affair was exposed. OMG that was right-wing partisan gold. Fox mined that vein of pearl-clutching moral panic like the professional emotional grifter they are. But still viewership per day was only 50,000ish—that was until the 2000 POTUS election and the "hanging chad." FNC viewership and online users leaped to 250,000 and pulled back to a steady 150,000.

Fast-forward to 2008 and Fox 2.0. Fox News transformed into a lethal white tribal identity amplification spiral machine in 2008 because of:

- The election of Barack Hussein Obama, which caused an explosion of white over-fifty-five-aged Retro American viewership of Fox News's white tribal identity activation and amplification content.

- The invention and exponential growth of a new industry we should have called "surveillance capitalism"—the hyper-targeted social media digital surveillance architectures which first exploded out of stealth mode in 2008 with Facebook and YouTube.

- The 2007–2009 Great Recession, which brutally destroyed the finances and primary wealth repository for many of FNC's 95 percent white Retro American viewers (their home equity). Viewers accurately perceived Metro Americans and elites and Wall Street got bailed out by the federal government while they were left to the wolves to fend for themselves. Embers of socioeconomic and class resentment were, by Fox News, fanned into raging fires (remember the Tea Party? Who put dozens of angry white Tea Party leaders on the air for thousands of hours? Fox News).

By 2010, Fox News and social media had become symbiotically conjoined. Social media engagement depended on getting free, emotionally engaging content from emotion-engaging media. Social media platforms used Fox News's emotionally radioactive white tribal fear and hate porn content as bait to surveil and then hyper-target consumers for digital advertisers (and Russian trolls later on—another unintended consequence).

Remember, Facebook and YouTube algorithms never send you *less* emotionally engaging content—they are programmed to send you (and auto-play) incrementally more emotionally escalating content. That emotional content spiral keeps your eyeballs and brain engaged to maximize their emotionally targeted ad monetization platform.

The power of the Great Recession produced the destruction of household wealth and jobs at a mass scale. It also delivered the final economic death blow to most of the regions within America's twenty-six mostly twentieth-century industrial and resource extraction base states we economists describe as "Retro America." At the same time, it supercharged the twenty-first-century economic base and balance sheets of many middle class and up living in the twenty-four states of Metro America as their digital and knowledge-based economies thrived.

The economic torpedoing of both Retro and parts of Metro America created a new, vast, and uniquely American socioeconomic class—America's working poverty class. In June 2018 we got the actual household economic data of this new massive American working poverty class economists call ALICE Households: "Asset Light, Income Constrained, and Working."

I've unfortunately come to label this new working poverty class as America's grievance and resentment class. What distinguishes America's new working poverty class? What makes them the grievance and resentment class? According to the latest Federal Reserve household economic data:

- Forty-two percent of Americans don't make $15 an hour.

- Forty-five percent of America's 155 million households can't scrape up more than $400 in cash liquidity in a pinch.

- Seventy-two percent of all American households live paycheck to paycheck.

- About 90 percent of Americans have experienced stagnant or declining wages since 1980.

- Working poverty households—ALICE Households—are defined as having a household income above the poverty line but below the median household income of $62,000. They are juggling (and sometimes missing) one or two payments a month of basic minimum middle-class life.

- This means they are one lost job, one injury, or one auto accident away from moving in with a relative or going on State/Federal assistance.

- This means about 115 million Americans now experience chronic economic trauma.

- If you add the additional 14 million households in actual poverty, twenty-first-century capitalism is not working for nearly two-thirds of American households.

Where does all that grievance and resentment anger in Foxholes come from? Where does Fox News driven populist Trumpism come from? It comes because in 2019 nearly two thirds of Americans are bringing a twentieth-century skillset to a twenty-first-century knife fight.

Not surprisingly, many of the folks whose inflation-adjusted wages have not risen since 1980 or earlier are scared, angry, blameful, or all three. Their life expectancy (depending on age and where they live) is about fifteen years less than a person the same age living behind my gated neighborhood in Metro America. They don't have a stock portfolio or financial cushion to get past what the top 20 percent of American households simply cover with savings or a margin loan on their investment portfolio.

What does this massively spread out economic carnage and trauma have to do with Fox News? One hell of a lot—it's played a major role in the real story behind the Fox News ascension. The descending income and wealth of the American working poverty class fueled the ascension of Fox News's powerful tribal blame, resentment, and victimization narratives—which in turn fueled the ascension of the Donald Trump's Presidential Apprentice TV reality show.

The Fox News tribal identity grift was from its beginning intended to build the most psychologically sophisticated and emotionally powerful 24/7 right-wing tribal activation and propaganda infomercial ever created. The original grift was that we disguised this content under the cover of a cable "news" network geared to people who were used to trusting the news. As *Rolling Stone* journalist Tim Dickinson reported in 2012, Fox

News co-founder Roger Ailes was able to "pioneer a new form of political campaign—one that enables the GOP to bypass skeptical reporters and wage an around-the-clock, partisan assault of public opinion."

Dickinson even got the metaphor right. "The network—at its core— is a giant soundstage created to mimic the look and feel of a news operation, cleverly camouflaging political propaganda as independent journalism." And thousands of free seven-minute political ads watched by tens of millions of Americans changed a whole lot of votes at the margin.

It should not come as a surprise that in my time at Fox News, the real Fox News agenda was known around the New York City headquarters offices as "the Liberal Death Star." Since I left Fox News 2.0 in 2013, the Liberal Death Star morphed into Fox News 3.0. It has created an entire American Foxocracy ecosystem enabled by a set of extremely powerful unintended transformations in technology, in political content regulations, and in the new economics of twenty-first-century America.

IT'S THE FOX NEWS GRIFT, BABY

If you are great at the art of the grift—and with the possible exception of Donald Trump there was no better emotional grifter ever born than Roger Ailes—the grift feels so good that the griftee (in this case, a cable viewer or online streamer) doesn't even mind being grifted.

In fact, they don't mind being grifted: For the average Fox News viewer, who feels they are in a constant mental state of siege, traumatic victimhood, and cultural persecution, their visit to Fox News's tribalized right-wing righteousness confirmation bias mental health spa is the best part of their day. And that tribal confirmation spa effect happens by careful design.

But just like any porn, the Fox News safe place for self-identified conservatives or Deplorables is a seduction to get you into the Foxhole tribal identity spiral. The tribal identity porn spiral is similar to the softcore-to-hardcore sexual porn spiral. They both deliver the same powerful and pleasurable neurochemicals we humans have in our massive brains. They also both create and activate conditioned emotional response (CER) pathways which are easily activated again and again.

What is a CER? Simple—if you are a committed conservative, how do you feel the nanosecond you see a picture of Hillary or Obama? If you are a committed liberal or NeverTrump conservative, how do you feel the nanosecond you see Mr. Trump speaking?

Revulsion? Hate? And hate's half-brother, sentimentality for a past age when everything made sense? That was the plan, man; that was always the plan. If you know how to manipulate and cynically exploit mankind's hardwired involuntary emotional and cognitive vulnerabilities, you can do just about anything. In my years at Fox News, what I came to see as our tagline should have been "Raw emotions cynically manipulated to achieve maximum audience engagement and profit."

Tragically on March 15, 2019, my message of how mentally dangerous it can be to marinate our emotionally sensitive minds for six hours a day or more in the most emotionally corrosive and traumatic emotions in humankind—fear, hatred, outrage, resentment, and blame—came to far-off New Zealand. It came from a white supremacy terrorist who was radicalized on the dark web subculture as well as on Instagram and YouTube.

I am not saying that daily binge-watching of Fox News opinion content will turn you into a white supremacist—don't go there.

But in the case of the New Zealand Muslim massacre, the young man marinated his already deranged and psychotic brain binge-watching undoubtedly in thousands of hours of offline and online interaction with extremist ideological content. Call that separate extremist media ecosystem white supremacist version of the Fox News white tribal activation Hot Pot.

But most worrisome to me—most of his radicalization came from within the world's most powerful political and cultural identity amplification Hot Pot—algorithmicized and hidden identity social media. This tragedy was unfortunately an extreme but real-life example of the white tribal identity amplification spiral on steroids.

While the murdering white supremacy terrorist was not a tribalized Fox News hyperpartisan by any means, the political and cultural digital radicalization spiral effect is exactly the same.

And it was working for more than a hundred years before it was digitized.

THE FOXHOLE SPIRAL EFFECT IS NOT NEW—JUST THE TECHNOLOGY IS

The psychological construct of the digital tribal identity amplification spiral I now call the Foxhole spiral goes back to the 1960s "Deviancy Amplification Spiral" and South African sociologist Stanley Cohen. Cohen noticed how the UK tabloid press at the time took a small story about a set of dueling teenage gangs and amplified the little nothing story into a big national invasion story that induced what he called a "moral panic."

This thoroughly contrived panic spread like wildfire in the press and emotionally traumatized people to the point of Brits hating either one or both of contrived narrative protagonists: the "Mods" and "Rockers."

Voila! The fake contrived moral panic turned into real emotional trauma—"What are we going to do about these hoodlums—they are ruining Great Britain—we have to stop them from invading our homes!!"

Later on in 1967, prominent sociologist Leslie Wilkins came to more accurately describe the power of mass media to amplify marginal news into a national moral panic as the "Deviancy Amplification Spiral."

As journalism commentator Matt Taibbi writes in his book *Hate, Inc.*, the deviancy amplification spiral was "an academic term for using invented problems to drive people actually crazy."

Taibbi reports the Deviancy Amplification Spiral worked like this:

> LESS tolerance
> Leads to
> MORE acts defined as crimes
> Leads to
> MORE actions against criminals
> Leads to
> MORE alienation of deviants
> Leads to
> LESS tolerance of deviants by conforming ingroups

In other words, the self-reinforcing nature of a contrived moral or tribal panic—when fed by breathless, contrived political or cultural media reporting—can amplify and "spiral up" small incidents into national panics.

Britain's tabloid newspapers dreamed up these moral panics because they discovered they sold a ton more newspapers during the half-life of these contrived crises. In other words—they manipulated and abused their sacrosanct "news reporting" status with a contrived illusion to monetize fear by selling more papers and more ads.

Hmm . . . that grift sounds familiar doesn't it?

And who owned the most tabloid eyeballs in the UK?

Fox co-founder Rupert Murdoch of course. He invented the modern tabloid newspaper, and his editors perfected the deviancy amplification spiral.

WHAT IS NOT NEWS ABOUT THE FOXHOLE SPIRAL?

Media sophisticates understand the original sin of America's tribal political warfare-as-entertainment complex was when we chose to convert America's political and cultural nervous system (the independent news and journalism media) into a tribal warfare-as-entertainment product. That occurred when the FCC canceled television's Fairness Doctrine in 1987, the last year of the Reagan presidency. (I'll get to this important regulatory transformation in a bit.)

It is not news either that Nicole Hemmer, an assistant professor of presidential studies at the University of Virginia's Miller Center and the author of *Messengers of the Right*, a history of the conservative media's impact on American politics, says of Fox, "It's the closest we've come to having state TV." Neither is it news that in America today it is not possible to know where the commercial enterprise of Fox News 3.0 ends and White House policymaking starts.

It should not be news to anyone with a reasonable grasp of media that, according to Jane Mayer in the *New Yorker*, Professor Hemmer argues that Fox News "acts as a force multiplier for Trump. Fox is not just taking the temperature of the base—it's raising the temperature. It's a radicalization model." For both Trump and Fox, "fear is a business strategy—it keeps people watching."

Professor Hemmer is dead right—the rigged outcome opinion programming I performed at Fox News for more than a decade was conceived and produced from the beginning as a "right-wing tribal partisan radicalization model."

But what she missed was how the FNC radicalization model works— and that is Fox News's tribal warfare playbook described in this book combined with hyper-targeted social media redistribution. She also missed the now massive reach of the tribal activation and validation porn Fox News still calls its "opinion programming." Professor Hemmer also missed the increasingly faster tribal partisan conversion speed.

Reality? The scale and scope of the American cultural and political battlefield expanded a hundred times or more from 1995 when Fox News started.

These once every hundred year tectonic shifts in digital communications created an enormous multiplier in both emotional force and audience reach.

WHAT'S NEW IS WHAT'S OLD IN TRIBAL ACTIVATION PORN

When you think about it, tribal identity capitalism has been with us since the printing press. If you define it as "the business of finding, activating, amplifying, and monetizing political or cultural partisanship via various media forms and content" you could say it goes back to the early transcriptions of the Bible.

The idea and strategy of tribal identity content is by no means new—it just reinvents itself with every new information technology. National newspaper printing and distribution was a new information technology—and America went to war with Spain over a right-wing war fever created by major newspapers (remember the "Remember the *Maine*" fiasco?).

The sinking of the USS *Maine* on the night of February 15, 1898, supposedly from hitting a Spanish mine hidden in Havana, Cuba's harbor, created the opportunity to unleash a huge moral panic storyline that lasted months. "Remember the *Maine!*" was headline news in newspaper articles that urged the United States to "do the only moral thing we can do" and go to war against Spain.

Because of that newspaper-driven moral panic, we did go to war with Spain. We also destroyed seven-eighths of Spain's navy (of which one unintended consequence was the Spanish Civil War in the early 1930s).

There have always been serious unintended consequences from media-based tribal identity activation and amplification spirals.

Until the end of World War I, newspapers were highly partisan and the leading player in tribalized political or nationalist identity. A syndicated ten-week-long story on the rise of the KKK in the Deep South intended to warn people about the KKK actually helped the KKK recruit more than 100,000 new members. Before daily regional newspapers, there were "pamphleteers" who produced highly partisan arguments for the American Revolution. Ben Franklin was, among other things, a printer for crying out loud.

But then came electronic mass media. Electronic tribal identity capitalism started with the dawn of radio and was first mastered (not surprisingly) by Adolf Hitler and Joseph Stalin—but also by a Catholic evangelist from outside Detroit. Father Charles Coughlin. In the 1920s and 1930s, democratic governments all over the world suddenly found themselves existentially challenged by this new information technology.

Both Hitler and Stalin discovered this new broadcast radio technology could be powerfully used to provoke tribalized anger, resentment, and violence. Father Coughlin in the USA took a different path. He started as a zealous supporter of Franklin Delano Roosevelt, going so far as to call the New Deal, "Christ's Deal."

Hmm . . . sound familiar?

Later, however, Coughlin became disenchanted with Roosevelt's leadership and began to espouse extreme right-wing views. By the late 1930s, he'd become an outright Fascist sympathizer with an audience of more than thirty million every week. He was eventually forced off the air in 1939 because of his pro-Fascist and anti-Semitic rhetoric.

So you get the point—Fox News's tribal identity porn is not America's first media-inspired mayhem or tribalized political partisan monetization rodeo.

Shoshana Zuboff, a professor emerita of the Harvard Business School and the author of *The Age of Surveillance Capitalism: The Fight for a Human Future at the New Frontier of Power*, captures the context well. "Originally there was a way to marshal radio for the purposes of improving democracy. One answer was the British Broadcasting Corp., the BBC, which was designed from the beginning to reach all parts of the country, to 'inform, educate and entertain' and to join people together, not in a single set of opinions but in the kind of single national conversation that made democracy possible. Another set of answers was found in the United States, where journalists accepted a regulatory framework, a set of rules about libel law, and a public process that determined who could get a radio and TV station license."

TELEVISED WHITE TRIBAL IDENTITY PORN PROGRAMMING USED TO BE REGULATED?

In 1949, America saw the dawn of a new national broadcast technology that sent televised video through the air into your one TV in the living room (yes, if you are under the age of forty-five I must inform you that only rich people had more than one TV and your dad was in charge of the one TV).

Anyway—after seeing the immense political power and cultural impact of radio, Congress did not wait to regulate TV (the medium Roger Ailes told Richard Nixon in 1968 was "the most powerful thing in the world").

Congress passed strict laws that highly regulated television content via local spectrum licenses that had strong "follow our public affairs debate rules to the letter or you lose your valuable TV license" teeth. The three national TV networks, ABC, CBS, and NBC, were even prevented from owning more than a few local "affiliates" to ensure that no political partisanship bled onto the American airwaves.

But Congress did more than just regulate. They also established a public interest standard that mandated companies using the public's airwaves produce a significant amount of noncommercial "public affairs" content for the good of the citizens. They also mandated a Fairness Doctrine "label" that required news media journalists to seek out credible representatives of different viewpoints and political power for this clearly labeled editorial content.

In fact, both political sides had to be represented by spokespeople of reasonably equal political gravitas (which means no former US senator squares off against a twenty-eight-year-old Democratic strategist).

Furthermore, all the political or cultural back and forth—ironically labeled the "fair and balanced" rule—had to be included in one or more continuing segments and not one-minute sound bites. These public affairs editorial interviews had no commercial advertising and up until the late 1970s were performed live.

What happened? Well jeepers—all this TV regulation worked. The rates and size of political polarization and tribalized partisanship (according to social and political scientists) stayed within normal healthy ranges (that is, a normal percentage range of political hyperpartisans on both sides).

The late 1960s and the 1970s of course brought us cultural disruption and economic disruptions (did you ever wait two hours in a gas line?). A US president resigned in shame and a wimpy, cerebral Democratic POTUS ended the 1970s by losing the US Embassy in Tehran and a second term to a "disruptive DC outsider" named Ronald Reagan. Before he became the governor of California, Mr. Reagan was best known as a movie and TV star that played off of a chimpanzee in the movie *Bedtime for Bonzo*.

Man, history does repeat itself, does it not?

Reagan of course stepped up and eventually won the Cold War. But by far the most powerful political and cultural impacts in the 1980s came from the creation of three new information technology systems—national cable TV, the personal computer (which brought in the real information distribution and communication disruptor the World Wide Web in 1994), and the introduction of wireless digital voice and text communication devices.

So here we are in 2019. All this disruptive information technology did its job—it's being used to create and distribute unimaginable amounts of emotionally destructive and tribally activating and validating content for hundreds of billions of dollars in profits every year.

This content and technology is as powerful and culturally disruptive as the printing press was back in the day but yet massively dispersed and distributed at the scale of running water.

Note: For you history buffs—Johannes Gutenberg died in 1468, a little over a decade after inventing movable type. But his invention set in motion a gold-rush-like fever for printing press entrepreneurs who opened print shops basically everywhere to cash in on his technological and culturally disruptive earthquake.

Why does this matter? Because we are seeing in real time what has to be considered close echoes of Gutenberg's printing fever in the political and social tumult all around us, says Jeremiah Dittmar, the lead author of new research published by the London School of Economics.

According to Dittmar, the rise of tribal partisan activation and amplification media turned out a lot like the gold rush fever caused by Gutenberg's press itself. Look at the major cultural transformations that followed that technology earthquake of movable type—the Reformation, the Scientific Revolution, and the Industrial Age.

You know—what we came to call the Enlightenment.

Today it should be as obvious as Donald Trump's spray tan that we are in the middle of our own major disruptive and tectonic political and cultural reformation that is driven by three major technology earthquakes and two major economic and regulatory events.

In the biggest understatement of the twenty-first century, Margaret O'Mara, a historian at the University of Washington, says that the wave of tribal partisan activation and amplification content in America is a key driver of the current political and social chaos we have in America. "The (internet and social media app) technology is an accelerant," she says.

Wow—give her a cookie. I like my Hot Pot analogy better.

But most worrisome to me, I continue to find that most Americans have no idea how they are being played and exploited or that these massively powerful and destructive emotional, political, and cultural digital amplification spirals exist. They have no idea how the FNC tribal warfare playbook, which comes right out of the propaganda and direct response advertising playbooks, came to exist or why it is so powerful.

For some reason, most Americans somehow also fail to understand that it was the very same FNC tribal warfare playbook that was adopted by a seventy-something-year-old ex-reality TV star who, in 2016, simply added the previously taboo conversations about class and white supremacy to the Foxocracy playbook—and it tribally activated sixty-five million Americans to make him the single most powerful human being on the planet.

With our attention spans and emotional reactions captured, measured, intensified, and then amplified by social media (in return for selling $100 billion of digital ads), the good old Fox News run-of-the-mill televised tribal fear and outrage porn it pioneered turned out to be like that movie where a little yellow VW bug morphed into "Bumblebee" with destructive power that now reaches at least one hundred million Americans monthly.

Yes, in 2019 the media still reports the canard that Fox News is just a "niche cable network with only 2 percent of voters." For mainstream journalists to suggest that there have not been major consequences from the emergence of a nuclear powered and fully integrated American Foxocracy is ludicrous.

And what about the total emotional targeting and manipulative reach of the complete American Foxocracy ecosystem? Well, friends—when you combine:

- The cable, online, and social media reach of Fox News's nightly unabashed right-wing cultural and political televangelists.

- Outrage and clickbait mongering right-wing digital streaming media now competing with Fox News.

- Conservative radio's forty million daily listeners.

- The Evangelical megachurch evangelists and televangelist culture warriors who reach the one-in-four Americans who self-identify as "Evangelical Christians."

The reach and scope of American Foxocracy is now jaw dropping. We now have for all intents and purposes a completely separate country-within-a-country that is digitally interconnected with God, guns, megachurches, and political, cultural, and religious evangelists and Fox News televangelists spreading the good word of white nationalism.

The actual size and audience reach of the American Foxocracy is hard to imagine. And now with Fox News 3.0 making it impossible to determine where Fox News ends and Trumpism starts—that self-reinforcing Foxhole spiral feedback loop now includes Bible study, Sunday services, and the White House briefing room too.

One person in the mainstream media who understands the very real dangers of the Foxocracy's tribal fear and hatred-as-entertainment-mongering reality in America is Margaret Sullivan, a media critic for the *Washington Post* who wrote recently that, "Democracy, if it's going to function, needs to be based on a shared set of facts, and the news media's role is to seek out and deliver those facts." To that, I'd add that news media is a vitally important Fourth Branch providing checks and balances against the three branches of government. The news media should be the nervous system of democracy, to inform the citizens of the democracy with unambiguous facts and analysis in a nonpartisan manner.

Sullivan continues, "Most news organizations take that responsibility seriously," even correcting themselves when in error with, "editor's notes, lengthy corrections, on-air acknowledgment, suspensions, and even firings of errant news people."

Is Fox News among the responsible? Nope.

"The rule at Fox," Sullivan writes, "is to stonewall outside inquiries and to double down on its mission, described aptly by my colleague Greg Sargent: 'Fox News is fundamentally in the business of spreading disinformation, as opposed to conservative reportage.'"

And it's not just any kind of disinformation. It's propaganda. Damn near "Trump TV," as she calls it.

Finally, she adds, "Despite the skills of a few journalists who should have long ago left the network in protest, Fox News has become an American plague."

Is Ms. Sullivan exaggerating? Am I?

Fox News's GOP tribal white identity propaganda is almost perfectly manufactured and published according to the formula and rules of creating great propaganda that the late Nazi propagandist Joseph Goebbels wrote in his perfectly named book, *How to Make Great Propaganda*.

BTW—my favorite parts of Joseph Goebbels's self-published twenty-point propaganda playbook, as reported on psywarrior.com but with my comments here in parentheses, are:

10. Material from enemy propaganda may be utilized in operations

when it helps diminish that enemy's prestige or lends support to the propagandist's own objective (e.g., hacked or stolen emails).

11. Black rather than white propaganda may be employed when the latter is less credible or produces undesirable effects (e.g., WikiLeaks and birtherism).

13. Propaganda must be carefully timed.
    a. The communication must reach the audience ahead of competing propaganda.
    b. A propaganda theme must be repeated, but not beyond some point of diminishing effectiveness (would someone advise the Donald Trump of this rule—the "lock her up" chant has gone stale).

14. Propaganda must label events and people with distinctive phrases or slogans (e.g., "libtards, snowflakes, liberalism is a mental disease, Pocahontas").
    a. They must evoke desired responses which the audience previously possesses.
    b. They must be capable of being easily learned.
    c. They must be utilized again and again, but only in appropriate situations.
    d. They must be boomerang-proof.

16. Propaganda to the home front must create an optimum anxiety level.
    a. Propaganda must reinforce anxiety concerning the consequences of defeat (cultural, racial, or political defeat).
    b. Propaganda must diminish anxiety (other than concerning the consequences of defeat) which is too high and which cannot be reduced by people themselves.

18. Propaganda must facilitate the displacement of aggression by specifying the targets for hatred (oh boy—that could be a book by itself).

19. Propaganda cannot immediately affect strong counter-tendencies; instead it must offer some form of action or diversion, or both.
Fortunately Joseph Goebbels never had Facebook or YouTube, or

Germany might have won World War II. And Ms. Sullivan has missed the important difference between political propaganda and tribal identity activation and validation porn.

The key point is this: When combined with social media, existential tribal fear and PC-based scorched earth shame and outrage porn spreads like a viral plague. In 2009, with the election of Barack Hussein Obama and the Great Recession, tribal identity porn went digitally viral. That is when Fox News morphed to Fox News 2.0 or what many of our contributors referred to as the "OBN—the Obama Bashing Network."

THE NATURAL SPEED OF TRIBAL CONVERSION AND RADICALIZATION WAS DISRUPTED TOO

What most in America have also failed to connect is that when you add tribalized cultural and political video content and powerfully engaging memes to social media, the entire feedback loop is like my pressure cooking Hot Pot analogy—what used to take tribal hatreds decades or more to fester now takes a few years—or less. We now are just realizing again as a culture founded to wipe out European tribalism that the existential tribal virus never left us—it just became dormant in the Baby Boomers after World War II (with a few short periods of exception) until we made fomenting American tribalism a $100 billion industry.

The massively important difference today in America is this—in the old days of generational tribalism, before digitized tribal identity activation porn went viral, it could take much of a lifetime or more for a real and not imagined existential tribal enemy narrative to take hold. The tribal enemy narrative had to be passed down from clergy to grandparent to parents to children and then a cultural spark was required to ignite ethnic or cultural or political tribalism before it became activated (e.g., the Catholic/Protestant "Troubles" in my native Northern Ireland).

Today, FNC's tribal identity activation and validation porn, consumed via hundreds of millions of 4K digital devices and 4K high definition TV screens streaming massive amounts of tribal identity social media, is both the accelerant and the spark—and Fox News is lighting that fuse as a for-profit enterprise every day.

And of course, this digital tribal identity activation spiral is not only happening in America. From the "Spring Awakening" in the Middle East, the UK's Brexit, the rise of white tribal supremacy groups in Europe, and even to the digital recruitment of tens of thousands of ISIS jihadists, evidence of the tribal identity activation power of digital fear and hate tribalism propaganda is in nearly every country in the world.

Cultural or political tribalism is still a dormant virus in many—but for many more in America it is now an activated virus. Video that delivers the perception or actual reality of tribal oppression and disrespect involuntarily activates innate tribal hostility, bad feelings, and animal spirits. That is what right-wing tribal TV does—it shows you a new way how you are being disrespected and made fun of by the left every day. How you are victimized by malevolent elites who grow stronger every minute while you grow weaker and more vulnerable.

Ms. Sullivan has it right—it is high time to take Fox News's destructive role in America seriously. Maybe we should call the Foxocracy an emotional weapon of mass destruction and a plague on agree-to-disagree democracy.

When good old political propaganda evolved into tribal activation pornography, we missed that jump to emotional hyperspace. We also missed the unintended social and health consequences.

Key Point: Our human psychology has a backdoor, and it is very hackable—by fear. Fear suggests loss. Fear involuntarily causes stress. Fear paints a picture of necessary response; thus, stress also involuntarily induces a strong desire to do something. But much of Fox News induced stress is nonactionable—you can't throw a brick through the TV, as much as you would like to. You can't drive down to the Mexican border with a shotgun and protect America from invasion. You can't even stop those "wetbacks" from hanging around the back of Home Depot and stealing good American jobs or fly to China and get your steel foundry job or auto assembly job back (mostly because with twenty-first-century technologies, those jobs don't exist anymore in China or Japan or Mexico or anywhere else).

So what? So this: when you add up those thousands of hours of unresolved stress and fear for tens of millions of Americans, the psychologists I consulted with on this book say this amount of constant and unresolved fear and stress can create a condition that's a cousin to a PTSD—post-traumatic stress disorder.

And for tens of millions of self-identified "proud conservatives/ Deplorables/Republicans"—especially ones over age fifty-five living in the 2,626 counties in Retro America that voted Trump—the unintended consequence of them living constantly inside the digital Foxocracy are almost all mentally and physically negative.

So yes—for Fox News and its incarnate offspring Donald Trump and

Trumpism, "fear is a business strategy—it does keep people watching."

But *why* does fear keep self-identified conservative people watching? And what are the negative mental and physical health outcomes that are compounded for a person over sixty experiencing three or more hours of abject fear every day?

Well, the latest data from ten separate neurological research projects on fear-induced trauma since 2005 has proven that fear works especially well with self-identified conservatives because they are neurologically hardwired with up to 25 percent more intense reaction to fearful images.

Did you know that? There are right and left wings in all countries and democracies—and the data is the same. People who self-identify as "conservative" have brains actually wired to be up to 25 percent more sensitive to fearful or disgusting images (more on this important finding in its own chapter).

Now you understand partly why the saturation coverage of a manufactured "immigrant caravan" on Fox News Channel or an Evangelical televangelist going on for two hours about how you are going to hell if you don't vote for Donald Trump in 2020 happened—it's physiology—and it friggin' works. It captures iris-widened eyeballs and fast-beating hearts—it keeps those eyeballs jacked up so they can be sold to adult diaper companies or collect credit card donations to buy televangelists bigger and newer Gulfstream private jets.

FNC WHITE TRIBAL IDENTITY ACTIVATION CONTENT WAS ALWAYS THE PLAN

The outstanding *New Yorker* journalist Jane Mayer also captures well my understanding of the genesis of the Fox News fear and rage based tribalized "opinion content" model. She reports that while "[Rupert] Murdoch could not have foreseen that Trump would become President, he was a visionary about the audience that became Trump's base." She reports in the same article that "in 1994, Murdoch laid out an audacious plan to Reed Hundt, the chairman of the Federal Communications Commission under President Bill Clinton. . . . [H]e planned to launch a radical new television network. Unlike the three established networks, which vied for the same centrist viewers (the broadcast news model), his creation would follow the unapologetically lowbrow (the contrived emotional manipulation spiral model) of the tabloids that he published in Australia and England, and appeal to a narrow audience that would be entirely his. His core viewers, he said, would be football fans; with this aim in mind, he had just bought the rights to broadcast NFL games."

The FCC had done a "deal with the devil," and with the cancellation of America's Fairness Doctrine we, as we now are finding out, sold our soul to the devil.

Anyway, Mayer also reports that Blair Levin, at that time the chief of staff at the FCC and now a fellow at the Brookings Institution, says, "Fox's great insight wasn't necessarily that there was a great desire for a conservative point of view." More erudite conservatives, he says, such as William F. Buckley, Jr., and Bill Kristol, couldn't have succeeded as Fox has. Levin observes, "The genius was seeing that there's an attraction to fear-based, anger-based politics that has to do with class and race."

Levin argues, "Roger Ailes confirmed (and activated) all your worst instincts—Fox News's fundamental business model is driving fear." The formula worked spectacularly well. By 2002, Fox had displaced CNN as the highest-rated cable news network, and it has remained on top ever since.

As Hundt sees it, "Murdoch didn't invent Trump, but he invented the audience. Murdoch was going to make a Trump exist. Then Trump comes along, sees all these people, and says, 'I'll be the ringmaster in your circus!'"

Alyson Camerota was a colleague of mine at Fox News for many years and co-host on *Fox & Friends*. She notes that for years the show's producers would "cull far-right, crackpot websites" for content, and adds, "Never did I hear anyone worry about getting a second source. The single phrase I heard over and over was 'This is going to outrage the audience!' You inflame the viewers so that no one will turn away. Those were the Fox News standards."

Yes, those were the standards I worked under for fourteen years, and yes, they still are today. All those journalists and more have done great work digging into what Fox News was actually doing under the protection of the First Amendment and the false flag label from the FCC as a "cable news channel."

What I am reporting for the first time is different. What I am reporting and sharing is what those deeply troubling and amazingly powerful psychological and behavioral manipulation tactics and techniques actually are—and why they are so incredibly powerful.

Fear is just the opening act. What I learned, decoded, and practiced during my fourteen-year tour at Fox News will (I hope) leave you appalled and shocked no matter what your political or cultural perspectives.

America's big problem today (okay, one of our big cultural and political problems—my bad) is that for my entire fourteen years at Fox (and to this day), 99 percent of thousands of people over the years who would constantly approach me in public have zero media sophistication or Psychology 101 basics.

My journey to discover why this mass behavioral event had taken place in front of my eyes for years led me to discover the psychological answers to my basic question. Then, when I added my economic and technology background and experiences, I discovered a much darker and much more disturbing truth.

That truth shook me to my core. We now have an entire generation of Foxholes who have consumed thousands of hours over more than twenty years of FNC white tribal identity porn. For context, Goebbels got the angry disenfranchised everyday Germans to hate Jews and go to war with Europe with his propaganda in just eight years with nothing more than a book, radio, and movies.

No one until this book has identified and reported in any depth on these much bigger societal issues, save the brilliant documentary film by Jen Senko, *The Brainwashing of My Dad*, about how her father lost his mind after innocently falling into what I now call "The Foxocracy" ecosystem.

The fact is in 2019, the downward gravitational pull of this traumatic negative feedback loop for the most emotionally vulnerable Fox News viewers/streamers has never been seen before at such a mass scale. It has never been seen before because a 24/7 fully digital tribal identity activation and amplification feedback loop located in your car, your PC, and your handheld digital device never existed before.

In short, many important teachable moments have been missed. But for me, the most important lesson on the emotionally and psychologically toxic Fox News's format of tribalized right-wing political and cultural fear-and-hate based high def video is as follows:

When Fox News tribal fear-and-outrage based cable TV content became magnified by thirty times the reach and intensity by emotionally targeted social media, the reality for tens of millions of almost exclusively white, over-sixty-aged working and middle class Americans was this: They began to exhibit all the classic behavioral and neurological signs of chronic emotional trauma, behavioral addiction, or—in far too many cases—both.

But worse, what we failed miserably at is identifying the mental health risk to millions of Fox News addicts (Foxholes) defined as a person who has watched three or more hours a day of FNC's purposely rigged outcome fear and hate based opinion "debate" performances for ten years or more.

As many behavioral psychologists I consulted for this book will attest, there is a very real negative behavioral cost that results from their chronic binge-watching and inundation of weaponized tribal fear, hatred, and rage based TV. For many it leads to desocialized behaviors and cultural and political zealotry—that is, becoming a Foxhole. Worst, Foxholes result in many cases the estrangement from family and longtime friends for tens of millions of Americans who are not similarly possessed with such zealous feelings of rage and revenge.

Truly—the American Foxocracy is so powerful today because nobody addicted to anything wants to consume a less-powerful drug. The new competitors to the Foxocracy have to, by definition, attract eyeballs by providing even more powerful and fearful/disgusting/shocking tribal activation content.

We all know the drill—you start with one OxyContin pill, then two. If you don't quit them, you need a higher dosage for the same pain relief. And so on—you build a tolerance level that requires higher dosage to dull the pain.

The FCC would properly label Fox News as an adult entertainment channel *if* the FCC actually had a clue about what Fox News is actually doing with its tribal partisan warfare-as-entertainment product. I mean, really—the FCC finally figured out the WWE fixed outcome wrestling "match" scam in 1994 and made them change their name to "entertainment" and disclose their "wrestling match" charade.

The FCC figured out the fixed game shows in the late 1950s and shut them down. The FCC even kicked most televangelists off network TV stations and UHF channels (who then just regrouped to form Christian cable TV channels).

Why has the FCC not called out and fixed the Fox News "fair and balanced" rigged opinion debate scam?

FOX NEWS: THE OXYCONTIN OF TRIBAL IDENTITY MEDIA

Finally, the best analogy about viral unintended consequences of Fox News tribal ID porn I ever found was the real story behind the unintended consequences that created the OxyContin plague and epidemic. Now *of course* I am not comparing addiction to synthetic heroin to addiction to Fox News tribal identity porn—don't go there.

But hear me out on this because the parallels are very instructive. Both went viral for very similar reasons. Gambling, booze, drugs, Oxy, and heroin are all the same—if they are used as a coping mechanism, the neurochemicals and psychoactive chemicals involved are addictive. When the user develops a physical tolerance threshold and the normal dose starts to lose effect, you consume more or an even stronger painkiller to cope.

Originally, Purdue Pharmaceuticals' new synthetic heroin OxyContin was labeled by the FDA as a "short-term acute post-surgery pain relief agent" and was only approved for two days of usage. The reason it was only approved for two days was, like any psychoactive pain coping medicine, if you take Oxy for more than two or three days, your body begins to develop a physical tolerance for the drug. Mental health professionals call this a negative and degenerative addictive feedback loop because the more Oxy you take, the worse the side effects and possible addiction can get.

Let's be real—if you take Oxy at a dosage level that would drop a charging rhino, the odds go up astronomically that you will develop a physical and mental addiction to opioids.

Well gee—guess what? The makers of Oxy allegedly hired a bunch of FDA regulators to big fancy jobs as lobbyists and soon after Oxy was able to get a "label shift" upon receiving additional research (that Purdue Pharmaceuticals paid for). Yes friends, the FDA—which is just like the FCC—has a mandate to protect American citizens. But after lobbying, the FDA removed the "two-day only" label and made it okay to prescribe it for a longer period.

Why is this analogous to Fox News, you ask? Well for one thing, the FCC was heavily lobbied (the same way) by right-wing lobbyists to remove the Fairness Doctrine regulations and restrictions in 1987. By the time the FCC approved Fox News as a "cable news channel" in 1994, most had forgotten that less than a decade before the right-wing Reagan administration was successful in removing the "label restrictions" on the rules of conduct for televised news.

Like I shared before, in 1949, televised news was—shockingly—required to be news. The FCC "label" required broadcast license holders to broadcast news content under rules that, if broken, could cost the broadcaster its broadcasting license.

But the irony here (and analogy to the unintended consequences of changing the use label for opioids) is the Fairness Doctrine was created by the Congress in 1949 because they were so afraid that if one of the three major national networks were to be owned or controlled by a "political partisan," that network could imbue its left or right political and cultural view on a third of America and have undue influence on our democratic election process.

They gazed into a future of millions of Americans inundated with right- or left-wing propaganda and rightfully saw this type of partisan content would be unhealthy for our democracy.

The result? The removal of the Fairness Doctrine in 1987 was like the FDA removal of the two-day dosage of OxyContin. That regulatory shift set the table for the Fox News scam (perhaps better described as the audience grift). Fox could label and call the network a "news network" when, in fact, they made all their money and ratings on their tribal identity porn content. They could hire some unknown TV news folks to read the news, and the old people who grew up with TV news created under the "dosage" rules of the Fairness Doctrine would think the real content and engagement strategy was news—and think the talk show hosts were TV journalists like Walter Cronkite who were just giving the occasional editorial.

My point: Fox "News" Channel's off label content explosion from fifty thousand viewers to one hundred million users makes FNC the OxyContin of televised media for a whole bunch of reasons.

By the way, in 2019, according to the Nielsen ratings, twenty-four out of the top twenty-six shows on cable TV today meet my classification of televised tribal partisan identity activation and validation pornography. The tribal identity TV pornocalypse is already here, and we and our caveman brains did not evolve to be ready for it.

Fox News on the right and now rapidly catching up MSNBC and CNN on the left (both new to the tribal partisan identity porn industry but learning fast) already dominate cable. Tribal TV has had its OxyContin moment—and eighty million Americans and their families are already negatively impacted.

American society has devolved and turned out exactly as one might expect if you were aware that today over two hundred million Americans consume billions of hours of emotionally traumatic tribal warfare from both left and right wings as monthly entertainment.

I mean, really—what could go wrong, eh?

What else should a reasonably educated person expect would happen to a country of two hundred fifty million adults living in one constitutional republic which, for at least the last twenty years, economically and culturally is essentially two separate countries (Metro and Retro America) where each separate country shares common politics and federal government but is separated by different economics, territory, and culture (see the seminal 1995 Bill Bishop article on the dire implications of "The Big Sort").

To quote Mr. Bishop, "America may be more diverse than ever coast to coast, but the places where we live are becoming increasingly crowded with people who live, think, and vote like we do. This social transformation didn't happen by accident. We've built a country where we can all choose the neighborhood and church and news show—most compatible with our lifestyle and beliefs.

"And we are living with the consequences of this way-of-life segregation. Our country is so polarized, is so ideologically inbred, that people don't know and can't understand those who live just a few miles away. The Big Sort has dire implications for our country."

Fox News did not invent the Big Sort—but what it did for the Big Sort we now call Retro and Metro America is augment it into the Big Sort Generation 2.0 while profiting off it. Now we have a country where the adult residents of each separate Metro and Retro country consume billions of hours of highly powerful video tribal partisan identity porn content that validates and accelerate their Big Sort way-of-life cultural segregation.

Yet the only commercial objective for tribal identity porn publishers is to demonstrate and validate new reasons to fear and hate the other 125 million adults living in Metro America by literally objectifying and demonizing each other as cultural and political jihadists in order to sell them electric wheelchairs and gold bullion bars and to prepare them to survive either the coming rapture or inevitable American Civil War II—whichever occurs first.

Public health experts tell us an epidemic is "a disease that spreads exponentially among many people in a community at the same time." But the term epidemic can refer to something that spreads or grows rapidly, and the exponential growth of white tribal identity hate porn consumption from fifty thousand in 1996 to one hundred million or more today is an epidemic.

That's the grifter edge—every human brain, whether in Retro or Metro America, has the same innately griftable emotional and psychological vulnerabilities. This immutable fact of life is what makes media grifters so wealthy and their victims so unaware and then so surprised they got grifted.

It is one of the best media grifts ever—selling the eyeballs of old right-wing senior citizens has grossed Fox News nearly $3 billion a year with over $1 billion in profits every year since 2010. The value of the entire Fox News/Fox Business Network business of grifting old right-wing white people is worth over $20 billion.

CHAPTER 2

How I Broke the Code on the Rest of FNC's Tribal Identity Porn Conspiracy

Television is not the truth. Television is a goddamned amusement park. Television is a circus, a carnival, a traveling troupe of acrobats, storytellers, dancers, singers, jugglers, sideshow freaks, lion tamers, and football players.
—Paddy Chayefsky in *Network*

▪

How do you become a star host at Fox News? Talk, act, and think like you are a televangelist cult leader. The most successful Fox News hosts have become leaders of their own tribal identity cult that meets every weeknight at the same time for worship. "American conservatism" is just political fundamentalism. If you wanna have a successful Fox News show, watch an Evangelical televangelist—they have our program strategy down cold.
—What an FNC Executive Producer advised me in 2009 before I guest hosted my first FBN prime-time program

▪

I now realize Fox News is nothing more than a propaganda machine for a destructive and ethically ruinous administration [that is] wittingly harming our system of government for profit while assaulting our constitutional order, the rule of law, and fostering corrosive and unjustified paranoia among viewers.
—Lt. Colonel Ralph Peters (ret.), Analyst on Fox News Channel 2008–2018

▪

Three things cannot be long hidden: the sun, the moon, and the truth.
—Buddha

Fox News Lesson No. 2: If you understand geriatric psychology you understand why the tribal right-winger engagement-and-addiction formula works.

To understand this lesson, you have to understand the target audience (as described by Roger). The core Fox News conservative tribal viewer is a basically a clone of Donald Trump, minus the great education, the tossed hair, bone spurs, and narcissistic personality disorder.

For your edification, here's the most recent Nielsen television viewer data in general: "Television is particularly popular among men and is even more attractive to people who didn't go to college and to Americans over the age of seventy." In a highly related matter, up to 47 percent of America identifies as Evangelical Christians, depending how you choose to define the term.

That is an excellent description of a cultural and politically conservative tribal partisan. Remember, 50 percent of Fox News viewers are over the age of sixty-eight and, according to Nielsen, watch an average of more than seven hours of TV per day. And 65 percent of the FNC audience for any given show except the morning shows normally skews male.

Fox News's core viewers see the world through the eyes of an old, white, culturally and politically ethno-nationalist tribalism. Why more old white men? Because they are generally more culturally resentful and more prideful than older women, plus they have fewer close friend relationships.

"WHAT'S THE DIFFERENCE BETWEEN A RELIGIOUS CULT LEADER AND A FOX NEWS HOST? NOTHING"

In late August 2009 going into the Labor Day weekend, David Asman, the host of an evening show I regularly appeared on at Fox Business Network called *America's Nightly Scoreboard*, took the week off. I had been pitching myself to the executive producer of the show to guest host *America's Nightly Scoreboard* in David's absence.

By the end of my first decade in cable TV punditry I was addicted to the juice you get doing FNC cage match television. It always took a few hours and martinis to calm down after taping a show—the adrenaline was addictive. I watched other folks guest host our *Bulls & Bears* show, and in most cases I was sure I could have done a better job. So I started pitching myself as a guest host.

Note: In talk TV, you build your shot at your own show by staying around the studio during major holidays and guest hosting the shows where (1) the hosts are on vacation and (2) the show has the lowest ratings (the pitch to the executive producer is "What do you have to lose—I might even raise your crappy ratings!")

Hosting live TV without a net with people screaming in your ear while you are talking to millions of people is the only way to learn how to do talk

TV hosting well. In this case, the executive producer was new to Fox and FBN and came from CNN. I think he assumed I had guest hosted shows on Fox News before so after much badgering he said, "Okay, you're in—don't fuck it up."

Since in fact I had actually never hosted any live TV program before, I immediately went to the office of a well-known executive producer of one of Fox News's highest-rated evening prime-time programs that I occasionally appeared on and asked him, "Hey boss—so how do I become a star host at Fox News?" I was expecting some technical advice and such, but I got none of that stuff.

He said, "Sit down and listen. First you have to really understand the audience in the evening—they are much different than the Country Club/Capitalist Republicans that watch your Saturday morning show who have real money in the stock market. The evening audience is the core Fox News base—they are the (for the most part) more white working and lower middle class or retirees that are addicted to Fox News. Their main TV is on Fox News all day—we know this from the Nielsen reports."

He continued, "The best advice I can give you is what I tell the anchors at night—you gotta talk, act, and think like you are a religious cult leader. The most successful Fox News hosts have literally become leaders of their own Evangelical denomination that meets every weeknight at the same time. Their audience worships at the altar of the host's version of conservatism because conservatism in America is just a nice way of hiding the fact that tribal right-wing political fundamentalism is more like a religious cult than anything else."

"Really? Dude, I've seen *Elmer Gantry* a bunch of times—so what you are saying is I should I channel my inner Jim Jones and get 'em to drink my Kool-Aid?"

"Toby, I'm dead serious. You don't see the email and snail mail we get from our core viewers. Ever since Obama was elected and we added crazy ol' conspiracy theory dude Glenn Beck to the lineup at 5:00 p.m. along with all his millions of conspiracy theory kooks, our ratings are skyrocketing, but it's a whole new crowd."

He was dead right about the Glenn Beck conspiracy theory crowd. Beck took over John Gibson's 5:00 p.m. show in 2009 with about 500,000 viewers, and the ratings exploded to 1.5 million viewers. Bear in mind this is the toughest time slot for cable TV—potential viewers who aren't retired are mostly at work on both the East and West Coasts and not watching TV.

Beck's audience blast came from his huge daily right-wing radio show audience (more than ten million listeners at the time). Along with the conspiracy theory nutjob folks he attracted, he also had a large Evangelical audience. I hosted Beck's show one time (I was the only experienced guest host available in the studio at 5:00 p.m. on a Friday when his car was delayed as I remember), and the emails I got after the show were shocking in the extreme conspiracy theory dogma his viewers wrote me about.

A note on conspiracy theorists: Now that you understand tribal identity psychology, let's go to this important subset of conservatives. As a group conspiracy theorists are extremely insecure souls who need mass quantities of personal self-esteem building.

What drives conspiracy theory behavior and makes conspiracy cult leaders so powerful is the psychological profile of conspiracy theory fans—that they are among the most low self-esteem people on earth.

Let me ask you this—who is the most well-known conspiracy monger in America?

It's not Alex Jones of InfoWars or Glenn Beck. It's Donald J. Trump, of course! You know, the one who pushed the Obama "Fake Birth Certificate" conspiracy for five years among dozens of other debunked conspiracy theories.

Behavioral psychologists tell us all conspiracy theorists have a distinct psychological profile. They're almost always deeply insecure and are in some degree of an existential crisis. The conspiracies they hold onto are a tribal belief system or psychological construct created to mentally survive in a world they perceive to be haphazard, scary, and unfair.

Key Word: "unfair." Ever hear or read that term "unfair" in a speech or tweet from Donald J. Trump? Since his POTUS announcement in July 2015, he has spoken or tweeted the word "unfair" over one thousand five hundred times. So yes, dear friends—the behavior of the president of the United States and most powerful person in the world is the epitome of the classic conspiracy theory nut profile.

Reassuring, no?

If you deconstruct the word "unfair" regarding feelings and emotional context to an insecure conspiracy theorist like Donald J. Trump, psychologists will tell you the term unfair is indicative of high levels of insecurity and (not shockingly) highly narcissistic. To a person like DJT, any criticism of him, his behavior, his business record, or anything else that forms his delusional personal sense and construct of self-worth and importance is intolerable.

Sound familiar?

For an extreme narcissist with insecure conspiratorial delusions of grandeur, *no* criticism, however slight, is left alone. Just read reader comments on InfoWars.com or Breitbart.com; disagreement or name-calling is returned with an attack many times stronger than the perceived insult. That is why the POTUS sits in bed at 4:00 a.m. and counts up what he considers to be the most egregious personal "attacks" on him and returns tweeted grenades and insults back at *any* comment made on CNN or MSNBC or the mainstream print or magazine media or tweeted for that matter.

The level of insecurity is breathtaking for anyone, but for the POTUS and leader of the free world to turn petty slights into full-scale wars of words? The unfortunate answer for America is that behavior is *perfectly* aligned and correlated to the personality profile of a conspiracy theory addict.

Why? Because the actual act of believing in conspiracy theories is a psychological construct for these folks to seize back some semblance of control of their lives. It inflates their sense of importance—ring a bell? The self-worth building attraction is the key: By believing the conspiracy, it makes those people feel they are privy to "special knowledge" that the rest of the world is "too blind," "too dumb," or "too corrupt" to understand.

In other words, conspiracy theory belief is a special form of delusions of grandeur. Trump and other conspiracy theory addicts surround themselves with QAnon, "Deep State," FBI, and CIA conspiracies as routinely as a normal person acquires clothes or other things that make them feel more handsome or attractive. Conspiracy theory delusionists know something the world doesn't know, and that is a powerful shot of self-esteem mojo for the clinically insecure.

It's a manifestation of a lot of negative emotions, and not surprisingly the same emotions are shared by the crazy wing of the Trump Deplorables and the QAnon conspiracy believers. Yes, they are angry and frustrated, but psychologists tell us time and time again that conspiracy theorists also feel on a subconscious level that they are inferior, inadequate, misunderstood, and left behind by a system that "failed them."

Trump is like any populist in modern history: He stepped forward, validated the Deplorables' feelings, and in his delusional way promised them "only he" could and would make *all* their bad feelings go away. By accepting and buying into his delusional promises, they are tacitly choosing to believe their subjective feelings about empirical truth and facts vs. objective truth and fact.

The term for suspending empirical fact for illusion comes from WWE wresting fans: "kayfabe." Kayfabe is the psychological construct between the wrestler and the fan that they both know the performance is an illusion and rigged, but neither admits it because the fan came for the *feelings* and catharsis they get watching an immaculately staged and choreographed fixed outcome "match." (More on kayfabe, Fox News, and Trumpism later—it's just so fascinating!)

By definition, both conspiracy theorists and Trump cult-of-personality addicts are practicing kayfabe—their subconscious and conscious desire to feel better about themselves and cheer for their hero and boo their tribal enemies are much more important to them than the promises and statements that are made during the performance.

Of course the embrace and confluence of the psychological co-morbidities of kayfabe and conspiracy theorist make this person *highly* irrational and impossible to reason with. Presenting them with empirically proven facts or evidence or fact-checking evidence of Trump's 7.8 extraordinarily false and delusional statements per day doesn't even reach the logic part of their brains.

That is what a "psychological construct" of delusional conspiracies is: It's a way to see the world that makes the person feel more important, gain self-esteem, and inflate their self-worth and importance. When you combine conspiracy delusions with kayfabe and tribal levels of cultural or political partisanship, you get a very powerful cocktail of—wait for it—confirmation bias.

Now take a breath and get back to the story.

"So what do you mean by 'act like I am a cult leader'?" I asked my executive producer friend.

"I mean act like a cult leader/televangelist and write your scripts like you are a cult leader and only you have the answers to your audience's questions and fears."

He went on, "To kill it here at Fox News prime time, you have to understand the subconscious ID of the audience and get into their unconscious need for feeling pleasure and feeling better about themselves. Your brand is your right-wing, tribal cult persona—are you going to be a charismatic televangelist who makes them feel great or just another stuffed shirt talking head in a suit?

"Look—have you read Richard Hofstadter's book, *The Paranoid Style of American Politics*? If you haven't, I'll lend you my copy. Everyone in the opinion broadcast team at Fox News has read it. But the gist of what I am telling you is this: Ever since the days of Barry Goldwater, conservatism has more and more morphed into a sectarian version of Evangelical fundamentalism.

"With our audience now filled with Beck cult followers and God Squaders, the guys who are getting the best ratings treat their show like a cult meeting, and we produce the shows like they are a cult leader holding a cult meeting. Understand this: A high percentage of Fox News viewers in general belong to an Evangelical denomination. In fact, a decent percentage of Beck's viewers are Pentecostal—you know the speaking in tongues and faith healing types? If you want to be a Fox News host and have your own show, my advice is to attend a few Pentecostal services in Virginia and look around—that is what a lot of our base audience looks and thinks like."

I was stunned. For one thing, Beck is Mormon (okay, many folks do consider Mormonism a religious cult). But though the book he was talking about was printed in 1964, it read like it was printed as an audience profile of Fox News in mid-2009. As I thought about his words, I remembered I did speak at the very first Tea Party rally in DC earlier that year, and those old white folks were angry and had that sort of empty look in their eyes like they were at a tent revival and I was Elmer Gantry.

If you read the fabulous review of Hofstadter's research on how successful right-wing spokesmen apply the messages of Evangelical revivalists to US politics by University of North Carolina professor (emeritus) Robert Brent Toplin on historynewsnetwork.org, you will understand the tribal fundamentalist mindset of the Fox News audience better than I could ever describe. I should also mention again for context that (a) you now know that the brain of self-identified "conservatives" is much more sensitive and reactive to fear than the rest of us and (b) there are ninety-four million people in America who self-identify as "Evangelical believers."

Social scientists have long made the case that if you are a serious Evangelical believer you are the easiest person in the world to dupe and manipulate (because those who already believe in a thing that they can't see and for which there is no empirical evidence proves exists are the easiest people to sell ideas that require a leap-of-faith, ok?).

According to Professor Toplin, "Historians and pundits often refer to Hofstadter's ideas about the 'paranoid style.' Much-overlooked, however, is a subtheme in Hofstadter's writing. That discussion focused on the emergence of 'fundamentalism' in American politics. . . .

"Richard Hofstadter recognized that evangelical leaders were playing a significant role in right-wing movements of his time, but he noticed that a 'fundamentalist' style of mind was not confined to matters of religious doctrine. It affected opinions about secular affairs, especially political battles. Hofstadter associated that mentality with a 'Manichean [the ancient religion based on its belief in a binary world only comprised of darkness and light] and apocalyptic' mode of thought. He noticed that right-wing spokesmen applied the methods and messages of evangelical revivalists to U.S. politics. Agitated partisans on the right talked about epic clashes between good and evil, and they recommended extraordinary measures to resist liberalism. The American way of life was at stake, they argued. Compromise was unsatisfactory; the situation required militancy. Nothing but complete victory would do."

I went on to host more than fifty Fox opinion debate shows in my career, and I boiled down the Fox audience attraction and retention dynamic like this:

Modern conservatism is political fundamentalism + tribalism + cult. If you don't know how to preach, you don't have a future in hosting tribal partisan TV. If the audience does not emotionally connect with you as a fellow tribe member preaching the gospel of Fox News, go broadcast sports.

If you can't connect with the ID of the audience, you are just reading news or making commentary no viewer really cares about. Make their ID feel the pleasure feelings they lust over, and now you have an audience.

The American Foxocracy tribal right-wing media ecosystems conspiracy fantasies work because (a) an ignorant info-siloed audience is easily duped—as recent research shows Fox News viewers know less about the news than people who don't watch news at all—and (b) the FNC alternative reality is immune from facts because their fundamentalist faith—a personal belief that cannot be proven by ordinary empirical means—is easily substituted by a tribal TV cult leader like me for empirical reality.

Partisan tribal social identification is more important to everyday people than political ideology. When you understand the incredible power and potency of partisan identity politics, I could get anyone to believe just about anything I said as long as they identified *me* as a fellow conservative partisan. Most political science research tells us that partisan identity precedes partisan ideology in tribal/cult value—or what political scientist Lilliana Mason calls "identity-based ideology"—and that holds for either self-identified conservatives or liberals.

Most people don't watch tribal TV (or vote for that matter) for what they ideologically want. They watch tribal TV to validate and revalidate who they are, and for the binary that proves once again their chosen tribe is the light and the other tribe is darkness. That moral righteousness and superiority is self-esteem gold.

At the end of the day, identity politics is defined as "I am who I tribally label myself as," and trolling tribal identity is the only way to make it in tribal TV. It's really the only politics we've got in America.

Buck up buttercups—as the astute Kwame Anthony Appiah, a professor of philosophy and law at New York University, writes in the *Washington Post*, "To wish away identity politics is to wish away gravity. Successful politicians (and tribal TV hosts) know 'I'm with you' counts for much more than 'I'm for you.'"

CHAPTER 3

In America, Politics Are Tribal . . . Period

Americans—liberal elites specifically—deceive themselves into thinking that politics are rational and just adversarial, as if Rachel Maddow could just present the best slideshow set of facts and ideas ever and the left would immediately win the day.

I hate to break this to you, but American politics are not a college debate class. At the margins, they are tribal warfare and manipulated emotions—and have been throughout America's history.

Once I understood the power and psychology of televised tribal partisan hate porn and politics as a monetizable entertainment product, my other favorite topics of discussion with SVP Kathy was her take on the idea of politics as tribal warfare and on Fox News as weaponized military-grade political hate and social identity pornography. After all, she had worked with Roger Ailes and the famous dirty political tricks master Lee Atwater on the TV ad that blew up Michael Dukakis's presidential bid—among other forms of right-wing political warfare. (If you don't know the mind-boggling master of political dark arts, Lee Atwater, I suggest you read about or listen to a 1981 interview available on TheNation.com.)

You may remember the picture with Governor Dukakis in the tank. George Bush Sr. said he looked like Rocky the Squirrel. What Kathy (and others) told me about politics as tribal warfare opened my eyes to the depth of the Fox News conspiracy (and I am paraphrasing from multiple conversations): "News is just the 'beard,' or cover, for the real mission at Fox News. Conducting a televised conservative tribal war against liberalism and socialism is the mission."

When I learned this, everything I had seen in my time at Fox News finally made sense to me: Fixing the outcome of Fox News's opinion programming was right out of the Ailes/Atwood dirty tricks playbook.

As Tim Dickinson reports in his *Rolling Stone* article "How Roger Ailes Built the Fox News Fear Factory":

It was while working for Nixon that Ailes first experimented with blurring the distinction between journalism and politics, developing a knack for manipulating political imagery that would find its ultimate expression in Fox News. The reason was he knew his candidate was a disaster on TV. . . .

To bypass journalists, Ailes made Nixon the star of his own traveling roadshow—a series of contrived, news-like events that the campaign paid to broadcast in local markets across the country. Nixon would appear on camera in theaters packed with GOP partisans—"an applause machine," Ailes said, "that's all that they are." . . .

Ailes had essentially replaced professional journalists with everyday voters he could manipulate at will. "The events were not staged, they were fixed," says Rick Perlstein, the author of *Nixonland: The Rise of a President and the Fracturing of America*. . . .

As for actual journalists? "Fuck 'em," Ailes said. "It's not a press conference—it's a television show. Our television show. And the press has no business on the set." The young producer forced reporters to watch the events backstage on a TV monitor—just like the rest of America. "Ailes figured out a way to bring reporters to heel," Perlstein says.

To understand the Fox News tribal warfare playbook, understand that Roger Ailes and his team not only pioneered the idea of rigged political TV. They also pioneered fear and hate based TV attack ads.

So why does Fox News fix the outcomes of the white tribal opinion "debates" they produce and broadcast? The answer is the same—it's always been the same: If we did not control the narrative and outcome of the segment, the right-wing tribe member—even with his or her powerful built-in confirmation bias—was at risk of suffering the pain and confusion of processing noncongruent tribal evidence or information (tribal cognitive dissonance). If he did, he'd change the channel.

No "consistent conservative" tunes in to feel wrong or embarrassed about his political or cultural judgments. Have you ever met a person with strong feelings or opinions about anything that questioned themselves and found that they enjoyed being proven wrong? I never have.

Creating video content that by design allows viewers to see, hear and, most of all, feel their tribe's superiority to their tribal enemy and feel a climactic victory is the other white tribal identity porn superpower—and don't you forget it. Whether you are watching right- or left-wing tribal porn does not matter; by watching the porn, you are, either consciously or subconsciously, watching and listening to experience the exhilarating self-congratulatory self-esteem building feeling of your judgmental righteousness—and of course the dopamine and serotonin chemical hits that automatically turn your brain into a pleasure chest.

Let's look at some things I heard from my Fox News production colleagues, many of whom were masters of politics at tribal performance art. (I've condensed and paraphrased multiple discussions here.)

"Look, tribalism is just a code word for personal safety and 'us vs. them.' The ancient brain psychology is incredibly leverageable. Your in-group is safe, the out-group tribe unsafe." Check.

"Atwater taught that to win elections, you have to make your guy be the tribe that 51 percent or more of the electorate consciously and subconsciously—instinctively—wants to join. Which tribe do they want to join? The one that their subconscious feels is the safest for them and their family. Moral: Winning the war to the voter's subconscious is what wins elections." Check.

"One way to win elections is to make the opponent into an out-tribe that at least 51 percent of the electorate doesn't instinctively want to belong to, where they subconsciously feel less safe. In short, he or she with the safest personal-value proposition is the most attractive tribe to the voting electorate and wins." Said another way—personal attack ads work by making the other guy unelectable. Check.

"Politics and culture are all about the tribe, and therefore Fox News is all about the tribe and innate tribal instincts. We praise the tribal hero and vilify the tribal enemy. Tribal leaders play off of the same emotions of fear, hate, and blame. If they do the job well, hate and blame combine into an intense brew of tribal emotions that wins votes and viewers." Check.

Finally, I love this gem:

"In a political race, what you are selling is free membership into your candidate's tribe and the pitch is 'In my tribe, you and your family will be safer than the other tribe economically, physically, spiritually, culturally, and racially. In the other tribe, you will be less safe. In the other tribe, you will be dangerously exposed to unnecessary risk economically, physically, culturally, and racially. Dear voter, you and I have to keep that other tribe from power—by any means. This election is existential; your safety and your families' safety are at risk if we don't.'"

In other words, as I stated previously, attack ads don't make the advertiser attractive from an ideological perspective. They work when they make the other person more unelectable. For example, according to a *New Yorker* article written around the time of Lee Atwater's death in 1992: "When Mr. Atwater, President George H. W. Bush's young campaign manager, was contemplating how to defeat Michael Dukakis, he consulted *The Art of War*," by Sun Tzu, the well-known ancient Chinese political consultant. Among Sun Tzu's pithier bullet points: "Know your enemy." Atwater conducted a bit of opposition research, identified Dukakis's vulnerabilities, and gleefully promised to "strip the bark off the little bastard." The two TV spots ended Dukakis's political career.

I was taught at Fox News what you must learn: Yes, politics may be seen as the civilized way (in contrast with war) for organized conflict, but it's the reverse of the famous Carl Von Clausewitz bromide ("War is merely the continuation of politics by other means"): American politics and culture are merely tribal wars continued by other means.

Roger and Kathy didn't see political and cultural information as news; they saw it as potential ammunition to be used against our liberal enemy during opinion segments. I figured out later this was totally congruent with the Ailes political advertising strategy of "make 'em hate the other guy more than my guy" and the attack ad goal to make the other person more unelectable. It was Roger and Kathy's job to evaluate the political and cultural ammunition of the day for its potency and lethality because watching that tribal warfare and victory story transpire was entertaining to our audience.

What I learned was the genius of the Fox News "fair and balanced" grift: Under the pretense of news and patina of a traditional TV newscast, we could claim to our audience that ours was the only even-handed approach to politics and search for the common good via "reasoned adversarial civic debate."

But on the second floor (in the executive offices) and in the seventeenth-floor halls of opinion-programming production teams, those who needed to knew that we at Fox News were really just in the original business of the Atwater and Ailes political ad agency. Politics as weaponized, scripted, rigged performance art was not just politics as monetizable entertainment, but was also a call to arms for the right wing of America to fight back against "the darkness"—the hated and feared liberalism sold every day by the vile and evil liberal media.

"TOBY—DON'T GET WONKY—FOX NEWS VIEWERS AREN'T POLITICAL THINK TANK JUNKIES— THEY ARE IDENTITY JUNKIES"

The final lesson I got from my FNC executive producer friends was *after* I hosted a few shows on Fox Business Channel. At FBN I got to write my own live opening segment copy, unlike at FNC where I performed my Fox News hit man job according to how my segment producer wanted me to lay into our token liberal prop-of-the-day.

I had always thought of our Fox Business audience as somewhere high on the spectrum of political junkies. I simply thought that to spend so much of their time watching us duke it out with the liberal guests/props, they were into the big ideas and my job was to stone my opponent with fabulous policy and ideological correctness.

While a few Fox News viewers are, I am sure, legit right-wing political junkies, I was mostly wrong. What I learned from my executive producer friend was a very important lesson about the conservative Fox News tribal audience: They are old. They are more interested in validating the righteous superiority of their social identity as a conservative and me defining the inferior "otherness" of the enemy tribe than in listening to me being ideologically wonky.

This idea is what associate professor of government and politics Lilliana Mason of the University of Maryland describes in her paper "Ideologies Without Issues" as the "ideology of identity" vs. "issue-based ideology."

What another executive producer told me was pure tribal and cultural identity TV gold. "First off, the idea that people vote for or don't vote for what they 'want' is wrong. What they vote for is who they feel they are— who they consider their home team to be. White conservatives are proud tribe members, so they believe in all the same orthodoxy and liturgy they hear over and over and over again. If you know a person is a self-identified 'conservative'—you also know where they stand on guns, on abortion, on the military, on taxes, on immigration, yadda yadda."

Key Point: "Toby, you gotta write and preach down to who these white middle class people are and write to that persona—not up. For your sermon to connect you gotta stop writing to your country club buddies. Here's what I give my producers when I hire them so they can write compelling teases and emotionally powerful openings. I call this process 'Emotional Target Practice'—to aim your tease and sermon to where their emotional and cultural orthodoxies were and compare and contrast to how different and scary liberals and liberal orthodoxy are today. Because their cultural and political orthodoxies are so permanently affixed to their sixty-five-year-old psyches, hitting and triggering their emotional targets ain't that hard, pal!"

He was so right. That was the best description of the Fox News tribal identity porn production process I ever heard—emotional target practice. I define the process as targeting the audience's latest and rawest open emotional wound or deepest rooted and most sensitive cultural raw nerve and analyzing the current news flow for the widest delta or amount of change from the way the Fox News audience was culturally raised and most likely still believes.

After writing dozens of show opening "sermons," I came to think of my goal as panning for emotional gold. Here is Fox News's audience persona playbook I was taught to write and "preach" to as an FNC talk show host. The important issue here is this is FNC's emotional manipulation playbook for their Millennial and Gen-X aged segment producers to get their heads into the Fox viewer's geriatric emotional operating system. The idea is simple— these are the potential deep-rooted emotional targets for the emotional target practice required to find the cultural nerve of the day and hit it!

As mentioned, the segment producers get the Daily Target List that goes out to all executive producers and producers every morning—the new emotional heresies/issues of the day. Think of this audience persona guide as the "evergreen" emotional hit list—these are the deepest-rooted beliefs and cultural morals that people over sixty were born and raised with and, most important, still hold dear and believe in.

We at Fox News create and produce our tribal identity programming *specifically* to emotionally manipulate the most vulnerable people in America: elderly, red state, small city, and rural living folks who self-identify as political/cultural conservatives. Think of Fox News as the vote hackers that came *before* the Russian vote hackers!

The geriatric Fox News audience is unified under one global emotional umbrella: They viscerally feel the country they morally, culturally, politically, and economically understand isn't here anymore. They are both pissed off about it and, at the same time, scared existentially shitless about this sorry state of affairs they viscerally feel and perceive.

To understand how to produce weapons-grade right-wing tribal identity fear and hate porn, you first have to know how our age sixty-eight or older target audience are culturally imprinted and wired with the old school "OG" cultural rules of mid-1950s and '60s.

Back then, all of us WASPy white folk had the same baker's dozen of basic cultural norms, family rules, and off-limits taboos that you followed or your parents kicked you out of *their* house—and you went to hell too:

- You went to church on Sunday unless you were Jewish (like you knew any?)—and as Martin Luther King said, the "most segregated place in America was a church pew at 11:00 a.m. Sunday."

- You got confirmed Protestant, Catholic, or Episcopal. Some went to Bible Study and became a born-again Baptist or Evangelical. But no matter what, you learned the catechism and rules of your faith or you got the paddle. By the way, Cassius Clay was not Islamic to you: He was a fallen Baptist. You thought Islam was from the story of "Aladdin and the Forty Thieves."

- You got married before you had children and strived to stay married for their sake because kids came first and your marriage second. Unless you lived in New York City, if you got divorced you were shameful and shunned. If you got divorced twice you were a closet homosexual.

- You got the education you needed for gainful employment, worked hard, and avoided idleness. Vacations were a drive to see your relatives or camp in a national park. If your mom worked, that meant your father was a slacker and your family needed the money.

- You voted how your parents voted, and if they voted for FDR and Harry Truman, then you voted Democrat, or you were in the doghouse at family holiday events for a while.

- You went the extra mile for your employer or client—if you did you got a lifetime job and a full pension.

- You were a patriot, ready to serve the country, and you knew your family and neighbors would be proud of your service.

- You were neighborly, civic-minded, and charitable—God was watching and judging you.

- You avoided coarse language in public and never talked politics, sex, or religion at the dinner table or with company.

- You were respectful of authority and if pulled over by law enforcement you STFU except for "yes sir" and "no sir."

- Drugs were for ghetto thugs or jazz musicians.

- TV time was *after* a sit-down dinner with the family except for sports and for special occasions approved by your parents.

- LGBTQ was a string of capitalized alphabet letters. If you were gay or lesbian, tough it out and do that stuff somewhere else—I don't want to know. Oh yea—if you were homosexual, you're going to hell.

If you've ever watched Fox News opinion programming, now you know one of the core ways they produce tribal and cultural identity segments. They take all those core, old school 1950s and '60s cultural rules, values, and behaviors and then display in high-def living color how liberals and liberalism are destroying their beloved culture and country right in front of the viewer's eyes with lots of sounds and moving graphics.

Frankly, it was too easy to manipulate these old geezers. At its core, Fox News is just Russia's Internet Research Agency troll farm without the vodka and borscht.

Key Point: What Fox News shows its audience is the America Fox News wants them to see—an emotionally traumatic mirror image of the old-school world they knew, loved, desperately miss, and sentimentally wish they could return to.

In other words, the Fox News tribal warfare playbook was Trump before Trump. His white tribe supremacy normalizing shtick just expanded his brand by letting white ethno-nationalists take their masks off and be who they always wanted to be in public.

I really learned as a Fox anchor about writing and performing a live or "cold open" was what in 2019 we term cultural or political "trolling." My job in the first sixty to ninety seconds of every tribal identity porn show is an example of:

- their worst cultural and political nightmare.

- all the most current sociocultural and political disasters and societal pathologies from the most up-to-the-hour white ethno-nationalist tribal grievance list which we repeat and dog whistle like a digital bumper sticker every few minutes.

What are the right-wing tribal grievance classics, you ask? Here is the list my executive producer and producer friends helped me develop (in no particular order):

- Our working-class jobs are being stolen by illegal immigrants who live twelve to a house.

- Legal immigrants are stealing high-paying technology jobs by taking lower salaries than what "normal" white Americans are paid or willing to work for.

- Too few white Americans qualify for the jobs available today because the government spends the money that should go to retraining them for the twenty-first century on welfare and food stamps for lazy grifters.

- Male working-age labor-force participation rates are at Great Depression-era lows because we shipped the good manufacturing and assembly line jobs to China, Mexico, and everywhere else so coastal elites could pay for their private jets and country club memberships.

- Opioid abuse is widespread because the coastal and political elites sold white Americans down the river with their "globalist" hatred and lack of respect for the hard-working flyover America.

- Homicidal violence plagues inner cities because *those* people are inbred animals—let 'em kill each other but keep them contained in their inner-city kill zone.

- Almost half of all children in America are born out of wedlock because *those* people are inbred sub-humans who listen to rap music and smoke crack all day or are atheists who don't go to church on Sunday.

- Single mothers raise almost 50 percent of these out of wedlock half-breed children because white people pay for their food stamps, welfare checks, and subsidized housing.

- Many college students lack basic skills because we spend so much money educating and providing lunch for illegal immigrants and chain-family immigration that we don't have enough teachers for the real Americans.

- Our high school students rank below those from two dozen other countries because they take care of their *own* and they have *walls*.

- George Soros and other socialists fund *every* large protest in America.

- Under Obummer, we weren't even allowed to say Merry Christmas by the Obummer PC police.

- Also, if we forgot something, blame Saul Alinsky.

However, Fox News never fails to play the "Primal Disrespect and Payback's a MOFO" card: Watch the Tucker Carlson Show. *All* he does now is show the audience how the last of the good stuff remaining in their life is now being stolen, raped, and pillaged from them by their arch tribal enemies—those smug, disrespectful, and condescending know-it-all coastal elite libtards who brought you:

- The Great Recession in 2008–2009 and zero after inflation working-class household income raises since 1982.

- Bailouts of the bankers and mortgage thieves with nary a perp walk or jail time.

- Spending $6 trillion in nation building and wasting tens of thousands of their grandkids' lives and futures on never-ending wars.

- But looking the other way when eleven million illegal immigrants swam into America to steal working-class jobs.

In short: At Fox News, we turned emotionally manipulating, trolling, and tormenting the crap out of our disillusioned and tribalized white audience into a sporting event. All that's missing is a scoreboard on the direct hits and strikeouts.

At the end of my TV host training, I was pretty good at preaching the white and right gospel (if I do say so myself). I did over fifty shows as a guest host.

Key Point: Evolutionary psychologists tell us that all humans are encoded with an "immune system" against uncomfortable thoughts. So Fox News doesn't broadcast uncomfortable thoughts or tribal heresies much past the first liberal salvo in the segment. After the opening ninety second or so rant, the host and script blows up and exposes the opening heresy for the "lies" they are. This fear, depression, anxiety, then rekindled hope and ultimate triumph protocol is what I later learned was the Roger Ailes right-wing tribal identity engagement-and-addiction formula.

It turned out that addicting old white guys to tribal identity porn is pretty damn easy. Sitting at home all comfy in your favorite chair mainlining self-esteem building tribal confirmation biased news, commentary, and opinion debates is literally the perfect emotionally addictive product.

CHAPTER 4

My Road to Fox News Enlightenment 2000–2018

I traveled a nineteen-year journey to Fox News enlightenment.

It took me that long to get the actual answers to the questions I could never answer completely during my fourteen years inside FNC. I had to step outside and engage with my direct personal experiences meeting Fox News fanatics, had to observe the Fox News Rain Man act a thousand times to find answers: What on earth would drive a normal human being to watch six or more hours of fear-and-hate-based anything without a gun to their head?

What unmet emotional need were we fulfilling?

It wasn't news—as mentioned, Fox News viewers constantly rate as knowing *less* about American news than Americans who watch *zero* televised news.

Why did the thousands of people who have come to meet me in public over the years (and still do every day when I am out in public within a red state zip code) always say the same things to me, like a population of Dustin Hoffman's character Raymond in *Rain Man*?

Why did the people who seek to connect with me always act like we are all members of some cult?

Why did so many of them think they have a Spock-like mind-meld connection and psychic bond with me?

Why are the Fox News "newsroom," news staff, and news bureaus about 50 percent smaller than those at CNN and CNBC, where I had also performed?

Why did Fox News not have an ethics and standards/practices/retraction/corrections department like the other televised news operations I had appeared on (CNN, Bloomberg, CNBC, CNNFN)?

Why did FNC's opinion programming televangelists and their mostly twenty-something-year-old production staffers have actual offices on the upper floors of the News Corp. building at 1211 Sixth Avenue in midtown Manhattan instead of being jammed into shared cubes like the "news department?"

Why did every producer I ever worked with or met profess their fealty to right-wing politics as if they were trained seals afraid of not getting a sardine from their boss?

Why did we hire a real live World Wrestling Entertainment superstar to be a business and markets analyst on our business and markets show?

I mean really—what would you think if every time you got identified and stopped in public, you got the same identical routine from people who evinced almost no grasp of what they were actually watching and why they were watching it for six hours a day?

I just could not figure it out—why didn't they know or understand that Fox News's "opinion-debate" programming was just a scam—a very well-produced and professional televised grift?

It never made any sense to me until I broke the routine and my questions down and researched them one by one. These unanswered questions also led to other unanswered questions or conundrums:

Why were these Foxholes oblivious to the fact that their carefully programmed and choreographed climax ("Wow! That felt great to watch you put a body slam on that libtard idiot!") was derived from a successfully produced and directed tribal cultural warfare-as-entertainment performance? Couldn't they see that it depended on the producers of this scripted political or cultural shit show accurately following the Fox News tribal cultural warfare playbook and carefully selecting mostly white Anglo-Saxon heroes and hitting our marks and disemboweling our hapless "just glad to be here" liberal props?

Why were they oblivious to the fact that while performing that seven-to-eight-minute segment, our tribal fear-and-hate porn, we had made a quick visit to the viewer's brain stem—you know the part of our brain still equipped with the primal/primordial caveman fight-or-flight limbic system programmed via evolution (sorry creationists) to involuntarily spit out seriously powerful and addictive fight-or-flight chemicals that control our involuntary fear/hate reflexes and blast a massive dose of the heroin-strength brain chemical serotonin (which is partly what Foxholes are unknowingly hooked on)?

Can't the viewer/user/tribal warfare addict, ensconced in his favorite chair and drinking beverages in the comfort of his own home, understand why he always leaves the opinion debate segment with the same all-important self-esteem and ego building feelings of (a) smug intellectual superiority, (b) absolute moral and cultural righteousness, (c) the thrill of watching another stated gladiatorial bread-and-circus victory over "Them"—their Metro America, microaggression-and–cultural-appropriating, PC sensitive, latte and smoothie swilling sworn tribal enemy (as opposed to merely a person with a different political perspective and opinion)?

Did they really think this stuff happened by accident?

My dear, longtime friend and host of my weekly *Bulls & Bears* program Brenda Buttner answered me one night while enjoying our post-performance victory cigar and martini when I ignorantly asked her, "Hey B—why do we always get such liberal morons on our show, and why do the guys like me always outpunch and beat the shit out of those poor folks?"

Brenda told me, "Jeez, Toby—what the hell do you think our producers get paid for? It takes a lot of work to make you guys look so smart and our liberal of the week so dumb!"

She left out "token window dressing prop," but she had her reasons.

So there you have it. If you for some reason watched me on Fox News and had not yet figured out my whole act and our "fair and balanced" "opinion debates" were rigged, well, they were (and they continue to be).

We duped the audience, the guests, and many contributors too.

But until late 2012, I didn't really care enough to understand why this viewer *Rain Man* act happened over and over again with the elderly audience members I met. The fact that I got a $5,000 check every week for working a few hours, plus weekly first-class round-trip tickets from DC to New York City, was a very effective curiosity de-stimulant.

And honestly, for most of my years at Fox News I really thought our little faux debate programming charade was just harmless entertainment— you know, like a nerf-gun battle with words as the foam missiles. Nobody got hurt and nobody's eye got popped out.

But eventually, the result of my three-year journey into discovering why Fox News opinion programming had such a universally powerful psychological and emotional impact on our deeply and tribally right-wing enculturated fans led me to this conclusion: All my assumptions about Fox News's tribal warfare programming were dead wrong.

I first discovered how deeply ignorant I was about the polarizing cultural impact of Fox News on Retro Americans in early November 2012. I was on a Fox News personality speaking tour of south Arkansas the day after President Obama won a second term. There, over three days, I met and talked extensively with more than a thousand members of our core small city and rural Retro America audience. Those seventy-two hours were the very first time I had actually conversed with the Fox News Retro America core audience beyond the obligatory airport or restaurant handshake.

Also bear in mind that until Donald Trump ran for POTUS and won, for a number of reasons that we all now understand are highly correlated to FNC's tribal fear and hate programming grift, I considered myself apolitical and happily lived my entrepreneur/capitalist life behind my gated "one-percenter" bubble (which now I understand makes me hated by Retro America as part of the "elite." Who knew? I thought I was their hero!).

When I actually visited Fox News/MAGA/Retro America flyover country, it was to do a corporate speech to rich corporate Republicans, play golf, or hunt some great BBQ. When I talked politics for free, it was only with my rich country club conservative friends and not the FNC viewer hoi polloi. First rule of being a TV contributor/tribal identity mercenary—you never open your mouth near a microphone without payment.

But on that late 2012 speaking trip to south Arkansas and after many speeches and Q&A sessions with thousands of real, true blue Fox News folks of all ages, I discovered the other hiding-in-plain-sight truths about my adoring, virtually all white working and middle class Fox News followers.

My epiphany was this: The operative issue for understanding these fine Retro America folks whose eyeballs we sold to catheter and dried food end-of-days advertisers was not that they were just clueless bumpkins duped by our highly choreographed emotional manipulation grift or duped by our fake "fair and balanced" debate deception. What spooked me was that these adoring folks of all ages looked at me and talked to me just like the old white-haired people in the airport did—like I really was a living apostle from the hallowed monastery of hatred toward liberal latte sippers.

More shocking: After I told thousands of these true believers in the lecture halls and Q&A sessions time and time again that they (like the proverbial poker game) were being played as suckers in Fox News's fake fair-and-balanced opinion panel grift and all we were doing was a seven-minute pro wrestling match in $2,000 Brioni suits, they:

1. Didn't care.

2. Or didn't believe me.

3. Or didn't understand the concept of grifting.

And in most cases all three.

Like most said to me after my "big reveal" about Fox News: "Toby, what am I going to do, watch MSNBC or CNN?"

Why didn't they care? Why were they not outraged in the slightest about being lied to and manipulated by me and Fox News and monetized to the tune of billions of dollars every year in profits?

Why do these same mostly Evangelical people not care a lick about the integrity or mendacity or immoral behavior of the person they undoubtedly voted for POTUS in 2016?

Cue Vince McMahon, Dr. Phil, Joel Osteen, and Donald J. Trump—they all know the answer. Hell, any professional grifter knows. These tribalized Retro American Fox News addicts don't care because—well—it's complicated.

And *that* is what the rest of this book answers:

- What are Fox News's tribal warfare "plays" in the FNC tribal warfare playbook?

- What are the other innate human psychological vulnerabilities that Fox News's unfair and imbalanced grift preys on?

- Why do so many people fall for it hook, line, and sinker?

But to steal a great insight by political strategists Salena Zito and Brad Todd in their book on the 2016 presidential election *The Great Revolt*, "the history of the American electorate is not a litany of flukes; instead it is a pattern of tectonic plate-grinding, punctuated by a landscape-altering earthquake every generation or so."

Look, the introduction of a round-the-clock tribalized white conservative political/cultural TV channel was indeed a tectonic earthquake in America. The introduction of two hundred highly demographic and psychographic targeted cable TV channels in every home was a tectonic media earthquake. The demise of highly profitable city newspapers (that lost their want ads and classified ad cash cows to Craigslist and LinkedIn) was a news media altering earthquake that continues to send even stronger aftershocks today.

But what I found more than anything feeding the demand for the

Foxocracy Hot Pot of white tribal identity porn is the radical decline of the income, health, opportunity, and social fabric of the once highly functional Retro America. That and the creation of the working poverty class (the ALICE households we talked about earlier—Asset Light/ Income Constrained/Employed class). The creation of a 115 million strong American working-poor class is the biggest cultural and economic earthquake to hit the nation in a hundred years.

And by now you should understand this—*real* news and *real* journalism are not grifts—they are highly valuable services. That is why most people watch their local news station. They want to know what is happening with the weather tomorrow, who won the game tonight, and what parts of town are experiencing bumper-to-bumper traffic from road construction.

But the term "news" serves as the cloaking device at Fox News. In between the tribal emotions grift programming there *is* some real news broadcasting.

What makes the Fox News tribal warfare grift so successful is the audience demographics—many tests have proven old white people can't tell the difference between "the news" and "tribal fear and hate porn." Almost 80 percent of Fox News viewers think Sean Hannity is a "journalist" even though Sean himself will tell you he's a political talk show host.

That's how a great grift works—the person being grifted doesn't know it, doesn't want to believe it.

Most FNC viewers grew up with three channels of TV and authoritative high integrity news anchors—think Cronkite, Huntly, and Brinkley. Recent social media sharing data shows that the worst forwarders of truly fake news (from Russian trolls, etc.) are—wait for it—people over fifty-five! People over fifty-five are also the fastest-growing population on Facebook—see a pattern?

Does Fox News have a plan to target the younger Gen-X and Millennial "cord cutters" conservative audience? They have started a streaming Fox News Nation app with young glorious hosts and cameos from the older hosts. They do not release subscription data, but insiders I have talked to say the subscriber count is "a rounding error and mostly older 'super fans.'"

I visited a Fox News Nation event in Phoenix recently—I can tell you there was not a person under age fifty to be found.

Just like Donald Trump's electoral coalition smashed both American political parties to the chagrin of the political news punditariat, the media experts analyzing Fox News and Trumpism continue to blow it every time they predict the coming demise of each entity. Clearly something big was going on with Fox News—and all I read and heard was crickets and confusion from the journalists (with a few exceptions as noted).

To get some answers, for three years after the 2016 election I went on a personal journey deep into the minds and hearts of Trump's Deplorables and Fox News addicts to discover and define what we call in consumer marketing "the target audience persona." What emerged is a group of citizens who cannot simply be described by terms like "angry," "male," "rural," "bigoted," and "racist." Fox News addicts, defined by me and addiction professionals as people who watch more than three hours of Fox News opinion programming per day, span job descriptions but share income brackets, education levels, and geography.

What unites them is not their shared "isms and ists" but the innate DNA-driven need to:

- Build and feel positive self-esteem, and rebuild shattered or bruised egos in a world that does not fit their worldview and calls them scum for their non-PC sins.

- Feel they are part of an important cause much bigger and more important than themselves.

- Put traditional white culture and Christian Evangelicalism before Inside-the-Beltway "swamp dweller" conservative ideology.

- Put "localism" before globalism.

- Get respect for their Retro American culture, which is disrespected constantly by traditional political media, from Behind-the-Beltway Washington, from the "liberal" political news media, the television entertainment, and movie industry, and of course the higher education academic industry.

- And, most important, to have *all* their nonpolitically or culturally correct non-PC words/feelings/beliefs normalized and proven righteously correct on the most powerful thing in their lives—their home TV set.

Everyone in the media seems to think this "crazy right-wing Fox News uncle" syndrome and estranged family situation affects just a small group; but the actual data tells a much different and frankly shocking story.

It turned out selling white tribal fear, hatred, blame, and resentment as a cathartic entertainment product under the pretense of news was just what a whole lot of Retro Americans needed in a new century that many don't really understand.

It turned out that providing a hermetically sealed alternative digital universe where Retro Americans feel safe and sheltered from being stigmatized as bigots, racists, homophobes, or backward-thinking twentieth-century dunces by self-proclaimed "color blind" and heterogeneous "we're the all-inclusive party" liberals is one hell of a business model.

MY FINAL LESSON LEARNED

By the end of 2012, I had learned what the Fox News tribal warfare playbook was and how it worked. What I did not know is why it worked so well and what real damage it was inflicting. Truth be told, I still thought the whole Fox News thing was a harmless partisan World Wrestling Entertainment spin-off network: a highly choreographed show for lonely old flyover state right-wingers with nothing better to do.

With the median age of Fox News viewers at sixty-eight, I still felt like we were giving them a cheap thrill and a way to get their heart started and blood boiling again. But by 2016, I was fairly stunned that no veteran Fox News insider or investigative media had come clean and told the real behind-the-scenes story about Fox News and our powerful brand of tribal identity pornography. Like all journalists I'd read and studied Marshall McLuhan's 1964 book *Understanding Media*. I understood exactly what he meant when he said, "The medium is the message. This is merely to say that the personal and social consequences of any medium that is of any extension of ourselves result from the new scale that is introduced into our affairs by each extension of ourselves, or by any new technology."

I understood what McLuhan's "new scale" meant. I understood that he was specifically referring to electronic media, which shaped collective, "tribe"-based identities.

But what no one seemed to have yet grasped were the social and personal consequences and the sheer scale of this new ubiquitous feedback loop.

This massively scaled, self-reinforcing feedback loop is truly, as McLuhan said, a very real extension of us. More accurately, it reflects our cultural and political identities.

It was created and mastered by the king of red state psychological warfare Roger Ailes and company, which now reaches (via social media multiplier effect) the one hundred million self-siloed Americans locked into algorithmically selected echo chambers of their own cultural and political cognitive confirmation bias.

I'd also read and reread Noam Chomsky's classic book *Manufacturing Consent*. I thought any good journalist that had read his groundbreaking work was fully aware (to paraphrase Chomsky) that audience deception was baked into just about everything in American life. So why hadn't some smart media reporter figured out and reported on our little scam?

As Matt Taibbi points out—with my comments in parentheses—in his 2019 book *Hate, Inc.*, "*Manufactured Consent*'s central idea was that censorship (and embedded political propaganda and emotional manipulation) in the United States was not overt, but covert. The key to this deception (grift) is that Americans, every day, see vigorous debate going on in the press. This deceives them into thinking propaganda (and emotional manipulation) is absent. *Manufacturing Consent* explains that the debate you're watching is choreographed. The range of argument has been artificially narrowed long before you get to hear it. It's a subtle, highly idiosyncratic process that you can stare at for a lifetime and not see."

Tim Dickinson published "How Roger Ailes Built the Fox News Fear Factory" in *Rolling Stone* and described the creation of the most profitable propaganda machine in history.

Okay, so Chomsky, McLuhan, Dickinson, and Taibbi get it—but what happened to the rest of the media? At this point, you must understand that I knew a lot more than the average on-air contributor about the real behind-the-scenes story and FNC's programming shenanigans. I lived it, helped produce it, and I wrote it and performed it thousands of times. Also, since 2000, unlike other paid FNC contributors, I was required to be at the New York City FNC studios every week to tape my show, *Bulls & Bears*.

I saw up close how the sausage was made. I had a few insiders that leaked me the "forbidden" daily e-memos from Ailes and John Moody, our SVP of News at Fox News, that basically told the producers:

- What stories to cover and not cover.

- How Ailes/Moody wanted these big-emotion trigger stories covered.

- What was the right-wing slant Roger/Moody and the White House wanted.

- Who were the good guy heroes to praise and the bad guys to attack.

For eight years "The Memo" also told us what the Bush White House thought reporters, hosts, and producers should talk about.

I never asked why I was the only co-star of my weekly show required to be in New York City. I found out why later, and it will make sense, trust me. (It was not my stunning looks.)

I also learned a lot more than most about the Fox News tribal identity activation and validation playbook because I gladly served as a guest anchor for vacationing anchors. I wrote my own monologues for those shows—and I gotta admit that was a lot of fun.

And don't forget—by using the secret Ailes/Moody Memo and becoming a go-to guest host, it was actually part of my job to dupe the other journalists and liberal guests. Obviously, I had the whole tribal-identity porn-star televangelist act down cold enough for the producers to trust me to perform it on live TV. Still, with my real job as a financial journalist/equities analyst/newsletter publisher (www.transformityresearch.com), the analyst inside me was always curious to learn more about Fox's tribal ID TV production cult secrets. I knew there was so much more they were not telling me.

Money talks, too, of course, and I was hoping to position myself for a multimillion dollar cable TV hosting job when the next FNC opinion host blew himself up by saying something really racist or libelous on live TV and spooked brand advertisers (think Glenn Beck and his "Obama hates white people" gaffe in 2011).

About halfway through President Obama's second term, my snooping and quest for a full-time Fox News opinion anchor gig had grown into a mild obsession.

Note: Although the original big bang for Fox News tribal identity activation TV was the late 1990s Lewinsky scandal/Clinton impeachment run-up—when thoughtful political debate in America transformed from "Who do you believe" to "Whose side are you on?"—it was the day after Obama was elected POTUS that Fox News 2.0, "The Obama Bashing Network" strategy, started and the ratings exploded.

By 2013 I had sponsored hundreds of late night/early morning cocktails and conducted off-the-record conversations with enough Fox News opinion show hosts, producers, and executives (plus I had hosted enough shows by then) to finally decode the last of the production and content secrets they were all sworn to keep silent. Those stories and lessons I have recreated here, focusing on the most meaningful.

I even gave the whole rigged outcome programming production process a code name in my iPhone notes section—I jokingly called my tribal identity TV notes "The Fox News Playbook of Tribal Warfare."

I also reaffirmed that many of the other contributors I hung out with or performed with were as clueless as the audience about the Fox News/Roger Ailes grift and production dirty tricks.

None of them got the daily memo. Fox News personnel had grown increasingly paranoid of being turned in and fired for sharing the playbook or sharing the "opposition research" that came from the fourteenth floor of 1211 Sixth Avenue. Nobody was willing to send it outside the building, really. Note: The Fox News basement is where the cramped "news" pods were—the secret "Research" department looking for the next made-up or contrived moral or cultural panic bomb we could drop on Obama plied their trade from luxurious offices on the fourteenth floor. I am sure this psy ops team is still there today.

Most contributors that I worked with were only at Fox via satellite, rather than on set in the New York City studios where the production teams worked their magic. Those contributors were mostly just happy to "build their brand" and pundit bona fides performing on Fox News.

But then everything changed for me and America in July 2015.

On my office TV I watched in astonishment as a real life WWE Hall of Fame grifter and longtime, hard core binge-watching Foxhole (the same certifiable crazy blowhard ignoramus I, as a guest anchor, had interviewed multiple times for Fox Business) glided down a gold-tinged escalator in Trump Tower NYC just like the old Gorgeous George pro wrestling character I had watched as a kid.

I watched, mortified, as this real estate mogul who had inherited every advantage and now had become a low-rent reality TV grifter—the one and thankfully only Donald J. Trump—morphed into a professional Foxhole. Trump performed a flawless twenty-minute Fox News opinion host impersonation to the entire world—and without a Fox News opinion segment producer!

Worse, Trump had my unofficial Fox News Tribal Warfare Playbook down cold—and it was still only in my head, for crying out loud! Was he getting the FNC daily memo too? Trump's only deviation from our emotional grift was to dispense with the coded racial language and metaphors used at Fox News and actually call Mexicans "rapists and murderers!" *Holy crap— you can't run for POTUS and say that crap on TV!* I said to myself. (Okay, I did not say "crap.")

By the end of his POTUS campaign kickoff in NYC, to my utter amazement and chagrin, the Donald from Queens I knew as a long-time Big Apple liberal and Democratic Party member had performed the perfect grift. He morphed into a Fox News opinion televangelist clone and was channeling the highly trained conservative populist performance artist Pat Buchanan too. As a candidate, he said things and used words that if I used them on the air, I would have been fired.

He used every Roger Ailes/Fox News production trick you'll find in this book. And since this book that you are reading did not exist, he had amazingly absorbed the entire Fox News tribal warfare playbook via osmosis—and I am sure ten thousand hours of "executive time" watching Fox News.

To top this all off, at first even Roger Ailes hated Donald Trump! But truth be told, Donald Trump is truly a white tribal activation and validation grifting genius. He just switched political sides and morphed into a right-wing culturist and political populist because he, above all else, has a feral sense of the opportunity for a world-class grift. He never thought he'd win, as the truth tellers close to him have disclosed. He just thought he could build his audience and brand and who knows—a Trump TV channel?

Trump had learned what I had learned after performing in thousands of opinion segment appearances—how to inject the right-wing audience's bulging veins with the emotional stimulants of fear, hate, contempt, resentment, victimhood, and above all liberal/PC-induced shame.

It did not hurt him either that his Deplorables had suffered massive amounts of chronic economic trauma or that cultural and political resentment was overflowing from the psyches of old white working-class America and PC-hating business conservatives.

He spoke simply, at the fifth-grade level I was taught to use by Fox producers ("Hey Toby—you wanna take your rhetoric down about five notches to the real world and make your point in American?").

Most important—the Trumpian form of tribal activation and cultural validation had two amazing results for the traditional political news industry: he jacked up *both* right- and left-wing tribal identity and validation TV networks (and the social media giants who had become tribal identity programming distributors). With Trump performances to sell, they were all making a ton of money.

With Metro America and Retro America seemingly at war, we now had a self-reinforcing feedback loop on both sides: What was Democratic/liberal cognitive dissonance content was also Republican/Deplorable confirmation bias! The more fear, anger, and hatred sewn and fertilized by Fox News's fully weaponized tribal identity porn aimed at its Retro America audience, the more similar levels of fear, disgust, and anger grew in the liberal Metro America trenches.

Both sides were (and still are) in a manic race to the bottom of their partisan audience's brain stem to stoke ever higher levels of involuntary fight-or-flight reflex.

Trump not only tapped into his audience's deep reservoirs of shame, contempt, and resentment that had come into their psyches via Obama's scolding politically correct lectures ("Listen to me—let me tell you what it means to be American . . ."). Trump's candidacy gave birth to the "Foxocracy," a fully aligned, twenty-four-hour, TV-to-pulpit united front of hatred toward liberals.

Trump gave his mostly Fox News audience what they had only dreamed of: permission to break free. "Thank you, Jesus!" they exclaimed—and strangest of all, the most religious part of the Foxocracy really did say "Thank you, Jesus and God, for giving us this thrice married, porn star banging, pathological liar and all-around sociopath Donald Trump!"

How did that happen?

The Fox News/Trump TV/Christian televangelist grift sells right-wing cultural heaven on earth—a very real emotional day-and-night spa and safe place from being constantly shamed by Metro America.

Anyway, after hearing and meeting Trump's "base" up close (in the rallies I attended out of deep curiosity), I also could not help but notice that the #MAGA/"Lock Her Up" T-shirt wearing folks spoke exactly like Trump.

Why? Well now it's obvious—they had binge-watched thousands of hours of fake Fox News "debates." Those stadiums were packed with a lot of Foxholes. They also had been preconditioned for Trumpism from forty years of listening to right-wing talk radio in their cars and trucks. They loved all the "trumped up" accusations and half-baked truths he was slinging because he validated and normalized what they already had come to subjectively believe as objective "facts" for decades.

But psychologically more important, they wanted to believe his delusions and illusions as objective fact, like WWE wrestling fans do. Trump's Deplorables were on the same page because they spoke the same language, and he was selling a more intense version of the shows they'd been binge-watching on FNC for twenty years.

Wow, I thought in stunned silence, *Did I just see what I think I saw? Did Fox News spawn an incarnate version of itself?*

And why not? We at Fox News (and the entire partisan conservative political media ecosystem before FNC) had already prepped and conditioned a huge audience for the new Trump TV reality show. What I never expected was that the audience would soon number some 65 million, or 35 percent of all American voters in 2016.

Holy smokes!—Trump was doing our tribal fear-hate-rage activation shtick better than we were. He also, ironically, became the financial savior for the beaten-down "fake news mainstream media." Like I mentioned—the "failing" *New York Times* reached $1 billion in digital-only subscriptions in 2019. When Trump first went down the escalator in Trump Tower, they were losing money.

Soon, this mesmerizing WWE/Fox News/SportsCenter mashup cartoon character protagonist with his spray-on orange face and scalp-reduction hair-sprayed pompadour became ratings gold. He said everything I could not say on TV—overtly racist things on live TV and on Twitter. If I had said these things, it would have gotten me fired or kicked off Twitter.

But then, when social media cut up his left-wing tweets and trolling into three-minute racial and cultural fear and hate digital grenades, out blazed trillions of clicks and tweets around the world. People over fifty-five became the fastest-growing audience for Facebook and Twitter. Unfriending Deplorable "Trumpers" in a blaze of sanctimonious glory became its own glorious sporting event. I should have created a "Best Unfriended Deplorable Rant-of-the-Day" blog page!

Trump even out-sloganeered Fox News founder and televised tribal shame savant Roger Ailes—Roger's "fair and balanced" dog whistle—wink wink—had become "Make America Great Again" (read: "make America white and 1980 again"). He also stole "America First" from Charles Lindbergh and the "America First" isolationist party formed in the late 1930s on a platform of keeping America out of World War II.

Those white, small city, or rural Retro Americans I had met in Arkansas and my PC-resentful country club Republican friends connected and bonded with Trump as if he had just delivered his own sermon on Mount Fifth Avenue. (The key word and concept here is "psychically and emotionally connected"—more on that vitally important concept in a bit.)

They started using his words and terms. They did not care about his profound mental, professional, and moral deficiencies. They called the *Washington Post* and CNN and the *New York Times* and NBC and other media outlets "fake news" and "enemies of the people" as if they were all of a sudden living in some neofascist banana republic.

And then—just like Jesus of Nazareth—the Donald of Queens disciples did come and join him—although he taught them quite a different set of the Beatitudes except the eleventh one—"Blessed are you when people insult you, persecute you, and falsely say all kinds of evil against you because of me. Rejoice and be glad, because great is your reward in heaven, for in the same way they persecuted the prophets who were before you."

Holy crap, I thought—it was undeniable—these folks were just like the ones I met in southern Arkansas who binge-watched six hours a day of Fox News tribal fear and hate content!

They had finally found their profane anti-PC and anti-Obama messiah, and to mix metaphors, they flocked to see his unscripted shit show just to hear him say something that they knew their hated PC crowd would find outrageous.

To stay in the Old Testament, it was like Trump was a modern-day digital Moses who'd come to help these slaves of liberalism break free of their hated chains of political correctness. He led them in cursing the hated liberal pundits with digital locusts for all their constant PC scolding and chronic moral superiority beatdown.

It was breathtaking for me to watch from the context of a former Fox News personality . . . and, well, you know the rest. When The Donald became the Republican nominee for president of the United States, I knew what I had to do. I needed (at least for my own sanity) to finally connect all the tribal warfare-as-entertainment product dots and figure out why the Fox News tribal warfare playbook was so psychologically and viscerally powerful that it had turned this vile New York City con man into a working class everyman's Pied Piper.

All of the above events brought me to my atonement part—how much had I played a role in enabling the rise of this Trumpism/Deplorables cult?

To save my own soul, I needed to really dig deep, put my big boy analyst pants on, and get some real answers to the real question: "What the fuck just happened and why?"

I hoped to convince as many people as possible that the Fox News grift and the "Only I Can Solve America's Problems" Trumpian con were the same con but with different colored hair and makeup. I hoped I could help prove to anyone that would listen that Trump's shtick was just a nuclear-powered version of a Fox News host but with the added risk of an actual nuclear disaster. You know—to add more dramatic effect—"stay tuned till next week's episode and see if I drop the bomb on Iran."

In other words—I had a world-class case of Trump derangement syndrome.

I finally had a political tribe—the Never Trump tribe. I became a "Trumphole"—which is as obnoxious as a Foxhole, trust me!

By May 2017 I had collected my notes and Fox News memories and written a short essay published on Medium.com entitled "Fear & Unbalanced: Confessions of a 14-Year Fox News Hitman." When my social media following and liberal digital media discovered it, it went viral. Hundreds of thousands of readers later, I knew I had just touched the surface of the audience I felt I needed to reach. The article was named one of the best examples of journalism in 2017 by the Time Warner media critic (take that, Woodward!). I later crowdfunded a paperback expanded version of my article.

And then the good people at Diversion Books said, "Toby—you *have to tell* the rest of your story to the world. Think of the New England Patriots—how would the Rams have done if they knew the entire Pats Super Bowl playbook before they played in the dullest Super Bowl in history! We will publish the real Fox News tribal warfare-as-entertainment story and expose the playbook of the entire Fox News tribal identity activation grift for the world to see and judge. Your book will make a difference" (cue the angels singing and the atonement bells ringing).

So here we are—I present you the con men grifting behind and in front of the curtain and the grift they are working for the entire world to see and judge.

In the eighteen months since the original Medium.com article, in addition to my editing and publishing day job at www.transformityresearch.com making self-directed investors hopefully richer, I have researched, analyzed, and written "the rest of the story."

I hope *Foxocracy* in a small way brings some justice to the emotional and relationships wreckage I helped Fox News bring to millions in America and American families. I can tell you after reading dozens of social and political psychology research papers and books, and then interviewing more than a dozen political and social science experts and psychologists covering every aspect of the base psychology that is the driving emotional engine or tonic behind high-powered tribal identity activation porn, I feel like I earned a master's degree in "Foxology." Plus a minor in tribal psychology and maybe a concentration in involuntary limbic system neuroscience.

But in all seriousness, after the Medium.com article went viral, I also received a much more personal and compelling reason to complete my quest—I read thousands of gripping and tearful letters and emails from the people on my social media. All of these thousands of notes described people whose lives and family relationships had been literally destroyed by Fox News. I also met Jen Senko, the director and producer of *The Brainwashing of My Dad*, which tells the story of her own father's decline from what I now call Fox News brain.

Then I got an even greater sense of urgency in the fall of 2018. That is when America witnessed acts of political violence by extreme radicalized Fox News addicted zealots in Washington, DC, and a Pittsburgh synagogue.

I truly believe political and cultural activation media literacy has to be now considered essential for all voters. It needs to be spread throughout America just like basic "social media literacy" and knowledge of social media's powerful algorithmic emotional manipulation shenanigans were exposed by insiders from the social media industry (undoubtedly atoning for their sins against America too.)

I mean really—if Facebook is "dangerous to 250 million Americans" as was claimed in their congressional hearing for simply redistributing this powerful tribal activation media, what does that make Fox News and the other tribal partisan political arms merchants who are the ones who actually create and publish this powerful tribal political/cultural activation media?

Finally, for what it's worth, here is the point most people miss about Fox News addiction: The Fox News junkies I've come to call Foxholes are not addicted to "political news media." True inside baseball politics is addictive to a relatively small group of nerdy political junkies and political professionals. I lived in DC for twenty-four years—political junkies laugh at tribal TV commentators like me at their favorite watering hole as "retail politics."

As the saying goes, "Washington, DC, is Hollywood for ugly people" and not perfectly coiffed blond hair bimbos with perfect white teeth. Real political news media nerds get their dopamine jolt and serotonin high from scoring killer STFU argument points against adversarial contemporaries that they respect while drinking in bars on the campaign trail.

Fox News junkies, on the other hand, are definitely not addicted to right-wing tribal activation and validation porn for nerdy political policy fascinations. What I finally discovered was what they get off on by watching a faux Fox News "debate" are not the debate points—they get off on the wonderful feelings they get from:

- being in an ideological cognitive dissonance-free safe room especially created for self-identified conservatives/Deplorables

- and watching their smug, PC, holier-than-thou mortal enemy eviscerated on TV by their tribal hero/imaginary buddy.

Fox News addicts do not get off on feeling smarter—they get off on having their righteous conservative political and cultural worldview's superiority validated. They get high when they are carefully and artfully led to perceive they and their tribal heroes and teammates are winning a never-ending existential cultural holy war that is morally and intellectually righteous.

Mental health professionals tell me Fox News tribal activation porn is addictive because it:

- Replaces the very negative feelings of the self-esteem mutilation and resentment the average Fox News viewer gets from the various economic and cultural traumas they have endured.
- And is a psychological antidote and prophylactic that protects their feelings hurt by the endless cultural beat down they viscerally feel from "the liberal" media, entertainment, and academic world who can't help but rub their face in yet another of their moral or behavioral deficiencies.

The magic draw of the Fox News tribal identity activation and validation grift is that it delivers to the viewer the positive self-esteem feeling that measurably gives their damaged ego a genuine boost. The Fox News junkie gets that shot of self-esteem when they see their cultural hero prove their political, social, class, racial, and religious resentments are not only justified but righteous.

After I understood this reality, I had one more question to answer: "If right-wing talk radio was the gateway drug to Fox News/Trump TV addiction, what is high-def tribal activation TV porn a gateway drug to?"

Unfortunately, in the most extreme cases we now have the answer—letter bombs and synagogue murder. Full stop.

I hope *Foxocracy*, in a small way, gives Fox News advertisers a dozen or more undeniable reasons why they must run, not walk, their valuable brand identity away from their association with FNC's destructive lifestyle brand of political tribalism as well.

What we know more than ever today is this fact: If you have the tribal identity activation and validation playbook and have the money, there are billions to be made in the tribal fear and hate video porn business. The endless supply of emotionally traumatized viewers hungry for revenge and cathartic blame shifting is just too easy to seduce and addict with the ultra-powerful drug of self-esteem salvation.

Let's be real about this—these are huge for-profit public corporations; creating and distributing tribal activation video content is now extremely profitable.

And at the very least, let's all finally admit that when nearly a third of American adults have stopped speaking to hopelessly estranged parents, brothers, sisters, and longtime friends, we have a large and genuine cultural crisis (and a public health crisis too) in America of our own making.

CHAPTER 5

Why the Emotional Impact of Fox News Is Ten Times More Powerful than Conservative Radio

First, I don't mean in any way to deny the political power of traditional conservative radio—it is a large wing of the American Foxocracy. I had a talk radio show for many years and did a lot of radio with the one and only Steve Bannon before he went bat shit crazy—I know the impact of talk radio—but it pales in tribal impact and mind share comparison to Fox News.

Many people have asked me, "Yea Toby—I get your Foxocracy thing—but man—Rush, Mark Levin, Glenn Beck, Sean Hannity, Michael Savage—those guys are on for many hours every day. The ratings say they cumulatively reach forty million. Rush has been on since 1988—he makes $70 million a year—even O'Reilly at the top only made $8 million a year. Why isn't conservative talk radio the real powerhouse?"

The number one reason for the smaller emotional impact is that most talk radio is consumed in a car while the driver is driving. Obviously performing the most complicated activity the vast majority of human beings perform in life while listening to Rush Limbaugh is different than sitting in your favorite chair watching a wide screen TV with an adult beverage.

Second, there is little or no social media redistribution or retargeting—and that is where 90 percent of Fox News content is consumed and how they get to one hundred million Americans per month. If you see Levin or Beck in your social media feed, it's from a TV program.

ADDICTIVE POWER AND SOCIAL NETWORKS

To be fair, Fox News is by no way the first entertainment company to gamify its content for user addiction. (Can you say *Candy Crush* or *Words with Friends*?) In fact, Sean Parker, a co-founder and former CEO of

Facebook, admitted in late 2017 that the entire premise of Facebook was explicitly to exploit the well-known vulnerabilities of human psychology.

As this book points out in significant detail, Fox News was engaging in mass exploitation of our psychological flaws and human nature a long time before the first line of Facebook code was ever written. My beef with Fox News is unlike Sean Parker of Facebook, no one from Fox News has ever owned up to its exploitation scheme.

Parker also revealed that the addictive premise of Facebook—he too calls it a "social-validation feedback loop"—is "exactly the kind of thing that a hacker like me would come up with." A like or a comment on a post sends users "a little dopamine hit," he said, encouraging them to post again. "The inventors, creators—it's me, it's Mark Zuckerberg, it's Kevin Systrom on Instagram, it's all of these people—understood this consciously. And we did it anyway," he said.

Parker's Big Point: "I don't know if I really understood the consequences of what I was saying, because [of] the unintended consequences of a network when it grows to a billion or two billion people and . . . it literally changes your relationship with society, with each other. It probably interferes with productivity in weird ways. God only knows what it's doing to our children's brains."

I'm certainly not God, Sean, but I can tell you the magnitude of addiction to the Fox News tribal hate-and-blame-porn feedback loop and what that addiction is doing to the brains of millions of mostly elderly white right-wing viewers: It's addicting and desocializing them by the hundreds of thousands.

Third, Nielsen says nearly 58.8 million people listen to AM radio per week. About seventeen million of them listen to at least one conservative talk show according to Arbitron ratings—which is about 80 percent less reach than the combined cable/online/social media platform for Fox News.

Fourth, as mentioned before, cognitive science research for decades has found that when it comes to emotional intensity, TV is ten times more emotionally impactful than radio because humans communicate emotions through facial expressions and gestures, not voice (conservative radio jocks aren't singing!).

Control of our expressions and gestures lies in the brain stem and the amygdala which are beyond consciousness (and we will get to the big role the amygdala plays in Fox News's fear-based engagement strategy in a few pages). Even the tiniest of facial cues are important—60 to 80 percent of people can recognize an emotion just by looking at the eyes of another person. The most powerful emotions recognized by most cognitive scientists are fear, anger/hate, sadness, joy, surprise, and disgust. Voice only discloses an anger/hate emotion and in a significantly less impactful way.

Fifth, our brain has "mirror neurons." When we see our tribal hero happy or distressed, it makes our mirror neurons cause similar feelings. That is why the Fox News host in the cold open almost always has a look of distress and unhappiness on his or her face.

Sixth, the conservative talk radio demographic is aging. It's the seventy-year-old, white, Protestant farmer in a small-town Retro America who's listening to these guys because he's driving in his car.

But from a psychological level, the most important difference is seeing the eyes, facial cues, and gestures of your partisan enemy that ramps up the emotional engagement a hundred times. Conservative talk radio is a monologue—with a few fellow angry right-wing callers. All the right-wing anger jocks may sound like demagogues (because they are), but there is no antagonist on set and on the air. It's seeing the tribal enemy's face and observing all the emotional cues that make the Fox News white tribal identity performance art so impactful to white tribal partisans.

From a political, cultural, and now White House mindshare perspective, there is no contest. Congressmen and senators and the Beltway Foxocracy members are not listening to talk radio unless they are driving to work or home. And certainly no conservative radio hosts have the ear of the POTUS like Fox News hosts—except Sean Hannity and Laura Ingraham, who have daily radio shows. But to left- and right-wing politicians and political operatives, they appear on Fox News as a free branding event.

Why do Rush and Hannity earn so much more money than top Fox News hosts? Because their programs are syndicated to more than two thousand radio stations. Syndicated means that each radio station pays a monthly licensing fee—but more importantly, the distributor for Rush or Hannity's radio show gets an allocation of radio ad inventory to sell nationally. Those national spots go for a much higher gross cost than a local pizza joint with a two-for-one pizza special ad.

The big radio syndication networks have relatively low production costs—a jock and a mike—and their biggest cost by far is the revenue split with their syndicated radio hosts.

But here is the biggest issue of all that separates tribal radio hate porn with TV: There is no Foxhole offline/online tribal identity porn spiral. I have messages from many Foxhole victims that say "yea my dad or brother listen to Limbaugh or Savage while they are driving, but they don't come home talking about the show. The show keeps them company while they are driving. But after the nightly Fox News binge-watching, my dad/brother/mom is on fire—they are all spun up and loaded for libtard bear. Then they get on social media to chat with their Fox News buddies and vent more steam."

This is the enormous difference in conservative radio and the Fox News white tribal partisan identity activation and amplification radicalization spiral—it's so much faster and has so much more intensity in general.

And look—I am not even talking about the Alex Jones conspiracy nuts or Breitbart.com "alt right" counterculture groups. I am not talking about the white supremacist hate groups—they too have online radicalization spiral feedback loops—but they are extreme zealots. America has always had significant counterculture conspiracy nuts and KKK and more extreme white supremacy hate groups.

What is most striking with the Foxhole white tribal partisan intensity spiral is how normal these people were before they fell into the predatory Fox News seduction. Here is again the Foxhole spiral in real life.

I first saw the scope of the epidemic of family isolation and estrangement caused by Fox News brain in the 2016 documentary *The Brainwashing of My Dad* by filmmaker Jen Senko. When I saw this movie, it sickened me that I had been a part of the Fox News "fair and balanced" scam for so many years. As David Alm of *Forbes* concluded in his review of the film, "*The Brainwashing of My Dad* isn't really about Frank Senko or even the media that hijacked his mind for thirty years. It's about all of us, and how easily manipulated we can be under the pretense of information."

The massive difference in the emotional and behavioral impact of conservative angry rant monologue radio and Fox News white tribal identity porn is:

- The FNC white tribal warfare performance production playbook.

- The emotionally powerful impact of seeing the face of your white tribal partisan hero and more importantly your mortal tribal enemy.

- The cumulative power of consuming thousands of hours of emotionally predatory white tribal identity porn.

- The cumulative emotional power of the offline-online Foxhole Hot Pot moral, cultural, and political digital spiral effect.

And finally, conservative talk radio does not produce sad stories like these for millions of American families living with Foxholes:

> "My mother is hooked on this tribal hate porn stuff. She lives alone and watches Fox all day every day and it has changed her so drastically that it has made my brother and I essentially cut off all contact. Any remark counter to the right-wing media narrative will cause her to turn into a vengeful crusader on a quest from God to purge those thoughts from her children.
>
> "To explain the depth of the hold this stuff has on people, especially older people, I'm an Iraq vet (2003–2004) and she called me a conspiracy theorist for making the entirely true statement that there were no WMDs there. What would I know, right? Sean Hannity apparently got more classified briefings than me, or something."
>
> —Christopher Cramer

> "Brother and Dad. And Mom and other brother. And extended family. It started with my brother, but he kind of infected my parents with it. My mom got more into it when she learned to use email and communicated with my Aunt, who is completely slavishly devoted to Fox News. They say I'm the brainwashed one, yet my brother bought every one of Glenn Beck's books. Both my father and my brothers bought guns after Sandy Hook. I've never given a dime to any political organization. It's hard to see them manipulated so easily. Just today my dad started laughing at his own insinuation that a housekeeper was an illegal immigrant, I couldn't say why.
>
> "It's been the most painful thing in my life watching this happening to my family."
>
> —Mick Smith

> "I lost my mother and brother to Fox News. Dad, thankfully, seems unscathed, but he's always been more logical, whereas my mom and brother are much more emotional. I love my family, but I find it difficult to interact with them. We have an unspoken agreement to never bring up politics and religion, but sometimes

one of them will go off on me, call me a 'stupid unthinking liberal,' and proceed to lecture me on how Obama is a Muslim
intent on 'destroying the glory of America.'

"It's frightening and incredibly sad. I've had to hang up the
phone on my mom once, when she started screaming at me
because I couldn't see how Obama was using 'illegals' to bring
Ebola into America so that he could wipe out all good Christians.

"I miss my family."

—Danielle

As mentioned, in researching this book and in response to my blog
article "Confessions of a Fox News Hitman," I have read thousands of
comments from people with geriatric parents or relatives telling a story
about the destructive impact that Fox News social derangement syndrome
had on their families.

I find many Americans, like I was, are completely unaware of the extent
and virulence of Fox News social derangement and the sheer number of
Foxholes.

A lot of elderly grandparents and older parents are going to find that if
their choice is yelling along with Bill O'Reilly vs. having a relationship with
their children or grandchildren, well, it's a choice they've made.

I would only add that based on my own in-depth research on the issue,
Fox News addicts suffering from desocialized Foxhole syndrome truly are
not consciously aware that their desocialized behavior is the primary cause
for their estrangement from family and friends. In fact, my research shows
quite the opposite: These poor folks can't for the life of them understand
how they gave birth to or became friends with "such idiot libtards."

Reader John Dore talks in the same thread about how Fox News addicts
who turn into those with Fox News derangement disorder "flip a switch"
and accelerate from normal everyday conservatives to tribal-grade partisan
fanatics:

I deal with this regarding my grandparents. We were always
close and, despite being conservative, they never really brought
up politics—we always talked about history or art or the trips
they took or other interesting things. They volunteered in the
community, worked their gardens, supported NPR, and were
active in the church. Always loved hearing from them. . . .

The election of Obama timed with some health issues really flipped a switch. They now spend a lot more time at home watching Fox, listening to AM radio, and getting caught up in email forwards. I used to get one interesting, thoughtful, interesting, even funny email from my grandparents a week about family or whatever was going on in their life. . . .

I now get, no joke, 10–15 emails a day about the coming Communist takeover of the country, or how we're already doomed because of Hispanic immigration, or whatever.

The change in the child-parent relationship with a toxically radicalized parent is the most common theme in the letters I have received. This comment in the American Conservative thread, from "Another Matt," is prevalent in most forums and comments I have read:

It's understandable not to want to be around a toxically unpleasant person. It's even worse when that person has a temper or violent tendencies. My dad is one such person.

He's going through a divorce due to the Fox News playing 25/8, his now extreme religious views, and the temper and lack of care for any of my mom's thoughts or feelings. My brothers blame her for not putting her foot down or not going head to head with him; the latter always just made him angrier. . . .

In my dreams, though, we have fist fights.

In forum after forum, many readers have poignantly summed up the Foxhole derangement spiral and the brutal impact of learned tribal fear, rage, blame, and hatred on family dynamics.

Key Point: Foxhole social derangement is heartbreakingly sad. And worse, if our survey research is at all close to accurate—if one in five Americans knows at least one person who exhibits toxic Foxhole radicalized behavior as a result of their Fox News addiction—this degenerative disorder is far more present in the families of Fox News addicts than has ever been reported.

If pollster Frank Luntz's numbers are correct, nearly 33 percent of American adults report they are estranged from at least one close family member or friend over "irreconcilable political differences." That adds up to over eighty million adults in our country.

I cannot overemphasize that the comments and evidence I've shared above about the impact of the real-life toxicity of Fox News brain disorder in American families are hardly unique. Google the phrase "How to survive the holidays with a Trump supporter" and you will get 2.4 million hits.

Social scientists used to describe radicalized and militant political rhetoric on both the right and left as isolated extremism, but clearly, another reason for the explosion in Fox News brain is what I and others at Fox News have done to America: We normalized and mainstreamed radicalized right-wing political tribalism and brought the most powerful televised tribal identity activation porn to the most emotionally vulnerable people in America.

What did we think would happen?

Video tribal identity porn is massively more powerful than conservative talk radio—let's end that misunderstanding now.

CHAPTER 6

How the Fox News "Fair and Balanced" Tribal Warfare Playbook Works

Okay—now it's time for you to see the FNC white tribal warfare playbook and how it works and why it works so amazingly well.

"Toby you cry at movies and TV shows? Dude—do you have that liberal gene and did not tell me? Real conservatives don't cry at movies or TV shows. Real conservatives get emotional about their kids, their dog, when they hear "Taps" or the National Anthem or when their team wins the World Series or Super Bowl. Only liberals cry at make-believe movies, opera, and TV cultural arts bullshit." That's what a Fox News executive producer told me when I mistakenly told him I cried like a baby watching *Les Misérables* on Broadway.

Another veteran news executive producer asked me: "So Toby, did you go to a liberal arts college? Did you study liberal arts?"

Me: "Yes—and finance and marketing."

Executive Producer to me: "Well forget that liberal arts shit if you want to be a host on Fox News. As far as Fox News is concerned, there are two kinds of Americans: 33 percent who graduated from college and 66 percent who did not. By a large margin the majority of our audience did not either attend or graduate from college.

"Within our college graduates in America there are two basic kinds of educations—general liberal arts where you learn all that liberal airy fairy crap or specific occupational credentialing that gets you a good job. Very few of our audience attended a liberal arts college or took much (if any) college or post-graduate liberal arts or humanities courses in the first place. Only people who get to Fox News by hitting the wrong button are liberal arts majors." (In fact, most actual print and TV journalists go to liberal arts colleges and studied media or journalism at a liberal arts college/university.)

But here was the real kicker in what she told me: "If you want to understand our audience and see the world through their eyes, listen to classic and contemporary country music and go watch and listen to an Evangelical televangelist—to our primary audience, country music and TV televangelism *are* the 'liberal arts.'"

After a number of psychotherapists and PTSD treatment specialists read my first draft of *Foxocracy*, their conclusion could be summed up this way:

Toby you may not be aware of this, but the behaviors you describe and the real story your letters from people who have lost parents, siblings, and longtime friends to Fox News derangement and desocialization syndrome tell are symptoms of repetitive trauma syndrome—a cousin to PTSD. Post-traumatic stress disorder happens after a single major trauma or a series of repeated deeply traumatic events. What you describe are people who are currently traumatized by intense, repetitive, and ongoing economic or cultural traumas.

What you call "Fox News brain" is actually more accurately described as an ongoing unresolved cultural and economic chronic traumatic syndrome.

Fox News's Senior Executive of Political Affairs and former Roger Ailes employee Kathy Arleigh told me this fact of life early in my Fox News career (here I paraphrase many conversations): "Toby you gotta understand this—any video content that causes involuntary physical and emotional arousal or has an automatic conditioned emotional response is pornography. *Playboy* is in pornification of women business. To condition you to subscribe or buy their magazine, they weaponize physical female sexuality with a camera and Photoshop.

"When a guy grabs the magazine and has opened the centerfold a few times and gets sexually aroused, he has created an involuntary emotional and physical arousal response and brain pattern. He has been conditioned by opening his previous issues and *boom* gets a boner.

"We at Fox News are in the pornography of white right-wing cultural and economic fear and hate business—we weaponize images of fear and disgust and storylines that are fearful and disgusting to conservatives because by the time they get to watching Fox News, they already have developed a conditioned emotional reaction to a picture of Hillary or Bill or Harry Reid or Muslims. And if they don't, after watching enough of our right-wing porn or propaganda, they will—and then we own their brain stem.

"Here is the kicker: We are in a war with two hundred other cable and network TV channels to get and keep an audience's attention—but once we have made it to an old white folk's brain stem and we get a conditioned emotional response, we own their attention.

"Once we own their brain stem, we keep presenting them with more fearful or outrageous images and content until the segment ends and they experience the feeling of righteous tribal victory and a happy ending. When they shake their fist at their TV and put their arms up in victory when they watch you verbally shred their viscerally hated tribal enemy, we've won—that's the happy ending, and we know we will get them back after the commercial—which is how we monetize their attention. No happy ending, channel changes."

THE FOXOCRACY AND PORN

My guess is when you think of the term *porn*, you think of the traditional definition; filmed sex acts watched to sexually *arouse* the viewer(s). This definition and understanding is not wrong, of course. But in the context of Fox News the key words are *"emotionally arouse."*

Today the term porn (thanks to social media) is used loosely to mean any video or image that "arouses primal emotions." Thanks to the constant digital emotional surveillance machine that we *inaccurately* label social media, we now hop online and view three-minute emotionally arousing videos of kitties and puppies and baby elephants, depending on what Facebook's or YouTube's digital surveillance says *you* are most emotionally susceptible to viewing.

And of course we now call those social media images, videos, or the social messaging memes "kitty/puppy/baby elephant porn" for fun.

There is of course nothing sexual about those cute or funny videos, yet we call them "porn" because they are shamelessly produced and algorithmically streamed into your social media for one and only one reason: to evoke *an involuntary, conditioned emotional* reaction and mild cognitive engagement. Your "awww" and "how cute" reaction is a conditioned emotional response that is evoked involuntarily (unless you hate puppies or cats—how dare you!).

Another term for placing smiling puppy videos in your social media is "targeted emotional manipulation." Via digital surveillance (remember, you agreed to this in return for a free social media app!) you have revealed your personal interest in and emotional susceptibility (via clicks, likes, and shares) for puppy porn or kitty porn or whatever—and that is why it is in your social media stream.

But it is really there because this digital surveillance machine revealed your *exploitable emotional weaknesses.* Facebook or YouTube shamelessly provides you with a stream of ever cuter and more powerful puppy/kitty/

lion cubs/baby elephant porn until you forgot you just spent an hour on your phone or digital device.

And, of course, during that lost hour you were fed a dozen or more highly targeted advertisements.

And finally, this is my TED Talk that I plan on making after this book comes out:

You wanna know what the real incredibly powerful and amazing Jedi Mind Trick at Fox News is—you know the one that turns normal agree-to-disagree people into stark raving mad right-wing lunatics who watch five hours of Fox News opinion programming and never turn their home TV off of Fox News?

The trick is this: Roger Ailes and his team of right-wing attack ad producers used what they learned from twenty years of learning how to make people believe magical thinking or hate the other candidate more than they hated their client via their one-minute right-wing attack or propaganda ads.

At Fox News, the same team already were masters of how to make already scared and frightened, economically and culturally traumatized over-fifty-five-aged white people living in Retro America believe that Retro America actually still has hope of winning its economic and cultural war against Metro America.

Why is that an amazing Jedi Mind Trick? The Retro/Metro cultural and economic war is *over*. Retro America totally and unequivocally lost to Metro America twelve years ago. But when watching Fox News, they would never know it! Retro America has 42 percent of the US population but generates just 32 percent of the American economy. Metro America has 58 percent of the population but generates about 68 percent of the US economy: The economic war is over by a landslide, and Metro America won. Eighty percent of the entire United States lives in urban regions.

The incredible power of the Fox News Jedi Mind Trick is we make them believe they still have a chance to win the twenty-first-century economic and culture wars—when they in fact have

No chance of winning.

No hope of winning.

Are in fact losing more and more ground every minute of every day.

Now *that* is an amazing feat—and okay really, it's more of a Jedi Mind Grift!

But the most amazing thing? Donald Trump stole Fox News's Retro America con and made it his own! He stole our fantasy narrative and told Retro Americans that they could have their 1980s economy and jobs back if:

- We got tough with China and Mexico that stole their jobs.

- Mexico paid to build a wall on our southern border.

- We got rid of illegal immigrants who lowered their wages.

- We started and won import tariff wars with the rest of the world.

- We nominated enough probusiness Supreme Court Justices.

- And we turned Obamacare into Trumpcare with much lower premiums, much lower prices, and much better coverage.

The final battle of the Retro/Metro war for economic and cultural supremacy was when Metro America emerged from the Great Recession and soared and most of Retro America did not.

But really, the Metro/Retro America battle was over in 1994 when Metro America brought China and its eight hundred million sets of hands into the low-skill assembly supply chain willing to perform low-skilled manual labor work for $5 a day and room and board and this thing called "the internet browser" was invented and the entire world began to be become digitized.

Republicans didn't understand what happened—they thought "globalism" was gonna be great for white collar America (they knew it would be amazing for big corporate profits too). It turned out that the only globalism that benefitted working class America was Walmart. To middle and working class Americans, Walmart is the only globalism they know: They just don't know that Walmart's global supply chain cost them millions of low-skilled manufacturing and assembly line jobs.

On Fox News opinion programming, they have created this fake Retro America liturgy like that *Wag the Dog* movie where Dustin Hoffman makes people believe that the moon landing was fake only in reverse. On Fox News, Retro Americans never see or process that irrefutable fact that not only did Metro America win the economic and cultural war by a landslide in 2009, that economic and culture war is now turning into a slaughter.

In fact, Metro America pulls even farther ahead every day:

- a tech start-up is launched.

- that tech company is funded by Metro Americans venture capital.

- another Metro American IPO comes to market.

- a kid graduates with a STEM (science, technology, engineering, and math) degree.

- a famous Evangelical fundamentalist televangelist scares away another Metro American company from moving to Retro America

- or that minister convinces another Retro American kid that the Christian Bible is not a book of metaphors, analogies, and parables whose purpose is to teach you the ethics of evolved non-tribal humanity and a moral code via storytelling written by hundreds of people over hundreds of years but instead the inerrant creationist word of God and Jesus to be taken literally and not metaphorically.

- another Retro American dies a premature death (with 20 percent lower life expectancy relative to Metro Americans) because of poor access or inability to pay for healthcare, suicides, drug overdoses, gunshot wounds, obesity, alcoholism, and the most deadly disease of all: chronic visceral loneliness or hopelessness with all the mental and physical health destruction that they create.

That is now the entire Fox News format:

1. Rule #1. Never ever let them know their tribe already lost the Retro/ Metro America economic and cultural war in 2009 and are now getting slaughtered by Metro America.

2. Rule #2. Do everything you can think of to convince these Retro Americans that there is still hope to crush the evil liberal empire if they just pass more tax cuts and deregulations and let Retro American corporations crush the mental disease of liberalism and progressivism and let prosperity trickle down to the working and middle class again.

3. Rule #3. Never ever forget Rules 1 and 2.

CHAPTER 7

A Few Key Stories to Illustrate the Playbook

I'm going to share with you all the most important stories and lessons learned from my days at Fox News. I hope they give you the insight you need to understand how Fox News works behind the curtain. Then after you have seen the playbook, we'll talk more about the why—why the FNC tribal warfare playbook is so psychologically powerful.

My first story is about how the immense manipulative power of televised political attack advertising got baked into the FNC white tribal identity production playbook.

One day after watching one of our favorite TV shows that was saturated with political attack commercials, my Canadian born and raised wife Marjorie asked me, "Toby—how is it possible for a candidate to run these fear and hate based commercials on TV that don't talk about the issues of the campaign? In Canada these are not allowed." (Point-of-fact: they are not allowed in any other modern democracy in the world.) "These ads don't tell me why I should vote for the candidate—they just tell me why I should hate the other candidate. What kind of campaign is that? What kind of democracy do you have here?" (I should add that she eventually did become a US citizen, bless her heart.)

Pre-Fox News, I did not have a good answer for her question. I had become numb to these attack ads—they had been around for most of my adult life. What I was not aware of when I started with Fox News as a paid market/economic analyst and contributor in 2000 was that before there was a Fox News Channel, co-founder Roger Ailes was the father and master of political TV attack ads. Roger and his partner Lee Atwater literally invented and mastered the dark arts of the uniquely American political attack ad (just ask Michael Dukakis).

TRIBALISM

Tribal in this case does not of course mean you are a member of an actual ethnic tribe—like a Navajo or Tutsi ethnic tribe.

To be "tribal" means that, as a result of marinating your partisan brain in hatred, fear, and resentment media for thousands of hours, your proud political partisan identity has literally reverted to your primal caveman operating system. That means that as a tribal or tribalized partisan, you view your opposing political or cultural outgroups as an *existential* ("life or death") threat to you and your family.

Key term—*existential* threat. As a tribalized hyperpartisan you see opposing political or cultural tribes with a binary (all good or all bad—black and white—no gray), zero sum (for me to win, you have to lose), existential/life-or-death warfare (it's you or me brother—*and it's going to be me*) prism of logic.

Key terms here again are *existential threat* and *perspective*. If you are a tribal partisan animal lover, you might stand outside an animal shelter and spray paint the cars of people who brought in pets to take back to the pound. You might bring home half a dozen dogs or cats because they were at risk of euthanasia. You are a hard-core hyperpartisan, and you are proud of it.

If you are a tribalized hyperpartisan political conservative or liberal, you are politically and culturally hard core. You watch hard-core white tribal identity pornography—today at Fox News that means you watch Tucker Carlson, Sean Hannity, Laura Ingraham, or Judge Jeanine Pirro. You read *Daily Caller* and Brietbart.com when not watching Fox News. You literally can't stand to be in the same room with your political or cultural counterpart. You would practically (or actually) disown your own child over marrying a person who belonged to your tribe's political enemy. You cannot hold a civil political or cultural conversation with even a loved one (let alone a stranger) you consider your existential tribal enemy for more than a few minutes.

In short, there is not an agree-to-disagree bone left in your body when it comes to your social or cultural political identity—and you are very proud of all of this.

Now, if you continually bring home half a dozen puppies or cats (and they have to live inside) and your spouse or roommate was not like-minded, you will eventually become estranged from that person—trust me. Does the term "cat lady" ring a bell?

Same applies to tribal hyperpartisans. If you have devolved into a tribalized political hyperpartisan, unless your spouse, family, and longtime friends are all similarly hyperpartisan, you will eventually estrange the non-tribalized ones (or if you have a ton of cash, your loved ones will use it to stay as far away from you as possible).

We will talk a lot about this "tribal partisan derangement" syndrome because it is a big part of the Fox News dark side.

What I later learned from Fox News executives was that the Ailes/Atwood political advertising strategy was simple—use what Roger called "the most powerful force in the world—television" to broadcast images and words into the viewer's home that were never intended to make the viewer understand his client's policy positions better nor their big ideas for a bigger and stronger America.

The Ailes/Atwater political advertising strategy was to harness the enormous emotional power of the combined visual and audio medium of TV to simply get the viewer to fear and hate their client's opponent more than they hated or feared their client. As Chuck Todd recently observed in his "journalist call to arms" article against Fox News in the *Atlantic* magazine, "Ailes's greatest gift as a political strategist lay not in making his clients more electable, but in making their opponents unelectable."

Bingo—Chuck Todd gets it. Roger Ailes had never produced a minute of TV news. When Roger Ailes first proposed a Republican Party TV channel to Richard Nixon in 1974, and then pitched it again to Rupert Murdoch in 1995, it was the same pitch: "What if we took my emotionally powerful, fear-inducing right-wing political attack ads and turned them into mostly scripted, highly choreographed, and rigged outcome half-hour and one-hour right-wing political and cultural attack ads? We could call these 'fair and balanced' opinion debate programs" (but as Mr. Todd also pointed out in his article, what does balanced have to do with the presentation of facts?).

In my mental recreation of Ailes's Fox News sales pitch to Murdoch, Ailes says: "You see Rupert—one minute by itself is not enough time to emotionally manipulate and hook your average voter—we learned in political advertising it takes the cumulative effect of hundreds of minutes of tribal fear and hate attack ads to work. Here's the beauty of a politically and culturally conservative TV channel—what if we created thirty- and sixty-minute liberal attack ads, called them 'fair and balanced' news and opinion programming, and ran them all day and night? What if we reached over ninety-five million American households and then got TV distributors to pay us for our tribal fear and hate content and advertisers to pay to advertise on it? Can you imagine how much damage we could inflict against liberalism with sixteen hours a day of right-wing tribal fear, hate, and resentment attack ads disguised as TV programming? Can you imagine how much money we could make from monthly Pay TV distributor fees and selling ads every seven minutes into millions of homes? Conservative radio reaches forty million right-wingers a day (at the time) selling ads for almost nothing—we could net a billion dollars a year profit in just three million homes!"

Murdoch did imagine—don't forget he was already the king of tabloid newspapers in Australia and the UK. Fox News was imagined and created to be a mashup of Murdoch's tabloid journalism instinct and Ailes's fear and hate attack ads. The product was intended to become a conservative talk radio hybrid where the audience would actually both see and hear their tribal heroes and their tribal partisan enemy—it was psychologically brilliant.

With the FCC's Fairness Doctrine abolished by the GOP in 1987, there was nothing to stop Murdoch from investing nearly one billion dollars of public company money he controlled to build their mutual dream—a liberal-destroying Death Star that would indeed soon become the scourge of left-wing liberalism and champion of right-wing tribal activation the size and reach of which none of them could have ever imagined.

In July 2018, according to newswhip.com user engagement data, Fox News retained its top dog position on the social media giant Facebook with 38.6 million user engagements and increased its lead over second-placed CNN. Growth has been rapid: In 2010, Facebook unique user engagement with Fox News content was 95 percent less than 2018.

But now it is much more rapid: In 2019, total engagements in just forty days on Facebook eclipsed 2018.

When you add in (1) Fox News's daytime and prime-time cable daily viewers of 3.5 million, (2) FNC's digital platform reach of 78 million, and (3) the other 40 million or so Fox News social media engagements recorded on Twitter/YouTube/Reddit every day (and then subtract for estimated duplicate users), Fox News in 2018 engages as many as one hundred million Americans with its right-wing tribal identity activation and validation programming every month.

Fox News is, of course, a cable TV news channel in name only. But what most people outside of TV and advertising miss is that Fox News really is the first and most powerful commercial tribal identity brand in America. If you define a brand correctly, the definition is simple—it's a "valued emotional promise kept."

Fox News Channel is the first major white tribal partisan identity national media brand. Its promise and value proposition to its audience is "Watch Fox News and you are going to feel better about yourself via validation of your tribal identity superiority every day. You'll feel righteous about all your anti-PC beliefs and absolved of personal responsibility for your withered household economics. In fact, if you watch thirty hours of Fox News tribal identity porn a week, we'll take that wimpy self-esteem you arrived with and make it stronger than Arnold Schwarzenegger!"

The GOP's social identity brand has been fuzzy and shapeshifting for fifty years. Fox News's tribal identity brand has been pitch perfect for nearly twenty years.

WHAT DO A HYPNOTIST, A TELEVANGELIST, AND A FOX NEWS OPINION PROGRAM HAVE IN COMMON?

As I hope you understand by now, the sole mission of this book is to expose and teach you how to *not* let Fox News's predatory brand of white tribal identity porn infect your mind and soul and turn you into a desocialized Foxhole (or how to save a loved one who is). I also hope you will spread the news about Fox News's tribal warfare playbook-driven content to self-identified conservative fifty-plus-year-old Americans so they too can learn how to consume this psychologically predatory content in a healthy way.

PS—you are a mentally healthy consumer of Fox News opinion white identity content if you remain an "agree-to-disagree" or "Hey—let's change the subject, okay?" proud Republican or Intolerable. Multiple family therapists have reported and shared with me that Foxhole syndrome is when the person who used to be able to discuss his or her political or cultural views with someone who did not share those same views just no longer can do so.

The mentally healthy heavy Fox News viewer 1) knows when to stop, 2) knows when to call a truce and move on, and 3) in the healthiest scenario can say, "Hey I hear ya—I don't agree but I respect your right to your beliefs (no matter how idiotic I think they are)."

The mentally unhealthy Foxholes exhibit the complete opposite behavior. And like I said—unless their family and friends are all basically Foxholes, too, they are headed toward family and friend estrangement.

By now you understand how the FNC's playbook of tribal warfare was carefully developed and designed to hack and exploit our DNA-encoded psychological and emotional weaknesses and vulnerabilities. It starts with our constant need to feed or refill our ego/self-esteem reservoir and feeling of superior self-worth. How to feed the need? Through an audiovisual presentation of convincing visual and rhetorical evidence of our chosen in-group/tribe's intellectual and moral superiority over our out-group enemy (the other tribes). It's about our caveman and tribal emotions, instincts and reflexes for personal safety and protection from fearful people, places, and things.

FNC's plays trigger and manipulate our involuntary "fear reflex." Fear works because it causes stress, and stress causes the desire to do something. Fear suggests loss. Fear paints a picture and creates a mental state that seeks a necessary response. Fearful images tell and show the viewer how he or she will be damaged in some disgusting and unacceptable way—and this threat of your being damaged triggers feelings of imminent danger.

This carefully choreographed, fear-inducing imaging and rhetoric most importantly makes the viewer react and involuntarily move into his or her tribalized white identity state-of-mind—and at the very moment, Fox News owns your brain stem and thus owns your attention, as well.

In fact, in their study, *Age of Propaganda* (2001), social psychologists and authors Anthony Pratkanis and Elliot Aronson argue that fear based content is most visually and rhetorically effective when:

1. It scares the hell out of people (i.e., it's existential).

2. It offers a specific recommendation for overcoming the fear-arousing existential personal or tribal threat.

3. The solution or recommended action presented by the trusted authority figure is easily perceived as reducing the imminent existential threat.

4. The viewer believes that he or she can fight the threat and can personally perform the recommended action.

But now let's move beyond the fear card.

Let's dig a little deeper into some of the other core predatory manipulations I learned at Fox News.

In short, there are many powerful reasons other than personal or tribal fear that FNC opinion debate segments are so profoundly impactful and why it is so easy to manipulate FNC's self-identified conservative or Deplorable cable or social media audience into a basic hypnotic trance.

MEET MY FRIEND THE PROFESSIONAL HYPNOTIST

Speaking of hypnotic trances, meet my buddy Tommy G. He is among other things a professional hypnotist in New York City who does bachelor parties, office parties, and everything in between. People love him because he is so funny and so fast—it takes him about sixty seconds to put me under via just his soothing voice and technique—he is a total hypno pro.

But the reason to meet Tommy G is to gain his insights into how and why Fox News is quite literally hypnotic and renders many viewers into hours-long hypnotic trances. Tommy and I discussed this issue of TV hypnotic trances for years—here are my notes from his professional summary.

Hypnosis is a way of communicating with people too.

Here's the deal: TV is hypnotic, like anything where you focus your singular attention to the exclusion of everything else. If you stare long enough at a candle flame to the exclusion of everything else, that is a hypnotic state. If you open your Facebook app and realize later you just lost an hour (or three) of time, you were most definitely in a hypnotic state of mind.

This is why TV is exceptionally and inherently hypnotic. The fact is that if a person is watching a TV program that totally absorbs their consciousness, they will be unaware of people around them, the feeling of their shoes on their feet, etc. In fact they are in a hypnotic state of mind and a deep hypnotic trance—an eyes-wide-open trance.

Does this state describe anyone you know? I know I have walked past my aging father-in-law while he is in his TV room and favorite chair watching golf or football and you could explode a bomb in there and he would not flinch. If you walked by me watching the last 9 holes of the Masters golf tournament, ditto: I am zoned out.

People in this digital hypnotic trance state are everywhere; the fast food restaurant, riding public transportation, at school—people are fixated on their digital devices. If you are engrossed in watching TV, YouTube, digital games, or social media to the degree that nothing else matters, you are in the state of an eyes-wide-open hypnotic trance, my friend.

But according to Tommy G, when Fox News addicts are in that eyes-open trance, they are extremely suggestible to all kinds of bizarre and hard-to-swallow conspiracy theories and contrived propaganda brainwashing because their analytical guard is fully down. That is another part of the how and why the Fox News white tribal warfare production playbook is so powerful—especially with men.

I know you will find this fact just shocking, but it just so happens that men are the most easily hypnotized by 1) sexual fantasy, aka video pornography, 2) war/action movies, and 3) sports, which are in a psychological sense really just the experience of vicarious warfare to men.

Now look with a critical eye at FNC's white tribal identity porn. It really is not much more than a mashup of sexual fantasy (at least the opinion shows with sexy looking female hosts and guests) plus tribalized political warfare presented like an ESPN sporting event or televised gladiatorial warfare to the male brain.

Key Point: The other thing that gets male attention locked in is to show them that their family or tribe is in danger. Social psychologists tell us that men naturally scan the environment for potential danger at an unconscious level—that their caveman brain and amygdala/brain stem is always working and making threat assessments. It's our genetic heritage. Ergo our unconscious male instinct is to still protect the women and children of the tribe just like back in the old tribal days on the savannas of Africa.

As Aristotle points out many times in his classic analysis of persuasive performances, *Rhetoric*, this fact of male genetic predisposition to protect their women and children has been exploited through persuasive political propaganda for millennia (read: how to induce men to wage war writ large). This is just one reason why televised personal and tribal fear moments are so hypnotizing for men—especially older men with multiple children and women in their life to protect.

But understand that a hypnotic trance is also an amplifying state—that is the key to Fox News hypnotic states and Fox News addiction and becoming a brainwashed Foxhole. It's an amplifying state because when we humans focus our attention on just one thing, we are implicitly telling our brain that this is important—so our brains drive us innately to get more of what we focus on. Note to self—my golf game is in deep need of more trances!

Images of sex and violence and tribal or family threats grab our attention and then our brains fixate on them. That is why the Fox News tribal warfare playbook shamelessly creates these family and tribal threatening images—our brain is always looking out for potential danger at an unconscious level. As always, the deepest part of the human psyche's role is to keep you and your family alive and well.

The really key insight into TV trance induction is that 1) the more a person enters into these eyes-wide-open trances, 2) the more his brain will spontaneously go into them. After thousands of these Fox News induced hypnotic trances, one literally becomes a Fox News trance zombie—and the more time one spends in a trance state, the more suggestible in general one becomes.

Tommy adds, "Toby, the key with Fox News is that people do not let you put them in a trance unless they trust you. And guess what? The really hypnotic voices are the ones that are modulated up-and-down—monotones don't work. That is why the great FNC right-wing hosts like O'Reilly sound like a persuasive salesman—because they are!"

In other words, from a professional hypnotist's perspective, the entire Fox News tribal warfare playbook is an overt and covert exercise in mass televised hypnosis: trance induction and retention.

A Fox News hypnotic trance allows Fox News to communicate with a person's unconscious mind. That's the part of your mind that you're not aware of right now. Like—until I mention it—you're not aware of your breathing. Or heart rate. Or facial expression. Or posture. Or the elements of "reality" that you take for granted as real.

Now we're getting somewhere. Hypnosis is a way of communicating with the part of a person that takes care of all this important stuff (and most of your mental processes, too, like making choices, problem solving, imagining possible futures, and more). And hypnosis is a type of communication that does connect without needing to bring any of these things into conscious awareness—that's why it is so amazingly powerful and manipulative.

Did you know this important but unrecognized aspect of the FNC white tribal warfare playbook?

Yea, I know—I didn't either. Thank Tommy G.

BUT HOW DO YOU KEEP AN AUDIENCE WATCHING FOX NEWS? "JUST MINE THE RICH VEINS OF WHITE IDENTITY INJUSTICE AND GRIEVANCE, DUDE!"

This story is about one of the fifty-plus nights I was asked to anchor the live "America's Nightly Scoreboard" on FBN. It starts about five hours before show time. On this prime-time opinion program, the process was that the host opened the show with an in-your-face demagogic editorial that was expected to secure the interest of the audience at home and glue them to their seats.

Of course, as you now know, in the Fox 2.0 post-2008 America, this meant the audience engagement strategy was another cathartic hour of Obama-bashing and liberal strafing.

Since I had not been preparing to host the show that night, I really had nothing in mind to write for my opening monologue. I was nervous that I would not convincingly fulfill my role as head blame-shifter for the "I-Hate-Obama" Fox News audience. I'd frankly run out of outrage-inducing or cathartic blame-shifting ideas. Even the Daily Memo, aka Roger Ailes's topics of mass liberal destruction and outrage, that day was pretty weak. Nothing much on the memo hit me as particularly outrageous ammo. It was just a slow day of outrage and inflammatory injustice-inducing ideas for the Fox Hate Networks.

So as usual, I went to see one of my favorite Fox News prime-time producer friends looking for a few ideas—the clock was ticking. Gene (not his real name—he is still at Fox News to this day) came from a political science background and was what Roger would consider a Fox News philistine. Gene did eventually sell his soul to the devil to produce a number of the prime-time populist conservative televangelists, aka FNC opinion talk shows. After all, even a philistine has to pay the rent and eat.

What he told me that night, though, gave me about one hundred hours of Fox News-style outrage televangelism gold. He also reinforced the now-obvious truth that Fox News was doing Trump before Trump was doing Trump. Whatever America we are living in now, we and Roger Ailes got there first many years ago to set the unreality show stage.

"Toby," Gene said, "what you don't seem to understand is that the primary animating psychology of our core viewer is the psychology of grievance, which is a fancy way of saying they want to see the blood-sport of injustice payback. Grievance from a conservative political perspective is basically pathological; it's any widely held perception and belief of a cultural or economic injustice inflicted upon them by the hated liberal ruling elite class.

"The key part of understanding and leveraging this right-wing pathology is this: In the court of tribal justice, a tribal injustice requires tribal redress—what I believe you would call 'payback is a mofo.'"

The cocktails kept coming and he was rolling. "So listen," he said. "What you don't seem to understand is our basic core viewer carries an almost debilitating sub-conscious inferiority complex. They feel judged and so overwhelmingly disrespected every friggin' day of their lives by those terrible elites who do nothing but condescend and disrespect them twenty-four-seven. If you want to tap into the mass inferiority complex, you have to ask yourself two questions and then answer them well: One, what cultural or economic grievance has this guy pissed off most today? And two, how do I mine those feelings of deep-seated grievance and channel that anger for him like you are his mirror image on the other side of his TV screen?"

As a fresh Martini appeared, courtesy of Des, the owner, I asked, "So how do I do that?"

"Let me change the metaphor," Gene replied. "To get this right you need to find a hot ember of irreparable cultural or economic injustice buried deep in the good ol' conservative grievance woodpile—and fan that ember with a storm of righteous indignation!

"How dare they?!! If you want to get your audience's attention and keep it, your job is to find the burning, unfair, right-wing injustice of the day. Then stoke that ember and give them new reasons that validate their righteous grievance. And then pin that grievance to the 'here's another reason why you should blame liberals for all your problems' narrative.

"How? Do what everyone else does here! Go to the Foxnews.com pod and ask them what moral or economic injustice against 'real Americans' is trending on Foxnews.com. Or go to Breitbart.com and Drudge Report and see which white right-wing injustice story has the most ugly and angry comments and now you have a monologue." (PS—this is the reason why Drudge and Brietbart.com are on every Fox News producer's browser to this day.)

Gene was right.

When you call out a widely shared perception of the unfair and the unjust, not only do you reconnect with the Fox News audience by acknowledging the moral righteousness of it is valid, but you also give them a few more easy-to-understand reasons to make them feel even more righteous (building their self-esteem from an "I'm so much smarter than those stupid socialist libtards" fist bump) and of course morally just.

It's like Tony Montana's line in *Scarface*: "First you show the injustice, then you get the grievance and pile on a few more and then you get their respect and keep their eyeballs!"

PS Ol' Gene is the same producer who taught me that to become a prime-time host on Fox News, I needed to go watch a Pentecostal evangelist and learn how to deliver a hellfire and damnation sermon and learn to mimic their speech cadence. He also taught me that the basic evangelical fear-based grift and emotional manipulation are derived from another subconscious fear and reflex: that our species of animal is the only one that is cognizant we are going to die. For many people, that unresolved fear of death is resolved by a convincing evangelist selling the opportunity for everlasting life.

While hosting Fox News "fair and balanced" opinion debate shows I learned that mining true TV grievance gold comes from creating a new reason to blame the liberals for every economic or cultural atrocity narrative. The atrocity does not even have to be true on Fox News—as we all know now, subjective truth is objective reality to our entranced audience. The innocent victim narrative is embedded in our audience's psyche. It's a deep, visceral, bone-marrow feeling of not getting a fair shake from society and/ or the government (or even better both) like they did in the old days when life was fair and just.

Remember, too, I told you the half-brother of cultural hate and blame is cultural sentimentality? The Fox News audience lives on nostalgic overload. You know the drill: "In their day, you worked hard, you followed the rules; kept your nose clean, paid your bills, and you retired with a pension and fat belly and doted on your grandkids."

Our audience is deeply sentimental for that age gone by—to live once again in a country that has not left them behind. Obviously we did "Make

America Great Again" before Donald Trump. I am dead certain that El Trumpedo learned how powerful white identity nostalgia porn is from watching ten thousand hours of Fox News.

In short, to engage an audience at a primal emotional level (which is what white tribal identify porn is designed to do) you have to meet the audience where their perspective already is, not where you want to take them. The lowest hanging fruit on the injustice and grievance tree is the simplest: when Obama got elected the old rules went to shit and the white middle and working class got screwed by the financial capitalist elites blah blah blah.

That narrative has the added advantage that it is based on a lot of actual fact.

Then just play the "unfair and unjust greatest hits" of the moment. In my day they were:

1. The Great Recession hit and the fat cats not only got bailed out but they got richer—and the real Americans got screwed—it was unfair and unjust and hard to argue against.

2. When a righteous conservative American opens the paper, turns on the mainstream TV, or scans their social media, all they see is the libtard/socialists/mainstream media screaming to everyone in the world that they're racists, xenophobes, dopes, bigots, losers, and worst of all, whiners. That's both unfair and heinously disrespectful, too.

3. From the typical Fox News viewer I met on the street/bar/ restaurant/airport, they felt they were presented in popular entertainment and culture on TV as low information-ignorant rubes that don't defer to the expert Masters of the Universe who actually know how the complex world works and how to govern it.

When members of our audience became convinced liberal society violated the rules of the game and is not playing fair, they got insanely indignant. The implicit deal behind the American sociological and economic arrangement they understood was that the members of the American ruling and political class would create economic growth from which everyone would benefit.

But the reality is the flourishing ruling class and liberal elite drives home the message that their failures are no one's fault but their own. They deserve their sorry fate. The rules of success in America changed and they should've got the memo and gone to college like they did.

Bingo—I had a monologue.

That night was around the fifth year anniversary of the 2008 bank bailouts. I talked about why they should never forget the holocaust-like injustice on the white working and middle class from the trillion-dollar bank bailouts during the financial crisis for banks and fat cats.

The narrative was not difficult to conjure. Many real Main Street Americans of course did lose their homes and savings and were left for dead in an economic flood without a paddle. I emphasized how liberals constantly tell them the Great Recession was their fault—they are the ones that took out loans they could not afford.

I told them if they live in places without jobs, if their neighbors are dying from addiction to painkillers, if their houses are underwater and can only be sold at a loss, the liberals tell them they should just move (even though for most that was and still is impossible).

I told them that it sure is easy to look down upon real Americans when the elites were born on third base and they all feel like they just hit a triple.

But the greatest injustice? How Wall Street got a socialist solution where failure means a bail-out while Main Street got the cold-hearted capitalism medicine where failure means bankruptcy and foreclosure.

Boom. Long story short—ratings killed that night. I found a perennial ember of injustice and I ginned up a new way for the viewer to see and hear how they got screwed (socialism for the rich, cut-throat capitalism for the white middle/working class). It was the Fox News tribal warfare playbook played to perfection. I got asked to come back and host a whole week when the host went on vacation.

I was jacked—the playbook worked! It worked because human nature is indeed immutable and our primal emotions are indeed primary—they are just too easy to trigger, fan, and ignite into a self-reinforcing moral spiral *if* you know how to produce TV for that moral spiral result. The digital-video era of communication thrives on rage and passion—and passion is the enemy of objective analysis—that's another reason why the playbook is so powerful and so lethally entrances the FNC audience.

Maybe Donald Trump was listening that night. He may be a pathological lying, sociopathic ignoramus, but he has a much better intuitive and feral grasp of the psychology of grievance than his establishment critics do. Most

Fox News addicts are not just pissed off—they have an inferiority complex boulder building deep inside. They want payback and revenge—and many want to watch a cathartic blame-shifting TV show that delivers a very real "it's not your fault and here is why" cathartic moment.

Most of all, the economic bottom sixty to eighty percent of white America wants what Donald J. Trump was selling in 2015; someone who will take a stand against all the aforementioned entrenched and non-redressed injustices and unfairness of liberal America and fight the fuck back.

That night I learned another important play embedded in the Fox News tribal warfare playbook: a cathartic seven-minute TV segment that mines the raw emotions of class and cultural grievance and feelings of injustice. It's the conservative TV vein of emotional gold that never ends.

TOBY—THIS IS HIGH-DEF TV—PEOPLE SEE YOU—YOU HAVE TO SHOW THEM YOUR RIGHTEOUS RIGHT-WING I.D. BADGE IN EVERY SEGMENT

As mentioned, perhaps the most impactful audiovisual production technique within the FNC conservative tribal warfare playbook is the simplest one— the viewer at home gets to see your emotions via your facial cues and that of their cultural and political tribal enemy. Not so with audio-only radio.

Yes, eighty-plus percent of our emotions are communicated by our eyes and hand gestures. But there is another critical part of making high-impact white tribal identity porn; it's the casting of the right- and left-wing actors.

Social psychologists and anthropologists have for years told us we still have an innate caveman reflex for in-group/out-group bias and an automatic instinct for "ethnocentrism" (i.e., how we automatically evaluate other cultures according to preconceptions originating in the standards and customs of one's own culture).

This reflex is a) universal, and b) encoded in our reptilian brain. Thus it's instinctual and automatic. Nothing shocking here—walk into a cocktail party with people you don't know and see how you find people to talk with and gravitate toward.

But a big part of understanding the Fox News tribal warfare playbook is to realize that when it comes to creating must-see tribal identity TV, 1) each of us, in essence, occupies the center of a set of concentric social and cultural circles that we have created in our own likeness (i.e., an egocentric circle), and 2) all of us need to immediately recognize that someone on our tribal TV screen is a member in good standing of our social circles—and in the case of Fox News one of those circles is a white cultural and political conservative circle.

In other words—is Tobin Smith on my team or not? How do I, the viewer, know he's on my team? If the viewer does not sense immediately, does not consciously and subconsciously judge that we are on the same right-wing cultural, economic, and political team, the viewer's innate cognitive bias reflexes take over and they tune that segment (or me) out.

As social scientist Joshua Greene writes in his book *Moral Tribes,* "humans pay exquisitely close attention to where we judge people reside in our egocentric social universes." After the election of 2016, that may be the understatement of the year.

It turns out the primary way we make these instantaneous judgments of whom we trust and who we want to listen to in a cultural/political talk show comes to us via verbal or linguistic clues. Greene describes this process like a "social I.D. badge" in that people naturally look for reliable markers of cultural group membership. Greene reminds us of the Hebrew Bible and the term "shibboleth" as "any reliable market of cultural group membership" or, more plainly, in-group/out-group Us vs. Them tribalism.

Research by sociologist Katherine Kinzler shows us that this predisposition starts in early age and goes back to our most basic automatic instinct for protecting personal safety. Her research concludes that our caveman brain, even before we can speak, uses language cues to distinguish the trustworthy Us from untrustworthy Them.

What does this have to do with the Fox News tribal warfare playbook for opinion programming? The answer is: a ton.

First, if you understand this innate reflex, you understand how and why on Fox News the right-wing and left-wing panels are selected and why guys like me who understand right-wing role playing succeed and otherwise conservative panelists fail.

The members of a Fox News opinion segment are cast by the producers for their innate social-cultural-political I.D. badge. That "badge" must flash "right or left wing" with the first words out of their mouths and looks on their faces. In fact, before they say a word. It's their race. Their clothes. Their faces. Their voices. Their language usage—it all morphs into a construct that the viewer/streamer is judging us as either "he/she is safe and Us" or "a threat and one of *Them.*"

Producers know that if the viewer doesn't see and sense who the tribal villain is and who their hero is, the segment does not work. My point here is that people way underestimate how important selecting the cast is. It's highly choreographed and important to suck in the older right-wing Fox News audience. I cannot tell you how often I would hear from a Fox News addict in public: "I know I can trust you Toby to tell it like it is—I appreciate that."

What they did not understand is that this white Scots Irish 50-something guy who looks like them, sounds like them, speaks (mostly) like them is playing a well-rehearsed role in which I:

1. act angry when they are angry (cue my famous "scowl" look).

2. shake my head when they are shaking theirs (which the director instantly shows on screen).

3. roll my eyes at the same time I hear another tribal apostasy (cue my OMG eye-roll and forehead slap).

4. and widen my eyes when I am ready to lay into the tribal enemy.

It's my right-wing TV pundit performance art: it's all an act. From an acting perspective, my job on a Fox News panel is to mirror the look and the speech of the guy at home (or the husband of the woman who is watching).

If you can't play the part of the white tribal identity hero, you don't emotionally and tribally connect. As I mentioned, I had a very high Q rating (likeability). That just did not happen by accident.

I learned how acting the role was more important than what you said. The code words, the in-group smirk, and laugh. . . . Watch the longtime pundits on Fox News—there is a reason they have been there for ten-plus years.

The lessons here?

1. It is impossible to fool human nature—so Fox News, as a business model, manipulates and exploits the hell out of our innate human nature.

2. Deeply buried and repressed feelings and perceptions of class grievance and disrespect eventually ferment into emotional manipulation gold. They are the programming gifts that keep on giving to those who make their living producing and acting in white tribal identity porn programming. So, at Fox News we learned to mine those feelings and manipulate the hell out of them for our benefit too.

What I found meeting thousands of our audience members on various speaking tours in Retro America was that our Fox News audience in general carries a giant chip on their shoulder. They get it by being told for decades by mainstream television, media, movies, and entertainment in general that they are old fashioned, unsophisticated, out-of-touch dinosaurs who don't really matter (except for growing our food and raising our beef cattle) and that they are really second-class citizens relative to the Masters of the Universe in Silicon Valley and the East Coast Meccas of intelligence and sophistication.

On the other hand, if you mixed in Hollywood showbiz with right-wing propaganda, sexy women, and angry older anchors who mirror the viewer/streamer like they were an identical twin they never met, you could conquer the white tribal identity world.

I learned later in my career what the successful Fox News opinion programming producers had been taught by Roger Ailes: that one of the reasons Fox News is so addictive to fifty-five-year-old-plus aged men and women is that we shamelessly manipulated their conscious feelings of tribal disrespect and perpetual grievance. That constant cultural beat-down would eventually morph into one helluva inferiority complex and grievances for us to mine 24/7.

If we could flip that inferiority complex into feelings of tribal superiority for an hour or two, the self-esteem blast of neurochemicals would be as addictive to the Fox News viewer as crack cocaine. And better—once addicted they'd always come back for their next hit. The tough part was having to raise the intensity of our tribal fear/hate/blame and victimology rhetoric because like any addict they build a tolerance for "juice" and need a bigger dose to get the same feelings.

So we did. All Donald Trump did was take our Fox News white identity porn programming and add white ethno-nationalism with his "Get 'em out of here" and "Send them home" shtick, which unleashed levels of white tribal identity racism that even white identity tribalist Roger Ailes would not attempt to achieve.

CHAPTER 8

Your Eyes Do Not Lie: Fox News Is Good Old Soft-core Sex Porn Too

I am not disclosing anything remotely new in this chapter: The pornified look of Fox News takes about ten minutes for any first-time viewer to figure out and is done for the obvious fundamental reasons:

Conservative media competition for Fox News is sound-only radio.
The only other real competitor for right-wing geriatric talk show viewers is Christian TV televangelists.
Unless it's sports, most old guys will take looking at attractive women over an hour of hell-and-damnation TV any day.

But let me give you an inside look at what pornified Fox News programming means. First, a short conversation with Roger Ailes—who by the way never appeared on a minute of Fox News programming.

I was on the second floor because FBN had established a movie studio there—the rest of the second floor was Ailes and top executives and a movie projection room to watch Fox movies for employees. Roger came into the movie room with a few guests—they were showing the *Avatar* film prerelease.

He said hello and I asked him, "Roger—a friend of mine asked me 'Why are all the women in Fox News so hot?' He told me, 'Dude if I worked there, I would be an HR disaster!'"

Roger did not blink. He said, "Toby, tell your friend the reason our female talent are so attractive is that I am the audience, and no guy like me wants to bang Andrea Mitchell. You know our audience—they want a show, not a college professor."

Boom, shakalaka—Ailes's answer is almost everything anyone needs to know about the Fox News aesthetic—high-end escort in a short above-the-knee skirt on a SportsCenter style set.

I learned everything else you'll ever need to know about what matters most to the producers of Fox News opinion programming while on a remote hit from Fox's DC studios from a mighty executive producer.

It was a slow news day. In the New York City studio was Sandra Smith, a Fox Business Network anchor (now noontime daily host at FNC) who was just a few years out of college, statuesque, drop-dead gorgeous, and of course, a bottle blonde.

Steve Forbes, the heir to Malcolm Forbes of the *Forbes* magazine empire, and I were in the DC studio. Steve is a notable Republican who ran a Don Quixote-like presidential campaign on a flat-tax platform.

Fox purposely had no written rules about what they wanted paid contributors to say or talk about (so there was no evidence that could be leaked to the *New York Times* or Media Matters, for example), but it had lots of unwritten rules. For instance, when it came to business/economic panel interviews, FNC producers did not want a paid contributor to talk about the value of the dollar vs. another currency.

I learned this the hard way when I was scolded by an executive producer early in my career: "Toby, never talk about the value of the dollar on Fox. Our viewers don't give a shit about the price of the dollar vs. the Euro. Our viewers aren't jetting off to Saint-Tropez, okay?" Not coincidentally, I had just returned from Saint-Tropez, and the same executive producer had asked me, "Why go there? It's nothing but old buildings and smelly Europeans and women with armpit hair. Who cares?"

You have to love the worldly Fox News opinion-show producers!

Note: All of the opinion-programming executive producers I worked with at Fox were dyed-in-the-wool right-wingers. This is the complete opposite of the producers I worked with at CNN or CNBC (and of course MSNBC).

Anyway, this hit was the standard seven-minute interview segment with three "boxes" (live streaming video shots—in this case, of me, Forbes, and Sandra).

Steve Forbes opened the segment and launched into a four-minute tirade about the US dollar being weak against the Euro and twelve reasons why it was all President Obama's fault. Next to respond was Sandra, and she went into a two-minute report telling our viewers that the price of oil was dropping because of the weak dollar. (FYI actually, because oil is priced in US dollars, if the dollar goes down in value, the price of a barrel of oil in dollars rises because it takes more dollars to buy the same amount of oil relative to the other currencies.)

Then the interview swung to me. There were just about sixty seconds left, so, sort of laughing, I said to the anchor, "Well, first, I know what Sandra meant to say is that when the value of the dollar drops versus the Euro, the price of a barrel of oil goes higher and—"

Boom! In my ear, the executive producer shouted, "Wrap!" which tells the anchor and the paid contributor to end the segment immediately—and for me to shut the heck up.

I immediately texted the executive producer after the hit: "WTF? Steve Forbes goes on a four-minute rant about the value of the US dollar which you told me many times to *never* talk about . . . Sandra talks about the value of the dollar and its correlation to oil prices and gets it completely *backward* . . . and I was trying to not embarrass Fox News with such inaccurate reporting and *I'm the asshole?*"

The executive producer texted me right back with the lesson no one should ever forget when it comes to Fox News: "Toby . . . if you *looked* like Sandra Smith you could say whatever the fuck you want to on my air." (Excuse me for using the F-bomb, but in Fox News land, that word is used as often as people breathe air. Don't tell the Evangelicals!)

Fox News Lesson Learned: Not shockingly, on Fox News, how attractive a female host or guest looks from the chest up or how bright your GOP star power is will always be ten times more important than what you say. Over my fourteen years there, I heard the dumbest and least-informed on-air statements and opinions from ridiculously attractive women and powerful elected GOP officials—without the executive producers ever saying a word.

You understand by now that an opinion segment at Fox is indeed a performance art; it's another Roger Ailes rigged "debate" show without a fair debate. And of course, that means these politics-as-performance art segments start with a cast of characters who have to look and act their parts for the majority male audience. Roger Ailes also understood that to catch the compulsive male channel flippers sitting at home in their favorite chairs with the remote controls in their hands, Fox News needed as much visual glam as it could get.

If you could perform one of those roles with some energy and deliver fifteen-to-twenty-second sound bites, you got invited back, and if you played your conservative role very well, you became a paid contributor plebe at $500 per appearance. Once you'd made more than $200,000 in appearance fees in a calendar year, you went to a fixed $5,000 per week regardless of how many appearances you made.

Anyway, when it comes to the liberal pundits on Fox News, the casting rules were very different. First, they have to look and sound like stereotypical big-city liberals. Then they need to totally use the liberal talking points that the core right-wing audience hates. And the darker the liberal pundit's skin color, the better.

IT'S ALL SHOWBIZ, BABY

In October 2000, early in my career as a Fox News contributor, I received my initial lesson about a Fox News panel debate being much more about showbiz than a substantive economic or political debate. One day, while I was taping a live segment on *Your World with Neil Cavuto* with my mutual-fund manager friend Bob Olstein and my old *Bulls & Bears* market analyst partner, Scott Bleier, Scott made an on-air prediction: "Cisco's stock price is going to jump to $75 by the end of the year!"

When Olstein heard that prediction, I thought his eyeballs were going to pop out of his head. He looked at Scott and screamed, "For crying out loud, Scott! That would make Cisco worth $1 trillion. Even you aren't that stupid, are you?"

We went to commercial break and with the microphones dead, Olstein looked at Neil and said, "When Bleier made that Cisco prediction, I wanted to reach over and choke that son of a bitch!"

Without missing a beat, Neil told Olstein, "Bob if you do choke him during our next segment, I'll give you five grand cash!"

We all laughed, but Neil was dead serious. Even in the days before social media, Neil understood the real Fox News programming ethos, that these debate segments were performances first and foremost. Moreover, the mantra at FNC when I was there was, "Let CNN do the news. You see their ratings? We're in the right-wing geriatric entertainment business; don't forget it."

FOX NEWS IS SOFT-CORE SEXUAL PORN FOR OLD PEOPLE TOO

One Friday, I was in the New York City studio as I always was on Fridays. As I have mentioned previously, I was the only contributor at Fox News who flew to NYC every week to do my show in studio with the host, my friend Brenda Buttner. At this point, I did not understand why my contract required me to be in New York City every week while the other contributors could tape remotely from home or a local studio. Once I discovered the fixed-outcome tribal hate-porn formula, it made sense, because I knew I was the guy they could count on to deliver our right-wing tribalists the triumphant happy ending they tuned in to see.

Brenda kicked off her prerecorded cold open (the "tease"), which in TV land is the technique of jumping directly into a story at the opening of the show with a high-energy, rage-inducing teleprompter script. Like any opening for any TV entertainment performance, our show had about between ten and twenty seconds to hook the channel flipper. (You may not realize it, but in non-prime-time hours, channel flippers are a big key to cable channel ratings. Their effect on ratings is exceeded only by that of the core addicts of a particular channel.)

Brenda was about halfway through the cold open when the producer stopped the segment taping. Brenda asked the executive producer what was wrong. Then she listened to her earpiece and got up with a sour look before disappearing off stage.

The stage manager (who had heard everything said to Brenda in his own earpiece) told those of us on the panel desk, "Eh, she just got a call from the second floor. She is doing a little wardrobe fix."

The term "second floor" was Fox News's code for Roger Ailes. Roger watched every show—live or taped—while he was in the building. He had a literal wall of monitors in his office to see what was being recorded on every camera. In addition to making sure that his rundowns of what he believed were the most powerful emotional audience triggers for the day were being used by the executive producers, Roger also made sure that the hosts—especially the female hosts—looked Fox-worthy.

From a looks standpoint, as the media journalist Gabriel Sherman reported in a *Vanity Fair* article recently, "Every show was like an interview at Fox. If Roger liked your appearance, he told the executive producer at the next daily production meeting. If he didn't . . . he let you know it *before* you taped." (Very true, Mr. Sherman.)

To understand Fox News's carefully choreographed emotional manipulation process, you can think of the beginning of an opinion segment as the host holding a psychic dental drill in his or her hands. The script always starts with the host boring into the rawest, most painful tribal apostasy or conservative heretical desecration of the day.

Then it was the right-wing tribal blood brother's job to turn that despair and rage into the joy of ideological confirmation, affirmation, and a final glorious tribal victory over the viewer's hated tribal enemy. The on-air host and talent are the actors in this performance—and looking the part is just as important as delivering the lines (especially for the women).

Brenda came back to the set wearing the same top, but with one more blouse button unbuttoned and a lot more cleavage than when she had first tried the cold open. I looked at her and said, "Geez, B . . . vavoom! You have a big date after the show?"

She smiled, we did the show, and no one else said a thing about her wardrobe change.

After the show, Brenda and I walked across the street to our favorite post-show drinking hole, Del Frisco's. The fabulous and charming maître d', Felix, cleared our normal spot at the bar, and I ordered our traditional post-show martinis and then toasted her on a job well done. Then I asked her, "So, B . . . what the heck was that stop-down and wardrobe change? The only thing that looked different to me was you came back looking a lot sluttier!"

She said matter-of-factly, "Oh that was a call from the second floor. Roger asked me to go back to the dressing room and put on a water bra and show more cleavage."

A water bra? Really?

Later, I found out from my many on-air female Fox friends that receiving clothing, hair, makeup, and cleavage advice from Roger was standard operating procedure. Considering all that went on behind closed doors with Ailes and the platoon of female talent he sexually abused, this was not surprising.

BUT ARE YOU FOX-WORTHY?

On another Friday, I finished guest anchoring one of the episodes of *America's Nightly Scoreboard* I hosted on Fox Business Network (FBN). The show taped an hour before we taped *Bulls & Bears*. I had a female economist guest on the FBN show who happened to be a young and beautiful blonde, and she was going to be on the *Bulls & Bears* taping with me as well.

Not ninety minutes after my guest had her hair and makeup done in the FBN studio just down the hallway, I walked with her into Fox's hair-and-makeup room. When she sat down, the FNC hair-and-makeup person who was there asked, "Honey, how long do you have? This is Fox News, not FBN. We have to start from scratch to make you Fox-worthy!"

Fox-worthy is a term the makeup and hair artists use (among others) for the high-end escort aesthetic that Ailes required for all female conservatives. The left-wing women? Not so much—they were not there to be eye candy; they were there to beaten and if possible humiliated.

After the show, this same woman and I had a post-show drink at Del Frisco's upstairs bar. (See a pattern?) While we were chatting away, I noticed a big dude in the dining room staring at her, and I thought, maybe this guy is an economist fanboy? I later excused myself to the restroom and took a little time to say a few hellos to the staff.

When I returned to my table, the general manager, Scott Gould, was consoling and apologizing to my guest, saying, "I'm so sorry. We just kicked that jackass out of our restaurant. That should have never happened here."

What had happened? Well, it turned out the dude who was eyeballing my guest was an oil magnate visiting from Dallas and had judged, by looking at her makeup and hair and escort-like outfit, that she was a hooker. He had offered her "Five hundred dollars more than whatever that guy is paying you" to join him!

It was funny at the time, but I could see the guy's logic—she did look like a hooker . . . and not a $500 hooker either!

A few weeks later, I was visiting another favorite Fox News watering hole, Broadway Langan's, on Forty-Seventh near Seventh Avenue. (See a pattern?)

The hair and makeup artists from FNC who had made up the female economist guest weeks before were there, and I asked them, "So my economist pal just got off the air on FBN and you guys rebuilt her look from the chin up to the top of her head. Why?"

They both looked at me in wonder, and one of them said, "How long you been here, Toby? What is it about our job at Fox News that you don't understand? Roger has a Fox-worthy look he wants, and Roger gets what he wants. FBN is a different network, although we are starting to 'Foxify' it up a little."

Here is the kicker: "But at Fox News, our job for the on-air women is to get the tits up, get the tops down, and make the hair and makeup look like a porn shoot."

Key Point: If you are female and want to get invited for guest hits on Fox

News, you'd better not have a problem with them making you up and doing your hair like you're a high-rent escort.

AT FOX NEWS, THERE IS NOTHING LIKE GINNING UP A GOOD CAT FIGHT

Another feature of Fox News tribal hate porn is the ginned-up cat fights between female liberal and conservative panel members. After all, what male doesn't love a good girl-on-girl catfight in high-definition TV?

My longtime friend, *USA Today* conservative columnist Cheri Jacobus, shared with me one of her experiences in how Fox News producers are continually trying to gin up a "Battle Royale" between attractive left- and right-wing partisan female pundits (the WWE analogy is on purpose).

According to Cheri, "About twelve or fourteen years ago, I was blackballed (for several years) at Fox News because when I was asked to have a 'catfight' with 'democratic strategist' Kirsten Powers, I said I'm happy to have a spirited debate, but no catfight. Kirsten (then a paid contributor and thus expected, like me, to follow the orders of segment producers) had tried to start one with me a few days earlier on the air. When I refused to play ball, the Fox booker phone stopped ringing."

Catfights have always been a part of soft-core porn. Why should it be any different at Fox News?

CHAPTER 9

More Fox News Production Lessons Learned

There is a lot more I learned about producing rigged-outcome debate programs in my years at Fox News. Here are more that are not well documented or discussed in the world of media reporting.

WHY "DEMOPUBLICANS" ARE SO CRITICAL TO FOX NEWS'S OPINION-PROGRAM MELODRAMAS

Here's another way the opinion debates at Fox News are methodically rigged for the conservative tribal heroes to win. My old liberal friend Bob Beckel (now marooned from Fox News because of accusations that he made racist remarks) is an old-school Chicago blue-collar Democrat.

Most people don't know that when Bob wasn't on air and trying to be funny and glib on Fox News, he did research polling for FNC on the Q ratings of the various hosts and paid contributors.

A Q rating is a person's on-air likeability rating relative to all the others in the survey. On Fox, the higher the person's score, the more the core partisan right-wingers liked you. A high score helped a lot in getting contracts renewed. I was fortunate to get a top-10 percent Q score from our audience. When I saw my results, I learned that the audience liked me because (a) I tried to make the segments fun and (b) I was darn good at rhetorically disemboweling the token liberal our core tribal audience despised.

That was my persona at Fox News: The funny yet lethal hit man.

One afternoon before a show taping, I was smoking a cigar with Bob in the breezeway between the Fox News offices, and we start talking about the significance of Q ratings, especially for the liberal contributors.

As mentioned, part of the FNC fixed-outcome production playbook was for producers to select a liberal opponent—usually not nearly as experienced on the segment topic as I was but someone who fulfilled the character prop role for the melodrama we were performing that day. I asked, "So Bob, who are the most popular liberal contributors on FNC these days?"

In response, he gave me a lesson in producing right-wing tribal identity porn: "There is a fine line between being the 'right' kind of liberal pundit on Fox and being the wrong kind."

"What do you mean by that?" I asked.

"I can tell you from the Q ratings that the liberals they like the best are the least confrontational. Fox News does not hire gunslinger Democrats. That is not what the audience wants to see. The audience wants a DemoPublican like Juan Williams or me or Mort Kondracke for you to beat up on.

"Look . . . Mort, Juan, and I don't represent hard-core liberalism and progressives. We represent a soft-core adversary that any good right-wing conservative pundit can beat like a red-headed stepchild in the eyes of the right-wing nut jobs we call viewers."

He was right. From the beginning to the end of every opinion segment that any of us paid pundits participated in, Fox's paid lefty contributors all knew there was only one goal for the segment: to make the viewer at home have the righteous sanctity of his political and cultural conservatism mindset once again validated; they all knew the whole point of the segment was for the liberal to "get whupped" in the eyes of the typical Fox News viewer.

Fox employed Mort Kondracke, one of the nicest milquetoast "liberals" you could ever find, as the sparring opponent for the alpha-male conservatives on these rigged panels. Mort was a prim and proper professor type who was the perfect gentleman, always. In other words, he was a professional liberal Fox News opinion-panel piñata, and he couldn't care less. He was on air daily, so that was $10,000 per week he made, maybe $20,000, since he was so senior.

When I left Fox News, Juan Williams was making $2 million a year as a liberal Fox News piñata. I'd take a beating every day for $20,000 a week at thirty-five minutes of cumulative weekly airtime. Wouldn't you?

THE LIBERAL PANEL MEMBERS ON FNC ARE DELIBERATELY RHETORICAL MINOR LEAGUERS

Another big part of Fox News's "fair and balanced" opinion-programming scam is that the "Democratic strategist" label is often a ruse. Let's call them what they are: fake analysts. When you hear someone on Fox

News described as a "Democratic strategist," it is almost always code for a third- or fourth-string liberal wannabe paid contributor crash dummy/piñata.

For example, Kirsten Powers (now an experienced contributor for CNN) was promoted and touted in the early 2000s by Roger Ailes as a Democratic strategist with experience in the Clinton White House. In reality, she was a prime example of the fake political analysts Ailes launched with fudged or outright fake resumes.

This kind of fraud still goes on today. Fox News may have hired Donna Brazile as their new token heavyweight Democrat, but according to what I see on Media Matters (which tapes one hundred percent of Fox News programming) she is sparingly used to say the least. Anyway, although she claimed she worked in the Clinton White House, Kirsten had merely worked in low- and mid-level jobs in a non-cabinet agency called the Office of the United States Trade Representative. For years, I heard from actual Democratic strategists in my hometown of Washington, DC, that they had no idea who Kirsten was and that she had no significant political experience.

This blowback got back to Roger, so *voila!* Kirsten was given a column at the Murdoch-owned *New York Post* and was then introduced as a political columnist instead of as a Dem strategist.

Liberal female antagonists on Fox debates (known as "props") have always been selected for their looks or ethnicity, not for their rhetorical chops or subject matter expertise. "Democratic strategists" with dark skin are always desired and are seen as important to liberal/enemy typecasting; just about any African American liberal or Hispanic American who calls herself a Democratic strategist will get at least one call from segment producers for a segment tryout.

On *Bulls & Bears* our favorite third-string Democratic strategist for years was Jehmu Greene. (After years on Fox News, she became a first-string Democratic strategist, and when she got too rhetorically strong, she was, of course, let go by Fox News.)

She is now a CNN contributor. Jehmu was straight out of the casting for "smug ethnic liberal antagonist." She specialized in the sour look that the director would constantly show when I or another right-wing protagonist was chopping her liberal dogma to pieces.

But you understand her value to our highly choreographed fear-and-redemption melodrama. I'm not saying all our primarily white male audience was prejudiced or didn't care for black folks; what I am saying is after the Obama election, there were enough racists in our audience to make a difference.

In fourteen years and two thousand segments at Fox News, I had only one fair fight. It was with a whip-smart, left-wing hard-ass attorney named Julian Epstein from San Francisco. After beating us all up pretty well with arguments he had never disclosed to the producer before the show, he never came back on the show again (and soon was banned from Fox News altogether after a tiff with Editor-in-Chief Neil Cavuto).

FNC FIXES ITS WARRIOR AND INTELLIGENCE PANELS TOO

Rigged outcomes and the selection of demonstratively weak opposition is part of all opinion-debate programming at FNC, including military and geopolitical intelligence panels. The military opinion segments all follow the same script: The liberal antagonist spews ideological heresies in one TV "box," and the host directs the conservative protagonist to "clean up the liberal mess" and tell the audience the real truth.

My fellow Fox News contributor Bob Bevelacqua recently shared his story with me: "Tobin, I read your Medium.com article on 'fixed debates' at Fox. I can 100 percent say the same thing happened on the military analysts' side of the house and is the main reason I tore up my contract in 2005 with Fox. Thank you, Toby, for telling the truth!"

Many of the ex-military contributors I worked with quit when they finally figured out that Fox News used them as pawns in its predetermined-outcome performances.

Recently, Army Lieutenant Colonel Ralph Peters (retired), whom I have had the pleasure of interviewing many times for FBN, finally hit the wall after ten years (again, not the same as Fox News opinion programming, but getting closer every day with Trump bootlickers like Lou Dobbs and Stuart Varney). Ralph was an expert on Russia—trained on the history and culture, the language, and having met Russian intelligence officers in the Kremlin and elsewhere.

The conversion of Fox News into Trump TV from 2016 to 2018 was the final straw for him. When Ralph quit on March 20, 2018, he was quick to denounce the network and President Trump in a classic email to colleagues:

"Fox has degenerated from providing a legitimate and much-needed outlet for conservative voices to a mere propaganda machine for a destructive and ethically ruinous administration. Over my decade with Fox, I long was proud of the association. Now I am ashamed."

Join the club, brother.

He went on:

> Four decades ago, I took an oath as a newly commissioned officer.
> That oath did not expire when I took off my uniform. Today, I feel that Fox is assaulting our constitutional order and the rule of law, while fostering corrosive and unjustified paranoia among viewers. . . .
> To me, Fox News is now wittingly harming our system of government for profit.

Ralph, too, had been blocked by producers from expressing his opinion and sharing his primary field of expertise: Russian intelligence operations and strategy. As he shared in a 2018 *Washington Post* article after leaving Fox News:

> As early as the fall of 2016, and especially as doubts mounted about the new Trump administration's national security vulnerabilities, I increasingly was blocked from speaking on the issues about which I could offer real expertise: Russian affairs and our intelligence community. I did not hide my views at Fox and, as word spread that I would not unswervingly support President Trump and, worse, that I believed an investigation into Russian interference was essential to our national security, I was excluded from segments that touched on Vladimir Putin's possible influence on an American president, his campaign, or his administration.

You are not the only one, Ralph, who is ashamed of aiding and abetting Fox News's crimes against America—not by a long shot.

YES, MANY OF FOX NEWS'S WHITE GERIATRIC VIEWERS ARE A BIT RACIST

On one show in 2004 during Passover, for some reason, I used some Yiddish expressions. I grew up with a gentile mom who somehow loved Yiddish.

She would often let loose an "oy gevalt," an "oy vey," or some other Yiddish term. Frankly, until I was much well into adulthood, I had no idea what she was saying or trying to express—or even that the words were Yiddish!

Many years later, after living for more than twenty years in a very heterogeneous DC suburb (my Jewish friends used the phrase "living behind the Hebrew Highway" to describe my neighborhood), I learned what the terms meant and found myself using them all the time. We had many close Jewish friends in DC and New York City, and it just seemed natural to me to use the terms. On this particular show, for no real reason, I threw out, "Oy vey! Look, you're making me gevalt with all this mashugana," to one of our willing liberal piñatas, who happened to be Jewish.

The next week, I was sitting in our production area when my Jewish executive producer came over and said, "Dude, we got all kinds of email from last week's show. What was up with all the Yiddish? All these emails said, in essence, "Tobin Smith is Jewish? I had no idea. I used to like the guy." (By the way, the show hardly ever got an email. Our sixty-eight-and-older audience was not the emailing kind.)

My executive producer said, "Look, I'm Jewish, and I don't use Yiddish around here or in public. Take it from me—our audience ain't exactly the most progressive. If you want to stay here, lay off the Yiddish and stay with your Scots-Irish crap, okay?"

At the time, I'd had no idea. Until I started traveling around to Southern towns to give speeches as a Fox News personality, I'd never really met our core audience. Later on, my executive producer's advice and the rise of Fox News-led Trumpism made total sense.

OF COURSE FOX NEWS TALK SHOWS ARE GOP PROPAGANDA BROADCASTS TOO

In 2011, George W. Bush's press secretary Scott McClellan admitted publicly that the Bush administration coordinated with Fox News to give Fox News Republican talking points to be discussed on air. I can tell you this: Fox News had been acting as a GOP infomercial since the 2000 elections—most extensively on the prime-time Fox News partisan opinion programming—more than anyone outside Fox knew until McClellan fessed up.

In 2004, I was at Langan's Pub on Forty-Seventh (now sadly gone) after doing the then *Hannity & Colmes* show. One of the show's producers was there with me, and he had an envelope labeled "Office of the President." I asked, "BT, you get love letters from the White House?"

He answered, "Nah, I get 'em from Karl Rove. Whenever Rove wants to drive home a point or sell some new policy, he sends Sean a package. Sean skims it and hands it to me and says, 'Make this the open tomorrow.' We get envelopes from the White House all the time. It's nuts, but Sean is the boss and I produce what he wants to air—simple as that."

Several months later, still in 2004, I was in the producer's pod at Fox on our Friday taping day, looking for a desktop computer to check email on, and I saw another envelope with the "Office of the President" label. When the producer got back to the desk, I asked, "So, J, are we doing what George Bush wants us to talk about, or what?"

She replied, "Nah, that's for the O'Reilly show. I'm helping out. They have a few folks out." When I asked, "Is it a standard operating procedure that FNC gets talking points from the White House and puts that shit into our show?" she gave me that look like *what are you, an idiot?*

Then she told me, "I'm only going to say this once: For your own good, you did not see this, and we did not discuss this. Got it? You could call Fox News the White House press office. Half the shit we talk about comes from the RNC or White House or Karl Rove's office. It's friggin' insane."

Fact: Since 2000, Fox News opinion programming has always been nothing but an unpaid GOP infomercial—and that was before FNC became Trump TV in 2017. At least Fox tried to hide the fact before Trump; now the unpaid Trumpian infomercials on Fox News opinion programs are just insane.

And to think, in 1949, Congress was afraid of a television network "imposing its political bias on the general electorate" and created the Fairness Doctrine expressly to prevent the potential for this reality.

My personal experiences with the almost daily White House propaganda directives to Fox News producers and hosts continued after I left. In August 2019, a literal trove of Treasury Department emails with Fox News was released to the non-profit organization Democracy Forward and provided exclusively to the *Hollywood Reporter*. To say they "paint a picture of a close, friendly bond between the Trump administration agency and two news organizations, Fox News Channel and Fox Business Network" is like reporting that Donald Trump once met Stormy Daniels—there is a lot more to that story.

For example, on April 25, 2017, my old buddy Fox Business Network host David Asman advised then–Treasury Department spokesman Tony Sayegh (a former Fox News contributor) on how the administration should pursue a key policy goal: achieving a major tax cut. After sharing a quotation from Treasury Secretary Steven Mnuchin, Asman wrote in the email: "Take the BIG TAX CUTS NOW . . . a long-term deal with small cuts is useless. NOTHING IS PERMANENT IN WASHINGTON. Big tax cuts now give the economy the push it needs."

Four days later, Asman wrote to Sayegh to tell him that a significant block of his FBN show would focus on the administration's tax policies. "You'll like it," Asman told him.

"Awesome, David," Sayegh wrote back. "You're the man."

Democracy Forward concluded in their statement that "the Trump administration is a revolving door for Fox News personalities and our documents expose the network as the administration's communications arm. Trump administration officials revising Fox News tweets, and Fox News rewriting stories to suit the administration's whims are not journalism, it's propaganda."

Like I said, when it comes to being the State Media and Propaganda arm of a GOP White House, nothing has changed at Fox News since my day except instead of working hand-and-glove with the White House, that pretense is gone. Fox News is just a good old lapdog obeying its master.

CHAPTER 10

Why Fox News's White Tribal Superiority Shtick Is So Incredibly Powerful

Okay. Now you and I need get real about why you and I and everyone else with a political or cultural tribal identity are so susceptible and eager to consume content that supports our tribe. Until I became a NeverTrump tribe member, I really never personally understood the addictive nature and gravitational pull of seeing "just one more story that confirms my analysis and judgment that Donald J. Trump is the worst human being on the planet!"

In other words, why did I run video after video on YouTube about some new Trumpian apostasy and immediately exhale with "God it feels so great to see yet another brick of evidence that tells me how much smarter and better person I am than those schmucks in those stupid red hats."

The answer to that question is Social Identity Theory (SIT). In case you skipped social and humanist psychology in college—SIT says individuals in addition to a self-identity possess social identities—that part of their concept of who they are and how positively they see themselves is also derived from their meaningful group memberships.

Social identity theory is based on the fact that humans are hardwired and driven to try to improve and build their self-image/self-esteem/self-pride through two vehicles: self-identity or personal accomplishments and their social identities.

In other words, humankind has two paths to improving our concept of self and self-pride:

1. Your self-identity/image building achievements and psyche building status trophies (i.e., your family, friends, things, and achievements that you are proud of and make you feel self-pride when you see them or talk about them).

2. And your social identities or the groups you feel proud of (i.e., "I'm a proud ___").

Henri Tajfel ("Dodge-Fell") is a Polish social psychologist who created social identity theory in 1979. Tajfel proposed that the most important groups that people belong to (social class, family, alumnus, conservative, liberal, etc.) are an important source of pride and self-esteem. Tajfel's experiments proved our in-groups give us a sense of social identity: a sense of belonging to the superior groups in the social world. Key word here is *superiority*—the feeling of intellectual, spiritual, moral, or physical superiority over "others" is the mother's milk of social identity (and the psychological engine that powers Fox News tribal identity opinion segments).

Social identity in fact fills two core psychological needs. One is to feel the positive personal self-esteem that comes from group inclusion and the other is a more positive and meaningful sense of who you are and what you stand for.

Now here is where this SIT thing gets interesting and where Fox News's tribal identity porn programming strategy rocks the world of self-identified right-wing tribal partisans.

First, categorization of our "in-groups" as superior and "out-groups" as inferior is a big part of the self-esteem and self-pride building from social identity. In short, you get a big dose of feel-good superiority and self-pride from the exclusion, demonization, and objectification of out-groups or "them." But here is the key to the Fox News emotional tribal manipulation playbook: It's the degree of contrast that counts the most to your social identity based self-esteem boost. In other words, the greater and deeper the good/bad, smart/stupid, righteous/unrighteous contrast you see between your righteous in-group and your hated enemy's out-group, the greater the shot of self-esteem and ego gratification your psyche gets.

So in terms of Fox News's white tribal identity porn, the more the Fox News hosts, contributors, and guests demonize and objectify the right-wingers' tribal out-groups like "the libtards," the greater the contrast between "the good guys" and the bad guys. The bigger the contrast between your homogenous white right-wing in-group and the heterogeneous out-group of liberals, the more powerful the self-esteem booster shot you get.

Given that innate psychology trigger, guess what we did at the Fox Hate Network—of course we would go out of our way to demonize and objectify our white tribal audience's identified out-groups as much as humanly possible. If we did, our audience got the most powerful self-esteem boosts we could deliver.

This chapter has one intent: to help you get your head around the immense power of "tribal identity" and "tribal identity activation media." Too few people understand that our political and cultural social identities fill two very important, unstoppable, and powerful emotional and psychological drives which we all share no matter our political or cultural identity.

Maslow taught us that first we have a powerful innate drive and motivation to build and refresh our feeling of self-esteem—call this pride-in-self and feelings of prestige, accomplishment, and value.

Social scientists tell us that in prehistoric tribal days, women preferred the alpha male—the self-confident leaders bursting with self-confidence. So in other words, the self-confident male got laid.

But our basic primal social identity reflex is also part of our drive to build our self-esteem with our level of social capital. Social capital is created when we feel family and group inclusion and acceptance (the feeling of being a proud member of a group we call "us" or an in-group).

Unfortunately for our democracy, with social identity also comes the self-esteem growth and social capital creation we get from social identity *exclusion*. With our new social identity in-group comes the reflex to distinguish ourselves by denigrating "others" or out-groups.

Sounds like being in fifth grade again doesn't it? I feel better about myself by being included in one clique while making fun of those losers in the other obviously less-worthy cliques?

Yet the fact is the research says humankind does this social identity capital building innately—it is indelibly part of our human nature to do so, long after we're done with fifth grade. You could also correctly say that your drive for social capital is nature's way of delivering you the ingredients for a mild but constant superiority complex.

Yet the obvious problem with exaggerated dependence on social identity feelings for filling up your personal self-esteem gas tank is obvious: For you to feel that superiority and build your social capital reserves, you have to see others not belonging to your tribe as inferior. In other words, for me to feel a moral or ethical superiority hit from my in-group, I have to contrast my in-group against a morally or ethically inferior out-group. It's the in-group/out-group contrast that delivers my much-needed positive self-esteem and ego boost.

Don't get this concept? Have you ever watched a reality TV show like

The Bachelorette or *Hoarders* and said to yourself, "Wow—compared to these folks, I am a saint!" or "Man, my problems are nothing compared to this person."

Thus we come to the most important part of the psychological power of our social identities—and the other hidden superpower of Fox News and the right-wing conservative media ecosystem. Social psychologists tell us that we highly evolved Homo sapiens innately and implicitly judge our in-groups to be morally, ethically, and intellectually superior to other competing groups—regardless if they are objectively better or not.

It's logical, right? Who joins a group to feel inferior? Okay, except for a longtime Cubs fan. These feelings of in-group superiority and out-group inferiority are encoded in our primal instincts. They served a very powerful purpose in our prehistoric lives on the African savannas.

But why is social identity superiority and inferiority so important to my story about Fox News? Number one—because as a partisan, you know we naturally seek information that confirms the superiority of our social identity and the inferiority of our contrasting out-group.

Key Point: Social identity theory is the other core content strategy behind Fox News's white tribal identity porn. The business of arousing your innate feelings of cultural and political superiority (and proving the inferiority of liberalism) is Fox's core business and emotional manipulation model.

The problem with this innate emotion-based strategy is this: Once we become emotionally attached to a particular in-group identity, social psychologists argue that "these social identity in-groups are powerful enough emotional attachments that they transcend thinking or objective fact."

Think about that last paragraph for a second—the intensity of our emotional attachment to our self-identified political or cultural in-group makes us transcend thinking and embrace our in-group's subjective beliefs as objective fact (the word "belief" defined as any cognitive content that we hold true).

Really—you don't say!

Does this concept sound at all familiar to you in 2019 America? Now you understand another Fox News superpower that is prominently used and exploited in the FNC tribal warfare playbook.

In a recent study of political identity co-authored by Toronto University Rotman School of Management's Matthew Feinberg puts a button on this power: "It is not the policy preferences or the values that differ between people, but simply the labels (i.e., in-group social identity) they give themselves that count."

There is a ton of emotional power inherent in your self-identified social identity. That gives a huge amount of influence to your social capital providers—the people in your life that lift your heart and build your reserves of spirit and love that social science calls your social capital.

Really Key Point: because so many Americans today consider our political or cultural identity to be such a big part of our personal sense of virtue and critical to maintaining our social esteem reserves, when someone attacks our politics or culture, they attack our virtue and they threaten to diminish a large part of our social capital reserves too.

In other words, "Them is fighting words," and we defend our personal virtue and social capital reserves at all costs. This behavior is in our human nature—we don't control it—it controls us.

Again—here is the Fox News context. When you show up at my tribal identity activation TV show or click on and stream my tribal activation segment on a social media app, the mere fact you tuned in for more than one segment tells me everything I need to know to start you on a tribal amplification and radicalization spiral.

The reason for this should now be clear—the more intensely you value your tribal identity, the more your self-esteem and sense of superiority depends on Fox News to constantly provide evidence that supports you against your perceived tribal enemy and out-group.

Key Point: For many Americans, particularly older, lonely, and economically challenged ones, the Foxhole spiral is a positive self-reinforcing psychic feedback lifeline—you get that now, right?

Why are Fox News and Sky TV and other News Corp. white tribal identity porn media companies so influential and emotionally powerful to their audiences?

Answer: Because they deliver innately needed feelings of hope and self-pride to people whose lives in many cases are leaking a lot of self-esteem. They can feel like a lifeline to people whose lives are filled with existential fear and trauma.

Let's you and I imagine this real-life scenario for many older white Foxocracy viewers in America. First off, odds are great you live in the part of America where 60 percent of America's twenty-first-century economy is not working for you—and boy does that drain your self-image and inflate your level of economic fear.

Now if you are like 62 percent of Americans over fifty that report you don't have enough nurturing family and friends in your life, your social capital reserves are rapidly depleting as well. Then—if you find the scorched earth identity politics and PC dogma of the left-wing Libocracy chronically insults and disrespects your cultural and religious beliefs, that unresolved trauma has a negative drag on your self-esteem reserves too.

For many self-identified "committed conservatives" or Deplorables, they are living a perfect storm of personal and social capital depletion and have been living that perfect storm for decades. For them, watching Fox News white tribal identity content or attending a Trumpism rally is like injecting a powerful cocktail of self-esteem and social capital reserves. The more hours they watch, view, stream, comment, or generally engage, the better they feel.

For many, their dose of cultural and political pride is the only positive emotional injection they get in their normal day. They don't have enough positive self-esteem building moments in their everyday lives, and they don't have enough human contact with spiritually nurturing family and friends either.

To add insult to injury, the more tribally partisan you become, the more time you spend with your Fox News televangelist "imaginary friends." Many Fox News addicts spend 50 percent or more of their waking time immersed in the Foxocracy, leaving little or no time for emotionally nurturing and spirit supporting human beings.

For them, social identity psychologists I've talked with say Fox News can become, in essence, your primary self-esteem and social capital dealer.

Rupert Murdoch and Roger Ailes did not create an American capitalism that is failing for nearly sixty percent of American households—but they sell a coping mechanism for the pain and trauma from that failure. All you need to do is power up your TV or digital device. Becoming the primary self-esteem/social capital dealer for conservatives has been the business and programming objective of Fox News and Murdoch for generations.

If you understand how humankind innately seeks people and groups that bring them self-esteem and social capital reserves, you can understand the real Foxocracy superpower: For a growing number of older white conservative Americans, their Fox News addiction is the best few hours of their day. And many of them have few remaining alternatives.

Review: If Fox News can activate your tribal instincts and fan your normal-sized white tribal identity ember into a self-reinforcing "tribal intensity spiral" via a constant digital feedback loop, they own you because they own your psyche.

In other words, if your life outside the American Foxocracy bubble is in a self-reinforcing downward spiral depleting your self-esteem, if you have fewer human relationships in your life to naturally build the levels of social capital required for emotional stasis—Fox News and the rest of the American Foxocracy are there to fill up your empty emotional gas tank. And for many that fill-up feels so damn good you can't get enough.

Why are so many Americans' reserves of self-esteem and social capital being depleted so fast they run to the Foxocracy for a daily emotional booster shot?

Ah—now you asked the right question. Think of this—what if you can't get enough self-esteem or social capital feedstock in your life outside the Foxocracy because you are one of the 60 percent of Americans whose economic health has been in a self-reinforcing downward spiral for decades?

Maybe in your real life outside the Foxocracy you are living in a chronic and self-reinforcing downward social capital depletion spiral because you don't have enough nurturing personal relationships or reinforcing social fabric in your everyday life?

Maybe you also noticed (via social media or relatives outside your area) that many Americans who live in Metro America (the twenty-four states where incomes and life expectancy are in an upward spiral instead of down) seem to have opportunities that you don't? Maybe you watch this slow motion train wreck over and over every day and you grow to deeply resent these facts and the seemingly insurmountable economic and quality of life divide between you and "them" because for you it did not use to be that way?

One person who has correctly identified the largely regional self-reinforcing downward and upward economic and health expectancy spirals in America today which unfortunately provides the unending supply of economic trauma feedstock which Fox News and the American Foxocracy feed off of is Ray Dalio. He is a self-made billionaire and founder of Bridgewater Associates LP, the world's largest hedge fund.

He for years has taught me and others that twenty-first-century capitalism in its present form has developed into a self-reinforcing upward and downward feedback loop—there's that term again. Unfortunately the upward and downward economic feedback loops that Mr. Dalio's extensive research team has tracked for decades have now reached a critical mass of negative ramifications that are amplifying an ever wider wealth gap in

America which, in his words, puts the very existence of the United States at risk.

In the first part of a two-part series published on LinkedIn, he argues that American capitalism is now desperately in need of reform:

"I have seen capitalism evolve in a way that it is not working well for the majority of Americans because it's producing self-reinforcing spirals up for the haves and self-reinforcing downward spirals for the have-nots.

"This is creating widening income/wealth/opportunity gaps that pose existential threats to the United States because these gaps are bringing about damaging domestic and international conflicts and weakening America's condition."

"Feedback loop" and "self-reinforcing spiral" are, perhaps strangely for a media company, the other key concepts you need to comprehend to understand the incredible psychological power and societal influence of the American Foxocracy and Planet Fox. The technical definition of a self-reinforcing spiral or feedback loop is a "circuit that feeds some of its output back into the input of a system in a self-regenerating cycle."

But the term simply means the effect of the positive or negative outcomes feeds the size and power of the upward or downward cycle. The positive outcomes spawn additional positive outcomes (in economic terms the size of the economic pie), and the negative outcomes spawn more negative outcomes (in social terms, the negative outcomes enlarge the scope and size of deprivation).

In recent history, the negative outcome of World War I for Germany led to a twenty-five-year downward and negative self-reinforcing feedback loop. In America, the end of World War II led to one of the greatest economic and societal positive self-reinforcing feedback loops in the history of the modern world.

The problem America faces, and not-so-ironically what the Foxocracy and now the Libocracy all profit and feed from, is very much like the downward spiral of Germany which accelerated with the Great Depression of the 1930s. The creation of a positive feedback loop of growth for fascism in Germany was fed by the negative feedback loop of economic deprivation. Economic depression led to fewer jobs; fewer jobs led to economic deprivation; economic deprivation led proud but desperate Germans to seek a solution to end the economic decline and deprivation and to find a villain to blame; the hypnotically charismatic Adolf Hitler came up with an economic and cultural solution in his oratory and his book, *Mein Kampf*; he and his Minister of

Propaganda came up with groundbreaking ways to employ his charismatic oratory to sell his solutions via the new technologies of radio, talking pictures, and propaganda movies—and then you know the rest.

Does that combo of negative and positive feedback loops sound at all familiar?

Used in the sense of media, propaganda, and Fox News, the American Foxocracy is now a fully integrated and self-reinforcing tribal propaganda feedback loop. Today at Fox News, white tribal televangelists feed the Trump White House information and the Trump White House feeds it back to Fox News, which goes directly into its own media output. To call Fox News white tribal identity mongers "hosts" at this point is absurd and farcical.

This white tribal content is then rebroadcast on Fox News and then repurposed—chopped into three-minute propaganda segments for social media—and retargeted to social media users. As you know, these users are identified by social media digital surveillance systems as the most likely to emotionally engage with this white tribal identity porn in their social media stream and share it virally.

To risk stating the now obvious: the American Foxocracy is the most powerful self-reinforcing political and cultural digital feedback loop of the twenty-first century. Fox News was explicitly built to weaponize Roger Ailes's intimate knowledge of how to manipulate and monetize our innate mass psychology.

Full stop. To deny this reality in 2019 is akin to denying gravity or the shape of the Earth.

Next, in order to increase our personal self-image, we innately enhance the status of the group to which we belong. For example, if you are American you believe America is the best country in the world! But we also increase our self-image by discriminating and holding prejudiced views against out-groups which we don't belong to by choice or exclusion. For example, if you are a proud conservative, then liberals are a bunch of losers and liberalism is a mental disease!

More importantly, in this process of social identification, we divide the world into "them" and "us" based upon an innate process of social categorization. We naturally access and put people into social groups—think high school! Social identity theory states that the in-group or tribe will *innately discriminate against the out-group* purely to enhance their own self-image.

Aha! So Fox News fans hate on their out-group enemy to enhance their self-image and self-esteem? I told ya—if you self-identify as a "proud conservative" and on the good guy side of history, part of the identification is a visceral feeling of intellectual and moral superiority over liberals and liberalism as the bad guys who hate America!

For Fox News, this social identity power gets better while America gets worse. The entire central hypothesis of social identity theory is that members of an in-group will innately seek to find negative aspects of "them" in the out-group, thus enhancing their self-image via evidence of their in-group's superiority. You may not have thought about this reality, but when you watch a TV segment performance that declares your tribal opponent is obviously an evil and stupid loser, you are directly congratulating yourself and the people who agree with you for being the most intelligent, morally superior, the most righteous, or all three.

What does Fox News opinion programming do around the clock? It sells you a list of half a dozen *new* negative aspects/policies/behaviors of "them" (those libtard idiots!) as well as recycling the libtards' greatest blasphemies and desecrations of America.

When it comes to weaponizing the incredible power of us vs. them social identity manipulation, the difference between 1930s Germany and America today, folks, is that in America since the launch of Fox News, social identity weaponization is done under the cover of "free speech" and the First Amendment and it is now a $10 billion annual commercial enterprise.

So yes—I am suggesting strongly that allowing a for-profit commercial industry to weaponize the First Amendment into us vs. them social identity activation and amplification porn is perhaps the most damaging governmental mistake since allowing OxyContin prescriptions to become commercialized and weaponized.

At least we now acknowledge the stupidity of Oxy deregulation.

But the deregulation of tribal identity activation and amplification porn? It's just good fun—it will blow over.

But it's not. I suggest you also think of your degree of self-pride or self-worth as a psychic bank account with very real deposits and withdrawals. Social psychologists tell me running a combined social capital and self-esteem deficit is very psychologically damaging.

For one thing, it's the road to deeper emotional trauma and depression. Worse, when a person lacks meaningful personal or social identities and a positive and nurturing social capital account, Fox News or other social identity/social capital providing cults are happy to provide a social identity and virtual social capital for you as well. (Now you get why so many Fox News addicts consider Sean Hannity or Tucker Carlson as their literal "friend." Let's call that psychological phenomenon "virtual" social capital!)

Key Points: Forty percent of the nearly fifty million seniors over age sixty-five regularly experience loneliness, according to a University of California, San Francisco study. According to the ALICE Working Poverty reports in June 2018, forty-five million American households are living in working poverty. At three people per household, that is 135 million Americans. And that does not count the forty-two million Americans living below the poverty line. If 177 million Americans are in working or actual poverty in a country of 326 million, that is 54 percent of Americans. As Ray Dalio points out, the "haves" are separating from the "have nots" at an accelerated rate.

My point? To truly grasp the immense emotional and psychological impact, power, and manipulation embedded within Fox News's tribal identity activation and validation media and the American Foxocracy's self-reinforcing digital feedback loop, you had better understand this fact of life:

Mankind's ignorance of the scale and intent of the psychological manipulation in our daily lives is the feedstock that empowers the monetization of media illiterate people for billions in profits for tribal identity pornographers and the social media platforms.

I want to break the ignorance and mental chain reaction. This is not a Don Quixote quest—I know how to manipulate the world of social media too. The most important reason for this book is to help you break that negative but upward self-reinforcing partisan spiral that results for many in a downward self-reinforcing desocialization spiral—especially for the 54 percent of people who live in an America where twenty-first-century capitalism is not working (and that number is spiraling upward).

- Older Americans who are already suffering from an epidemic of chronic loneliness and the unhealthy co-morbidities that come with the chronic depletion of their precious social capital.

- Or those who live in the conservative culture and work in traditional nineteenth- and twentieth-century Retro American industries targeted for extinction by the ironically labeled "Progressive" and "Democratic Socialists." Somehow their definition of "progress" has little or no plan for how those people would make a decent living post facto.

Remember this fact of human nature and you will get the rest of this book: When you show a political or cultural media manipulation company your proud cultural or political social identity colors, you send up a digital flare that says "I'm yours—take my social identity pride and manipulate my cognitive bias and use them to make me feel great about myself as long as you can."

Again, I am *not* comparing Fox News social identity porn to Nazi Germany, so don't go there. But make no mistake: The Fox News tribal warfare playbook is 100 percent predatory. Its predation is all about seducing and converting as many vulnerable political and cultural conservatives as possible into hyperpartisan conservatives, okay? With Roger Ailes out of the picture, Fox News 3.0 is about money and power Rupert Murdoch style. But to illustrate how powerful well-produced social identity pornography and propaganda can be, it is fair to point out a comparable period of time where a significant percentage of citizens were exposed to constant social identity media programming, and that was Germany in the 1930s and '40s. According to the US Holocaust Museum historical website, "The high quality and impact social identity propaganda used by the German Nazi Party in their newspaper and movie media for the years leading up to and during Adolf Hitler's leadership of Germany was a crucial instrument for acquiring and maintaining power, and for the implementation of Nazi policies. . . . The Nazis were skilled propagandists who used sophisticated advertising techniques and the most current technology of the time to spread their messages. Once in power, Adolf Hitler created a Ministry of Public Enlightenment and Propaganda to shape German public opinion and behavior. . . . It incited hatred and fostered a climate of indifference to their fate."

I'll leave the relevance of this comparison up to you—but to me FNC's powerful social identity porn and GOP propaganda is like history; it may not repeat itself entirely, but it does rhyme. But I will say this: If the preceding paragraph does not put a shiver down your spine, check your pulse.

The power and impact of Fox News's nightly nuclear powered tribal social identity/tribal connection porn and the way it speeds up the viewer's conversion and radicalization into a highly intense tribal right-wing social identity is beyond most of our comprehension and life experience.

But for the millions of families that now have estranged family members they have watched with their own eyes convert from mild mannered "agree-to-disagree" conservatives to Foxholes and Fox News addicts, the power and outcome of binge-watching thousands of hours of tribal social identity pornography is very real and very devastating to their family.

All Donald Trump did in 2016 was put new packaging on Fox News's tribal identity and cultural connection porn formula—converting the existing out-group prejudices and cultural/racial resentments into a new form of American politics with a bull horn. Instead of Richard Nixon's famous "Southern Strategy," which required using code words appealing to white Southern racism without alienating white suburbanites who recoiled at overt racial language, he just skipped the code words and subtlety.

Fun fact: Who do you think Nixon's code-worded Southern strategy was designed and developed by? *Yes*, my new friends—it was indeed Roger Ailes and his political advertising partner Lee Atwater. Yea, I know—you can't make this stuff up, right?

Look—Like I said, social identity activation and ego-building is the same reason people watch reality TV; it's the ego and self-esteem boost that makes people watch *Cops* or laugh out loud when they read about some poor schmuck who is arrested running down the street naked after trying to shoplift a pack of Ho Hos from the local Walmart or Piggly Wiggly. Of course the article fails to mention the guy is off his schizophrenia medicine and is starving because he is homeless—but where's the self-esteem boost if you knew that?

Here is the difference between tribal hate and cultural superiority porn and trashy reality TV. The low-rent reality TV show *Jersey Shore* makes you feel great when you compare yourself to Snooki and JWoww—but you don't hate them; you feel fortunate you aren't them and feel (relatively) you are obviously a vastly superior person.

The visceral attraction of reality TV (you know—where Donald Trump came from) is also based on social identity theory—but it doesn't make you hate the characters—you just mostly feel sorry for some and root for others.

Right-wing tribal identity porn only works when you hate the "other"; you don't feel a bit sorry for them—you hate them because they are a threat to you and your tribe.

"MAN, YOU LOOK JUST LIKE TOBIN SMITH!"

Fast forward to my wife Marjorie and me walking into a restaurant in North Scottsdale, Arizona. We have a winter escape home there in a zip code reported to have the highest concentration of registered Republicans in America. The golf club I belonged to for many years had multiple golf courses and 125 televisions in its various facilities. All their TVs are tuned to Fox News during every hour the club is open.

If someone asks to change the channel, they get asked to leave—not the venue, but the club!

An older man walks over to me as we get near the restaurant entrance and says, "Do you know you look just like Tobin Smith from Fox News?"

"No," I respond, "who is he?" He looks me dead in the eye as Marjorie stands there biting her lip (she has seen this movie many times before) and answers, "Well—he is one of my heroes on Fox News. He hates those socialist liberals on his show as much as I do—as we all do up here in Scottsdale. I watch every Saturday morning at 7:00 a.m., and he just kills those libtards.

"Look, I'm retired—and I'm scared to death Black Jesus Obama is going to bankrupt America and leave me and my wife dead broke with no Social Security. Tobin rips those libtards a new one every time they prance one out—he's a true patriot and great American. Do you watch Fox News? You should watch him!"

"Well," I said. "Yea, he sounds like a hell of a guy. Just for the record, I am Tobin Smith from Fox News—nice to meet you." His face went ashen—like he had seen a ghost. I took my driver's license out to prove it was me, and he sat there stunned.

I asked him how much he watches Fox News. He replied, "All day—we never turn it off." Then he said, "You know, Tobin, I'm really scared about the future. These socialist commies have taken over our country, and I'm afraid my Social Security is going to go broke with all this new Obamacare spending. The stock market is slowly recovering"—this meeting was 2010—"but who knows what's going to happen with these people in charge. Thanks for sticking up for us real Americans—God bless you!"

When we sat down for lunch Marjorie said, "Geez, Toby—that old guy looked at you like you are a cult leader or something. Do all these Fox News addicts really hate liberals that much? Are they all that afraid of losing all their money and everything they worked for?"

My answer was that considering the fact that guy had, I am sure, consumed ten thousand segments of emotionally eviscerating Fox News tribal identity porn for more than a decade, what would be surprising is if he was not a blithering tribalized right-wing cult member afraid of losing everything.

By that time, I had had that same conversation five hundred times before with other cult-like, star-struck Fox News addicts. But for millions of the true Foxholes, Fox News is a cult of fear, blame, resentment, personal absolution, and self-esteem replacement just as much as any other cult I've ever heard about or studied.

Carolyn Lukensmeyer is the executive director of a conflict resolution group founded in the aftermath of the 2011 assassination attempt on Gabrielle Giffords, the former Arizona congresswoman. She was quoted in the *Wall Street Journal* recently: "Among the requests for conflict mitigation she has received recently: rabbis and pastors whose congregations are at each other's throats; Fortune 500 companies where productivity is down because employees bicker over politics; and a mother in New England who feared her family's holiday would be ruined because her two daughters who were returning from college had not spoken to each other since the 2016 election."

She ends her interview like this. "This [political tribalism] is now deep in our homes, deep in our neighborhoods, deep in our places of worship and deep in our workplaces," Ms. Lukensmeyer said. "It really is a virus."

When I talk about the untold stories inside the cult of Fox News, it's no exaggeration. I found the top producers, executives, and talent at Fox News acted and performed just like I would imagine cult leaders would. Later I found out that was not by mistake or coincidence. The entire production process of the fear and hate based tribal identity pornography was just a series of cult-like recruiting ads.

Okay, so here's a blinding flash of the obvious: For Foxholes, Fox News is by almost every modern definition of the term a cult. For that matter, the American Foxocracy has become nothing more than a new fundamentalist religious denomination competing with Evangelical TV and even church services. FNC's prime-time tribal identity porn hosts perform more like televangelists than political talk show hosts for a very good reason—they are televangelists for Fox News's religion of tribal identity redemption and blame shifting absolution—can I get an amen!

Roger Ailes was the master right-wing political ad man who had never produced a minute of TV news but had mastered the dark arts of tribalized, zero-sum tribal manipulation media. Fox News built its tribal social identity brand the same way all cult leaders build their cult brands: by making the public hate and fear the "other" tribes more and promising the only truth that matters is their truth.

After thousands of hours of tribal identity binge-watching, the cult of Fox News Foxhole spiral conversion is complete. I mean, how could it not be?

All of which brings us to our next big major Fox News tribal partisan identity porn playbook strategy: the power of tribalized fear porn.

CHAPTER 11

The Incredible Power of Weaponized Visceral Threat and Fear

Now you must understand the key part of the Fox News tribal civil war playbook—for self-identified conservatives, the easiest and best emotional hook is fear: fear of others, fear of destitution, fear of death by jihadist—there's a million riffs on conservative hypersensitivity to fearful images.

I learned this lesson in my first year as a paid contributor.

THE QUIET LADY ON THE SEVENTEENTH FLOOR

Near the coffee room that I visited hourly on FNC's spartan seventeenth floor (occupied by the Fox News opinion-programming team, far away from the basement hard news operations) was the office of a VP I had not been introduced to. I had no idea what she did. I was eventually told that her name was Kathy and that she used to work for Ailes at their GOP political advertising and TV consulting firm along with his infamous GOP tribal dark-arts partner and pioneer Lee Atwater.

Kathy came over to my cubicle one day with a print advertisement she had received in her mail for my investment newsletter at the time, ChangeWave Investing. She introduced herself and said, "So I got your newsletter sales pitch in my mailbox. When I read it, I thought, this guy is in the same business we are."

"How do you mean?" I asked.

"Well, you guys are in the financial fear porn business," she said. "Your sales-porn flyer here is full of FOMO—fear of missing out—we call that greed porn. You also use fear-of-financial-loss porn, or FOLM—fear of losing lots of money." Then she added this insight: "But the real emotional impact comes from your fear-of-losing-money story and how you promise to prevent major losses happening today for your scared-to-death investor audience." It was October 2000, during the dot-com crash, and investors were losing a ton of money. "I like it. Well done." Then she asked, "Who wrote this piece, may I ask?"

"I did," I answered. "You look at me like I'm a stock market guru, but for most of my newsletter-publishing career, I have mostly been a professional direct-response copywriter, editor, and marketer."

"Wow," she said as she looked at me. "So you know the secrets and superpowers of fear porn too, eh?" And then she stunned me. "Only a few people I have ever met"—I'm paraphrasing here—"understand that all purposely emotional and brain-stem arousing communication media is just another form of pornography."

Wow. I had never thought of Fox News opinion programming that way before. I also had not thought of my sales copywriting as fear porn, but, damn, I realized she was right on both counts. Doh! Not coincidentally, the primary customers of my investment newsletters are—wait for it—over fifty-five-aged conservatives!

"You're in the pornography-of-financial-fear business at your newsletter company," she continued, "and we at Fox News are in the pornography-of-right-wing-tribal-fear-and-rage business. Porn is porn. If it effectively arouses your emotions, it's a form of pornography. You obviously know and practice the secret superpowers of sales porn well. You will do very well here at Fox News—you're a natural!"

From this and other conversations, I learned the most important lesson about Fox News and what Fox News really is, as conceived by Roger Ailes (drawing on his prior partnership with dearly departed right-wing political advertising partner Lee Atwater):

Fox News was to fulfill the vision of the liberal-targeting killing machine Roger had dreamed of since 1974, when he wrote a secret memo to Richard Nixon about a "Republican TV channel." In this memo, he told President Nixon, "Today television news is watched more often than people read newspapers, than people listen to the radio, than people read or gather any other form of communication. The reason: People are lazy. With television you just sit—watch— listen. The thinking is done for you."

The Fox News iteration of this original vision would create and produce the most visually powerful and emotionally arousing right-wing tribal-hate-video pornography the world had ever seen, according to Roger's tribal-fear-and-hate-porn attack ad formula perfected in their production of GOP political attack ads.

With soft-core sexual porn video-production values plus careful hard-core scripting and gamified visual and topic orchestration, FNC would essentially hack and hijack the tribal partisan's brain while they sat hypnotically entranced to their TV at home. (This was before the on-demand digital streaming platforms and social media, of course.)

Because viewers watched while sitting comfortably at home (as opposed to listening in their car, where at least some of their attention had to be on the road) Fox found it ridiculously easy to frighten and manipulate the emotions of the mostly geriatric right-wing partisans.

By turning their one-minute attack ad formula into seven-minute "opinion talk show segments," the cumulative effect on a partisan conservative watching all that attack ad content over and over again for thousands of hours would be the eventual conversion of non-radicalized partisan into a radicalized hyperpartisan.

A big point to remember about Fox News is that it is not in the business of monetizing politics or tribal partisan engagement, per se. What Fox News is in the business of is monetizing mankind's native human psychological flaws—emotions, behaviors, and physiology hardwired into our brain which we have little or no control over.

Now it just so happens that the biggest tribal audiences are formed on the basis of politics, culture, and religion. That means non-college-graduate, social and political conservatives are by far the easiest to dupe and manipulate with this strategy. One of the reasons why liberals (until Trump) were hard to build a significant TV audience from is they never were big political hate porn radio listeners or TV watchers and are wired to not be very susceptible or reactive to fear-laden imagery.

HOW SCIENCE PROVED THE FEAR PORN FORMULA WAS BUILT-IN FOR CONSERVATIVES

Neuroscience discoveries on our brain's hardwiring are clear: Cultural and political conservatives are *much* easier to frighten and seduce into a cloud of emotions.

As mentioned, that "secret backdoor" to your brain is fear. Long ago, social science proved that personal-safety stimuli and fight-or-flight feelings, instincts, and emotions are prioritized to be delivered to the "switchboard" of the brain ahead of the other core emotions.

Televised fear-and-hate-porn content works fabulously well for ratings because it engages human beings both consciously and subconsciously. Why? Neuroscience tells us it's because our prehistoric fight-or-flight brain region (our "fear chip"), called the amygdala (ah-MIG-dahla), is specifically wired to process personal safety information first.

Conscious and unconscious fear for safety override all other stimuli to the brain. In other words, fear content causes the amygdala to react automatically and involuntarily, before the cerebral cortex (the thinking and rational part of the brain) can apply logic. That "secret backdoor" or wormhole to your brain is fear.

Fortunately for Fox News, self-identified conservatives are almost twice as reactive to fearful and enraging content than self-identified liberals—who knew? One group knew for sure: Roger Ailes and his merry gang of right-wing tribal fear and hate porn producers.

In twenty peer-reviewed scientific studies since 2005, cognitive and neuroscience researchers found that liberals and conservatives actually have different brain structures, different physiological responses to fearful stimuli, and activate different neural mechanisms when confronted with similar fearful situations.

Deep down in your heart you knew that, right?

What the neuroscientists found when self-identified right- and left-wing people were subjected to fearful disgusting images was amazing; they found in study after study that self-identified conservatives actually have a larger amygdala region in their brains than self-identified liberals.

This means that conservatives really do feel and react to fear far more deeply than liberals, and their fight-or-flight response time is actually faster. (Fight-or-flight response comes up a little later as one explanation why Fox News addiction and desocialization is so unhealthy too.)

Even more fascinating, in hundreds of blind tests of self-identified conservatives vs. liberals, researchers could identify the conservative 86.2 percent of the time just by how their brain reacted to fearful stimuli via the latest functional MRI (FMRI) technology.

So yes—neuroscientists and social psychologists have determined that right-wing conservatives' brains really are different than liberals' brains—and especially sensitive to feelings of fear and disgust! There is also significant amounts of research that show liberals have a much higher rate of the so-called "empathy gene" than conservatives do. That genetic fact explains a lot about how liberals react to events vs. conservatives too!

Now you know the secret to why right-wing tribal fear porn is so effective with self-identified conservatives: The larger amygdala in self-identified conservatives is vastly more sensitive to fearful images than left-wingers.

This neurology is the main reason Fox News emphasizes and leads with fear segments in its tribal "opinion programs." People who self-identify as conservative react almost *twice* as much to fearful images and content than liberals. As such, they are consistently terrified of Muslims and Islam and being murdered by jihadists and all the other tribal fear buttons Fox News hosts push a hundred times a day.

PS: This has to be why MSNBC and CNN do *not* emphasize fear program segments except for fear of Trump. Fear of Trump is visceral—but in general the liberal mind is not nearly as reactive to fear as the conservative brain.

Key Point: Tribal instinct is involuntary, and that is how the Fox News tribal social identity porn formula manipulates conservatives—producing involuntary emotional responses. There is no more powerful stimulus to your brain than fearful stimuli. That is why even though a Fox News "opinion program" is not in any way a hard news program, most of the highest prime-time tribal hate porn programs open with a "Fox News Alert!" in bold red colors with the anchor/host sitting behind what looks just like a hard news anchor desk.

Another part of Roger Ailes's genius was to not stop at just fear porn. Over the years, he added rage, blame, and plain old hate porn to the formula so Fox News programming would touch every involuntary emotion and reaction in the tribal partisan's innate portfolio of human emotions.

After the restrictions on partisan opinion broadcasting were lifted in 1987 with the revocation of the Fairness Doctrine and the end of personal anti-disparagement restrictions in 2000, Fox News tribal hate porn had the green light to produce and broadcast (and later stream) the conservative tribal identity porn that Roger Ailes had dreamed of thirty years prior.

But Roger's dream of converting his one-minute tribal fear and hate political ads into half hour and one-hour television programming really took off with the election of President Obama and the financial crisis of 2008–2009. Obama and the Great Recession created the Promised Land for right-wing tribal and cultural social identity pornography.

WHY FEAR IS THE CURRENCY OF CONSERVATIVE TRIBAL IDENTITY PORNOGRAPHY

Soon after my Fox News awakening about the power of fear-based images, I began strolling into Kathy's office every week to chat. I was fascinated to find her office jammed with hundreds of books sent to her by publishers. She primarily read the conservative political and cultural books, she told me.

My first question was, "So what do you really do here at Fox?"

She answered, "I do what I did for Roger and Lee at their old right-wing advertising agency. I let them know what issues are pissing off or frightening to right-wing conservatives today and how we should frame the narrative."

Later on, I figured out that what she really did was help Roger put together his daily segment talking points and ensure his emotional-engagement-angle memo was distributed and followed to the letter by all the Fox News opinion executive producers and production teams.

In essence, my take was she led the daily tribal fear patrol looking for the next big fear and rage triggers. The term "fear-and-rage porn" is a nice way of hiding the obvious: Whether you are a Fox News opinion-program producer, direct-response copywriter, or social media guru, we are all in the business of exploiting the innate human psychological weaknesses and involuntary instincts for profit.

The American Constitution was intended to act—and has indeed acted—as a restraint on humanity's darkest tribal impulses for more than 240 years. In contrast, Fox News opinion programming post-Fairness Doctrine was expressly designed and choreographed to encourage and monetize humanity's worst impulses toward tribalism.

How is that for a company mission and business model?

HOW DO YOU LIKE YOUR TRIBAL IDENTITY PORN: SOFT OR HARD-CORE?

Just like sexual arousal pornography, there is "soft-core" and "hard-core" tribal identity arousal porn. Here's a good explanation of hard-core tribal porn that I heard early in my career from a producer/drinking buddy after my inaugural appearance on *Hannity & Colmes* in 2002 (which in 2008 became just *Hannity* because the right-wing audience could not stand the liberal Alan Colmes any longer, I was told): "Toby, you gotta think of the [*Hannity & Colmes*] show like it's tribal snuff porn. Our viewers hate liberals and liberal politics and culture with a passion. My job is to make sure the viewer at home watches enough liberal shit-slinging to get their blood boiling and then *BOOM* watches that dude snuffed out on air. Watching liberal snuff porn frigging rocks our tribal right-wingers' world!"

Okay, class, why on earth would Fox News terrorize its own audience?

Now you get it—because that is the fastest way to bypass the rational brain and get to the amygdala! When people are afraid, they don't reason. When people can't think rationally, they'll believe anything, and they'll be afraid of whatever they are told to fear.

Leave it to the great screenwriter and director Aaron Sorkin to get this concept right! Sorkin brilliantly conveyed the innate power of tribal identity fear porn in his movie *The American President*. The monologue of POTUS Andrew Shepherd in this movie captures the Fox News tribal hate porn strategy in all its "glory."

In this scene, POTUS Shepherd (played by Michael Douglas) is fighting his GOP opponent, Senator Bob Rumson (played by Richard Dreyfuss), and Rumson's unabashed use of fear and rage to capture votes in national elections:

> We have serious problems to solve, and we need serious men to solve them. And whatever your particular problem is, friend, I promise you, Bob Rumson is not the least bit interested in solving it. He is interested in two things and two things only: making you afraid of it and telling you who's to blame for it.
>
> That, ladies and gentlemen, is how you win elections. You gather a group of middle-aged, middle-class, middle-income and blue-collar voters who remember with longing an easier time, and you talk to them about family and American values and personal character.

LESSON LEARNED: HERE'S HOW WE *KNOW* FEAR WORKS BEST

Social scientists tell us that the primary emotions are anger/rage, fear, joy/pleasure, sadness, and contempt/disgust. As you've now learned, fear is the key to the success of tribal hate porn in right-wingers because when someone feels fear or anger/outrage, that person is in tribal mode, not in rational mode. That is when they can get hooked into the segment.

But how do FNC producers know that fear-based content works best today? By looking at real-time viewer data from Nielsen and then engagement data (streaming, clicking, and comments) from Foxnews.com.

TV production teams know which segments are working because of the Nielsen two-minute audience ratings. Every two minutes while the program is broadcast, network leadership and executive producers get a read on the audience numbers. What they are looking for is simple. They want to know if the new show builds from the audience it got from the last program or if it loses audience count. They want to see if the first segment holds the audience it inherited. On Fox News, even on markets and economy shows, fear was more potent than greed.

One of the best examples of this was our opening and closing segments for many months after 9/11. After we got back to our regular programming, week after week after week, Brenda would end the opening segment by asking all the stock-market pros, "Given the terrorist risk in America, does the threat of terror change your trading on Monday morning?"

I was running a mutual fund and hedge fund at that time, and every week, I would say the same thing: "No, Brenda. Buying stocks when people are fearful of temporary events is a great time to make money. I use irrational investor panic and fear to make money off of irrational fear."

The next week, the same question. And the next week. And the next. Finally, after a month of the same question, I lost it. "No, Brenda! Only the idiots watching us scare the crap out of them will be selling their stocks on Monday! Please don't stop it. I'm making a fortune off Fox News ginning up our viewers' collective paranoia and them selling their stocks in panic!"

Boom! The show taping stopped because someone—me—had screwed up. I apologized, and when the segment was re-shot, I, of course, said what they wanted me to say.

Why did we start every opinion segment with a Fox News Alert and a fear/anger- or disgust-inducing B-roll video and script on terrorism? Because the first two segment ratings reports show that fear works.

I later found out that it was Roger Ailes who commanded that we end our first segment with the fear-of-terrorist-attacks pitch because the data said it worked. One day, to learn why some of my great segment ideas always wound up nowhere, I asked Brenda, "So, B—who do you have to sleep with to get a segment pitch approved here at Fox News?"

She responded, "Well, it's Roger, and you are definitely not his type!"

I heard the same thing from hard-core Fox News addicts for decades:

"Toby, I wanted to throw a brick through my TV at that libtard last Saturday, but you came through and handed him his head on a platter. Thank you for sticking up for capitalism/'Murica'/the good guys!"

Again—have you ever wondered why there is no moderate/centrist tribal cable TV network? Think about moderates like me. I don't have tribal imprinting and wiring—other than my visceral disgust with Trump and Trumpism—to be manipulated.

I want to know what's going on in my country and my world. But moderates, by definition, are not tribal; they consider themselves pragmatic and self-identify as not being part of either the left- or right-wing tribe, whom they hold in contempt as mindless partisan ideologues. But make no mistake: Our non-partisan tribe feels superior to partisan tribes simply because we think for ourselves versus becoming right- or left-wing "sheeple." Being a proud non-tribal is a social identity too and definitely a self-esteem booster for centrists/Independents. Trust me—centrists do feel superior to those grubby tribal right- or left-wingers.

Ailes's gift to right-wing candidates was creating TV advertising that carpet bombed their opponents with enough antipersonnel cluster bombs that they eventually were rendered unelectable. The building of Fox News's right-wing cult was more than just an attack in a congressional race—Fox News attacks "those people" or simply the "others" as an existential enemy that must be overcome in a great, white, right-wing tribal crusade.

Key Point: At the end of the day, Fox's tribal partisan identity porn is really just a hybrid mash-up of:

1. Ailes's attack ads.

2. low-brow reality TV.

3. a soft-core porn cable channel.

4. a rigged outcome WWE TV wrestling match.

5. a Christian TV network.

IS THIS THE TOBIN SMITH SHOW OR THE O'REILLY REPORT?

This story is about the power and nature of blame-based messaging with self-identified conservatives. FYI—blame porn (just like in the Evangelical pulpit) is another superpower of tribal TV because it is blame-shifting, and blame-shifting ("it's not my fault, it's their fault") is massively cathartic.

So here I am in DC waiting to do a TV "hit" about rising energy prices on the *O'Reilly Factor* show. I've been interviewed on every news and business channel over the last twenty years. Bill O'Reilly is the only talk show host who talks to the paid contributor talent before you go on air to basically tell you what he wants you to say.

Normally at Fox News as a New York City based contributor, my experience was it's the segment producer who tells you what they want you to say and the context in which they want you to make your argument.

Anyway, O'Reilly is in my ear with this classic O'Reillyesque exhortation. "Smith," he says—in dozens of segments on his air he never called me by first name—"here is how this is going to go. Last year you said oil prices were going down and now they are going up. I know that oil prices are rigged and manipulated by all the major oil companies—they short oil futures"—i.e., they make money betting on oil prices going down—"and make billions when prices plunge. Then they all get together and cut marginal supply and *boom*—the price of oil jacks up. Exxon, Mobil, Shell—they are all in this shit show together in a big worldwide conspiracy, and I know it and am going to blow the whistle on it."

I also must add that in my years of dealing with O'Reilly he always thought himself to be an economics and market genius—if you didn't put up with his pedantic, cult-leader-like pre-segment lectures on whatever was the segment topic, you were not invited back.

He continued, "So I'm going to call you out on being dead wrong on oil prices and educate the audience at home about how they are getting ripped off by big oil and Wall Street guys like you stealing money from their pockets."

I responded, "You know, Bill—my forecast was right last year—oil prices did go down with the 2009 recession. Now they are rising because actual end demand is rising. And the oil majors are colluding to raise oil prices? You mean OPEC right? Mobil/Exxon and Shell are not part of OPEC, as you know."

O'Reilly responds, "I'm confused—is this the Tobin Fucking Smith Show? Until it is, this is how we roll.

"You don't understand what I do—I scare the shit out of Joe and Mary six-pack sitting all comfy at home, and then I show them how you Wall Street carpetbaggers are to blame. You don't know what you are talking about and how Wall Street is nothing but a conspiracy against the little guy. Fear works—resentment works—blame works too. Me coming to their rescue and telling 'em I'm on their side and how the big guys work against them is what I do—comprende amigo?"

"Roger that, Bill—thanks for the education. I thought it was your good looks that made your show click."

There, my new friends, is Fox News in a tiny capsule: At Fox News, empirical fact is worthless; triggering our base emotions of fear, anger, blame, resentment, and hate is the currency of the tribal identity porn game and what the tribal performance art at FNC is all about. Subjective opinion flows like water into the minds of the Fox News fanatic because, of course, no empirically proven fact ever enters their self-curated digital echo chamber.

But the most important program issue of all? Getting the audience's addictive brain chemicals flowing if we choreograph and execute the fixed outcome "debate" game plan correctly.

If we do, there is a fist pump "Yea!" ending for our viewer—that's FNC's happy dance drug deal with the viewer (we will dive deep into the neurochemistry of tribal identity porn addiction in a while—I promise it will be exciting!).

You have to understand that the language of tribal TV is fear, righteous tribal victory, and cult-like social identity beliefs repeated over and over again until they stick. Linguistic scientists call this verbal technique "generics." Liberals hate America. Big oil is ripping us off. Liberals hate capitalism. In the tribal fear, rage, blame, and resentment porn business at Fox News, the entire performance art is built on the premise that if you scare the already frightened, lonely, disconnected, angry (and for most of the audience financially traumatized) people at home even more, you will get their emotional fight-or-flight brain chemicals involuntarily flowing. And that will give us a chance to addict you.

At its core, tribal identity TV is just a riff on Caveman Psychology 101, and evolution did not prepare your brain to ingest tens of thousands of hours of tribal fear, hate, and blame porn.

Episodic everyday tribal TV is different than seasonal episodic drama/comedy/sports TV. You may feel you are "addicted" to *Game of Thrones*, but you really just love the wondrous emotions and escape you feel watching adventure/romance/swordfights and those flying dragons. It may have felt like withdrawal when the show ended in 2019, but you have many other TV shows that float your mental escapism boat.

Prime-time politically tribalized opinion and commentary programs broadcasting every weeknight are different—they're on at the same time every day of the year. Like I have stated from the beginning, daily tribal TV is an appointment to feel tribal superiority feelings—a social identity self-esteem booster shot, if you will.

Instead of escaping reality for an hour or two, the Fox News viewer is actively rescripting the reality of their life.

Properly produced, tribal identity porn is psychologically addictive because the feelings we deal in are the core psychological social identity needs we all have—to replace depleting self-esteem by validating the superiority of our in-group and seeing yet another high-def example of the inferiority of our hated enemy out-group.

Game of Thrones is make-believe that takes you to a fantastical faraway place. Fox News's tribal fear, rage, blame, resentment, and hate programming helps you feel better about who you are right now and validates the righteousness and superiority of your right-wing social identity every day.

Eventually I learned from my producers at Fox News—via many late-night cocktails at the various Fox News New York City watering holes— that Roger's real dream and the actual mission of Fox News was actually much darker than just rigged opinion debates.

What we created in my years at Fox News was a perpetual emotion machine powered by nuclear bombs of tribal fear, outrage, grievance, and blame. Those nukes filled the TV rooms of our viewers with the very real fallout of vitriol and resentment. For many of those viewers breathing that toxic air for six hours a day, Roger knew their dormant virus of political tribalism would activate and soon their worldview and the Fox News worldview became one.

All of which brings us to Fox News's most powerful tribal instinct triggering technique of them all—the conservative's visceral hatred and resentment of liberal identity politics more often referred to as "political correctness," or simply PC.

YOU DON'T UNDERSTAND WHAT IT IS LIKE TO WORK IN WEST LA AND BE A CONSERVATIVE

I'm in the Fox News studio in West LA for a live hit for Sean Hannity on a Friday night. It's a 5:35 hit, and traffic in LA for you non-LA people is horrific—you might as well go find an adult beverage with a friend and let the traffic clear out. An FNC producer from NYC is in the LA studios that day, and since LA is my original home and I know the hood, I take him out to Santa Monica for drive time cocktails.

It turns out Bruce the producer had moved to LA from NYC, and the moment our adult beverages arrive he starts wailing about how brutal it is to be a conservative New Yorker in LA. "Toby you can't believe it. I go out to after work drinks with my wife's friends who are all West LA professionals in the corporate insurance world. Jesus—the river of PC bullshit did not stop all night—and they could not believe that I (a) work for Fox News and (b) did not vote for Barack Obama. In fact, they looked at me, shook their heads, and said, 'Bruce—you might as well go back to New York City—you will never make it out here. Everything you do and say is an insult to how we see the world in West LA.' And oh boy—every friggin' conversation was about how racist Republicans are and how bigoted they are versus the polyglots in LA who speak at least two languages and they don't respect their culture and heritage blah blah blah. I told them I was Jewish, and they said 'That might get you by in Beverly Hills—but not here. You Republicans are just so non-PC.'"

I have many longtime friends who self-identify as right wing or Republicans. In fact, virtually all my West Coast peeps are right-wingers minus the Bay Area.

What I have found is people use the term "PC" a lot but don't really understand what it means. Like most cultural or political terms, PC is just mental shorthand for identity politics. And identity politics is just the commonly used term for a group of people that feel their rights (as a member of an undefended or marginalized minority or culture) have been abused and need to be protected by law or receive special treatment.

For instance, the Civil Rights movement and gay rights movement were never a "zero sum" business; affirming the rights these minority groups already had under the Constitution did not give them something new or confer preferential treatment.

But for the purpose of understanding one of the most important ways Fox News manipulates, triggers, and radicalizes its culturally and politically conservative audience, you have to understand the searing, bone-marrow-deep resentment and hatred generated by liberal identity politics and its brand of political correctness for people like Bruce.

First understand this fact: PC is also just a synonym for cultural or political us vs. them tribalism. But I found that the particular brand of political correctness that makes self-identified conservatives' heads spin is the smug, scorched earth absolutism kind: "If you don't use this word or this phrase, or think the way I do, you are a (choose your favorite "ism," "ist," and "phobe"—it's a long list) which proves to me you are morally and intellectually deficient" (with the implication always that if they don't follow the PC rules of behavior, they are just a backward, gap-tooth hillbilly in a pickup truck).

The Dems/Liberals/Left apparently never read Dale Carnegie on how to win friends and influence people. "Criticism is dangerous because it wounds a person's pride, hurts his sense of importance, and arouses resentment."

Attacking a person's morality or intellect because they do not conform to your version of political or cultural correctness is like serving up criticism with a chlorine chaser. I'll use the favorite term of tribal right-wingers, "Snowflakes," to illustrate my point. Without a doubt in my mind, the most powerful driving force that drove Donald J. Trump to the American presidency was his skillful battle against cultural political correctness. He dispensed with the traditional racial and cultural code strategy and went right to his Trumpian anti-PC bullhorn.

Since he was born politically incorrect, he was a natural warrior against it.

Now to a self-identified liberal, the term political correctness refers to a commonly held belief that there is language, practices, and policies which could reasonably be expected to offend, marginalize, or disadvantage a group and thus should be eliminated or at least managed in a civilized and sophisticated society.

I am told the PC concept originally revolved around the core liberal drive for a color-blind America and a more fair and sensitive country that welcomes and respects the culture of all its citizens. PC was and is (in most cases) I think a noble pursuit—but with conservative talk radio first and then the vast growth of Fox News it's been weaponized against its noble intent.

Today, to a politically and culturally incorrect conservative person (especially from small city or rural America—not living in a racially and ethnically diverse urban community) who proudly identifies as a member of Trump's "Intolerables" tribe, political correctness means a way that we speak in America so we don't offend overly sensitive "snowflakes."

Don't shoot the messenger here, folks—just telling you how at least 40 percent of Americans feel about absolutist scorched earth political correctness—they despise it with all their being. Brian Ott, a political scientist who has studied Fox News/Trump TV's core audience, says that Fox News has an emotional and psychic "lock on 42 percent of the American public." He has concluded from direct research that this lock is "absolute."

Why is that? One common theme is the dogmatic approach of the left wing that preaches "inclusion" and how inclusive and color blind their big tent is, but excludes Americans that don't say the right words or believe in the "right" issues.

More graphically, my favorite dictionary and arbiter of all things American, the Urban Dictionary (urbandictionary.com) tells us that political correctness means, "If you are so pathetically weak that you don't have the balls to say what you feel and mean, you are a hopeless politically correct pussy."

All righty then—our urban and nonurban cultural divide is indeed deep and vast.

Furthermore, to be considered an upstanding member of the Intolerable tribe is to believe that political correctness is nothing less than a plot and method of liberalism to control and dictate public speech and thought.

One of the most common examples of succumbing to political correctness is the word "y'all." While I did not get this PC memo, I am told that using the term "y'all" is not politically correct anymore because some African Americans have decided that it is offensive.

Oy! My point here? There is no more powerful way to trigger right-wing heads to explode and induce all kinds of instinctive tribal behavior and emotions than to mount a discussion supporting political correctness. To even the non-tribal conservative, when they don't agree with affirmative action they are called "racists." When they don't agree with transgender bathrooms, they are called homophobes.

When they want to build a physical wall to keep undocumented immigrants and their young children out of America, they are racists and baby killers. When they want to ban Muslims or asylum seekers from entering the country, they are Islamophobia bigots, racist, and un-American—that's a near PC grand slam.

So gosh—what culturally and politically PC visceral heresy act does Fox News perform on a daily (and sometimes hourly) basis? They gin-up as many political correctness segments per day as humanly possible. From the "War Against Christmas" to using the term "snowflake" and "elite" as often as possible in referring to Millennial and Gen-Z aged liberals, ripping into

PC behavior exacts a purely Pavlovian trigger response in conservatives from basically everywhere.

My point: To a conservative (and most right-leaning Independents) engaging in political correctness is tribal activation and validation mongering on steroids. It's a "gimme" as we say in golf. When the Fox News producers are out of ideas for today's show, they just search "politically correct" and they have at least one segment.

As GOP Speaker of the House Paul Ryan was quoted recently on today's toxic environment of political tribalism and identity politics, "Donald Trump did not give us all this. Donald Trump is showing us what it looks like."

American politics, it has become painfully clear, is now driven less by ideological commitments than by our tribal partisan social identities— less by what we think than by what we are defined as by our chosen tribal membership. For cultural and political conservatives and binge-watching Fox News addicts in general, their bone-marrow-deep resentment of being labeled "racist, homophobic, Islamophobic" for their long-held beliefs and cultural differences from urban liberal America is *the* most powerful Pavlovian tribal trigger possible.

Remember—to many Americans in 2019, their political identity is their ideology.

In my opinion, it's now crystal clear that the Democratic Party and Progressives have done themselves no favors by creating so many identity politics issues and cultural PC checkboxes that that many mainstream Americans will never culturally fit within. They drive away a lot of good people who simply hate being demonized or stigmatized by how they see the world.

Can you blame them?

Because above all else—the power of anti-PC programming is to emotionally troll the hyper-aggrieved viewer to get a visceral tribal reaction. Luckily for Fox News, self-identified white right-wingers, after watching thousands of hours of Fox News, develop such a bone-deep and finely tuned feeling of communal victimhood that for many those feelings are never more than just slightly below their emotional reactor.

Feelings of bitterness toward smug condescending liberal absolutism, name calling/labels, and utter disrespect for how other tribes see the world is Fox News's bread and butter emotional trigger and hot button manipulation.

CHAPTER 12

The Untold Truth about Tribal Social Identity Porn

As social scientists **Robert Kubey** and Mihaly Csikszentmihalyi have written in *Scientific American*, "Perhaps the most ironic aspect of the struggle for survival is how easily organisms can be harmed by that which they desire. The trout is caught by the fisherman's lure, the mouse by cheese. But at least those creatures have the excuse that bait and cheese look like sustenance. Humans seldom have that consolation. The temptations that can disrupt their lives are often pure indulgences. No one has to drink alcohol, for example. Realizing when a diversion has gotten out of control is one of the great challenges of life."

They add this insight as well:

> The term "TV addiction" is imprecise and laden with value judgments, but it captures the essence of this genuine phenomenon. Psychologists and psychiatrists formally define substance dependence as a disorder characterized by criteria that include spending a great deal of time using the substance; using it more often than one intends; thinking about reducing use or making repeated unsuccessful efforts to reduce use; and reporting withdrawal symptoms when one stops using it.

Key Point: What distinguishes addiction to Fox News tribal hate porn from regular TV addiction is simple: TV addicts watch a bunch of channels. They make friends with their favorite actors, hosts, and news anchors all over the dial. Watching TV gives them something to do. Their imaginary friends are always there at the same time and place. Perhaps the most significant difference is that ordinary entertainment TV addicts (like me!) discuss their favorite shows and stars with their actual friends and family in friendly banter and debate. Far from estranging them, the mutually shared experience of a favorite TV show is a social bonding event like discussing the movie you just saw with family or friends.

In contrast, the average Fox News addict watches more than three hours per day of just Fox News tribal identity porn. Moreover, most hard-core Fox News addicts I have met and heard about from family members never turn the TV off of Fox News. (Cue the old couple with a Texas accent saying, "Oh, Tobin, we love you on Fox. We never turn it off at our house!")

Key Point: Just like addiction to sexual porn, video games, food, or sex, addiction to right-wing tribal porn is classified as a process or behavioral addiction.

Fox News addiction is very real.

The incidence rate of addiction to Fox News is much larger than anyone ever imagined or that has been reported. Frank Luntz's poll disclosing nearly one-third of American households have political estrangement issues occurring is the closest third-party research that corroborates our Fox News social derangement disorder incidence data.

You now know what "hooks" partisan tribal viewers—it's the feel-good brain "drugs" they get from watching yet another fixed outcome and rigged gladiatorial victory by their self-identified tribe.

In short, Fox News addicts get high.

TRIBAL BLAME PORN

In 2008–2009, I found that for many viewers, their new and growing Fox News addiction was more about Fox News as a powerful coping mechanism than the normal cultural or political warfare themes Fox News specialized in programming. Our new audience engagement theme? Lost faith and hope in their prosperity, their children's future, and white America.

Here is what I learned about tribal blame porn. Fox News ratings started to really take off in 2008 when a certain person won the American presidency. Apparently for many white Americans who suffered the brunt of the financial pain of the 2007–2009 Great Recession and then the heresy of a black Barack Hussein Obama as their president, the one-two punch put them over their tribal ledge.

After thousands of hours of reading about, researching, and interviewing Fox News addicts, the light bulb finally went off: My tribal "fear and hate porn" definition had missed an important other emotional target and trigger: economic *blame* and self-absolution.

After the election of Barack Obama in 2008 and the Great Recession of 2007–2009, Fox News moved from primarily creating and televising the pornography of tribal fear and hate into the much more engaging and insidious business of providing the more powerful and addictive tribal identity pornography of communal victimhood, blame, and personal absolution for a new, broader, angrier, and emotionally vulnerable audience. Fox's tribal fear-and-hate-porn strategy morphed into the business of packaging and selling a very potent production of communal tribal blame and victimization porn to the twenty-first-century post-Industrial Age victims of various villainous out-groups (globalists, Beltway insiders, pointy-headed elites) who sold them down the river.

In other words, after the financial wreckage in Fox Country, we had a new large and politically/culturally engaged tribal market in America. Broke, angry, and resentful white working-class Americans, living mostly in the 2,626 Trump-voting counties, would channel their tribal, cultural, and racial hate and resentment into watching Fox News to see the faces of the hated East and West Coast elites who they deeply believed had screwed up their lives.

Key Point: Fox News's new audience was already fearful about the continuity of their jobs, their way of life, and their future when they discovered Fox News post-2008. Our job at Fox News was to give audience members a name and face to blame for their economic trauma, their anguish, and their fears. When we did, Fox News viewers got the most powerful feeling and drug of all: permission to stop blaming themselves for the downward trajectories of their families' lives.

Ah, relief and endorphins. You know that great feeling of relief you get when you find out you did not do that stupid or careless thing you thought you did (you know—like leave your kid in the car)? Or better— that the dumb thing you did or said did not have the bad consequences you feared?

Well—that feeling of relief actually comes from a rush of the brain chemical endorphin. Endorphin is nature's pain relief chemical—it's stimulated by physical or mental pain. It evolved for survival; we needed it to switch on when we got hurt but need to scramble out of danger, for example.

Neuroscientists tell us the addictive power of an endorphin rush is second only in power to the opiate-like power of serotonin (released when you feel your judgment and belief is proven right). Here is a perfect example of how Fox News produces a tribal fear-and-blame pornography segment.

HAZLETON, PA, AND THE FEAR-AND-BLAME PORN DELUGE

Yes, the election and Great Recession came in 2008, but I see FNC's wall-to-wall coverage of the Hazleton, Pennsylvania, "Immigration Act" in 2006 as the watershed moment for Fox News's new kind of right-wing tribal porn programming.

For what seemed an eternity, one segment we did over and over and over again on the Saturday shows and prime-time opinion-porn programs was, in effect, various riffs on the fear and blame theme of, "Is *your* small city about to be Hazletoned?"

In case you don't remember, Hazleton was one of the many small towns in the Steel Belt that lost its steel plants and good-paying hourly middle-class wage jobs. Hazleton was merely emblematic of the end of America's twentieth-century economy and of the rapid ascension of America's post-industrial economy; we could have used two thousand other small Steel Belt cities as examples.

In Hazleton in 2002, the mega-meat processor Cargill Industries opened a large beef-processing facility near the town along with some distribution centers including an Amazon distribution center. In 2006, Hazleton's mayor, Lou Barletta, championed an ordinance—the first in the nation—penalizing employers and landlords for dealing with illegal immigrants. The courts blocked the ordinance from taking effect, but Mayor Barletta became an overnight folk hero in upstate Pennsylvania. For weeks, Fox News loaded TV screens with pictures of this small town because of Barletta's actions. Other small-city mayors looking for Fox News face time followed the same script.

In a *National Geographic* story about the incident, Michele Norris of *All Things Considered* radio fame dug into some of the feelings that white Americans expressed to her:

> It is an indisputable fact: All was not fine and dandy in Hazleton before legal Hispanics started moving to Hazleton from New York and New Jersey to take the low-paying meatpacking and warehouse jobs.
>
> But by 2006, the town had been rescued from economic disaster by lawful and much-needed out-of-state immigration. Lo and behold, new jobs begat new home purchases, which begat new service stores, and then Dominican and Puerto Rican dining establishments opened.

The problem was the original white townsfolk not only did not share in much of this new prosperity, they "felt they did not recognize their hometown and were not safe downtown." (The townspeople in the late nineteenth century must have felt the same way when those dirty and disgusting Irish, Italians, and Germans—the great-grandparents of the 2006 white Hazletonians—first emigrated to the city for the brutal steel-working jobs, but I digress.)

The good Lord knows we showed the same damn Hazleton stats and B-roll video every week on Fox News. These stats come from Binyan Appleton's *New York Times* article on Hazleton in 2016: "In the 2000 census, just 4.9 percent of Hazleton's population had identified as Hispanic. A decade later, that figure was 37 percent. By 2016, the most recent data available, 56 percent of the city's population said they were non-white Hispanic. Hazleton today is now a majority-Hispanic city, just like the nearby cities of Reading and Allentown."

Look at the fear and blame themes in the Hazleton story. This is pure tribal-fear-outrage-blame-porn gold at Fox News, as reported in a recent NPR article.

On change being uncomfortable, no matter where it's coming from: "When people talked about it, it was often the notion of suddenly being outnumbered—that's a word that I heard over and over and over again. Going to the doctor's office and suddenly looking around and realizing that everybody else is Hispanic. Going to the local Walmart . . . and realizing that, 'Boy, the things they're selling in the produce aisle are different,' or 'There's a whole aisle where everything is in two languages, and I never noticed that before.' . . . 'Suddenly it feels like this community that I knew so well'—so what they were saying is that they don't feel like it's 'theirs' anymore."

On race as the subtext: "They wouldn't necessarily say 'those brown people,' or 'those Latino people.' There would often be sort of proxy for that—'the food is different, the music is different, the town feels different.' There was a large 'threat' narrative—safety is a big issue here."

Hazleton became the poster child for the next twelve years of Fox News fear-and-blame-porn segments in all its living brown color. Tucker Carlson even did a whole show in early 2018 on Hazleton eighteen years later. For Fox News, Hazleton is the tribal fear-and-blame-porn gift that keeps on giving.

Note: Despite my lengthy macroeconomic background, as a paid analyst and contributor on Fox News I was expected in our right/left opinion debates to toe the right-wing line on this "terrible injustice of immigrants taking the jobs of white working class Americans" (read: white working class Americans).

From an economist's perspective, I argued the side of "creative destruction" and how the natural regeneration of blighted regions is the normal process in free-market capitalism, in which new, hungrier immigrants are willing to take hard physical jobs that the establishment citizens don't want.

To my dismay—but not surprise—my contribution time to these segments was always cut short by the segment producer and EP. Many times, the "Hazleton again" segment producer would tell me, "Tobe, I need you to play ball on this segment. Tell your viewers how this economic horror is coming to their small town soon too. I need ya to play ball with me on this one."

My fellow former FNC contributor Linda Chavez tells the same story. Although the former Reagan White House official was a longtime Fox conservative contributor, Linda told me that as a paid conservative Fox News contributor, she basically became a nonperson if she made a case for an ideologically heretical position on live Fox News TV.

Linda took a position in favor of more legal immigration—a position that had been consistent for more than thirty years and that was based on what she told me was her "strong belief in markets over central government planning."

As Linda told me the story: "One producer basically told me that it was 'confusing' to have me on to discuss the subject because conservatives were supposed to be for less immigration and liberals for more. Another time, O'Reilly spoke in my earpiece from New York when I was in the DC studio to warn me not to confuse everybody with a lot of facts and statistics. 'You have your facts and I have mine, so keep it general.'"

Key Point: If you are paid to be a conservative Fox News contributor, you are expected to play your role in Fox's performance art episode. If you are an unpaid conservative and don't speak the accepted conservative talking points on air, your number is lost and your career as a Fox talking head is over. Period.

QUICK KEY FOX NEWS LESSON LEARNED: "THE BALL GAME"

Now is a good time to take a break and get into the ways Fox News producers fix the outcome of our "fair-and-balanced" debates for the right-wing contributors to win the "debate" in the eyes of the home viewer.

On the seventeenth-floor hallways of the FNC opinion-programming cubicles, I would constantly hear the phrase, "So here's the ball game." At Fox News, "the ball game" is the institutional euphemism for the conservative-vs.-liberal debate set up to ensure the conservative side wins by making sure the viewer hears what the producer knows or was told the audience wants to hear to feel the self-esteem rush from being once again tribally validated and victorious.

Yes, folks—you could say FNC tribal identity porn is really nothing more than highly scripted and choreographed confirmation bias performance art with introductory notes of fear and blame added to the recipe.

The Hazleton segments are a perfect example for a basic overview.

In order to have an optimal ball game—a segment in which the left-winger comes off as a bleeding-heart liberal the Fox News viewers *love* to hate and watch us right-wing heroes mop the floor with their snowflake's liberal tears—the producers manipulate a set of multiple outcome levers.

The first lever of rigged opinion program production is the selection of the liberal crash-dummy prop du jour. One key to the stacked-deck Fox News opinion panel ball game is that the segment producer at Fox News is not trying to find the world's expert on labor economics or post-industrial economics to debate us right-wing tribal heroes. The producer actually does the opposite—trying to match the weakest and lamest but most stereotypical "libtard" crash dummy prop against the most reliable conservative contributor possible (or sometimes against an unpaid right-wing guest who is on the show because she is a bona fide expert on the topic). This strategy is all about setting up the right tone and cadence for the choreographed emotional roller coaster of fear followed by tribal validation required to deliver the right-wing happy dance. It's fair to say that one of the big differences between tribal identity porn on MSNBC or CNN versus that on Fox News is the quality of the opposition.

Key Point: At Fox News, the liberal is always just a prop for the scene that has been carefully written and choreographed. Remember, a big part of the Fox News opinion-panel scam is not just the strategy to never stage a fair fight: The strategy is to make sure the stereotypical liberal character is beaten before the segment ever airs.

Take the normal Hazleton debate segment. The cold-open B-roll video shows the town overrun by Hispanic businesses, and audio plays of the mayor spouting off to the effect of, "We will not let our town be taken over," followed by a few shots of Hispanic-looking young men sitting around doing nothing. In tribal TV these images are called the "racial dog whistle shot." Dog whistle shots are meant to silently communicate non-PC things that the producers believe many partisan audience members believe—in this case that Hispanic men are mostly lazy and prefer to sit around doing nothing.

In this sequenced performance art segment, the host turns first to the liberal pundit and asks, "How can you defend the hostile takeover of Hazleton by outsider immigrants from New York and New Jersey?" Before the segment is taped, the panel members have submitted their points of view (POVs) on the issue, which the producer has theoretically distributed to all the participants so they know what both their competition and their allies are going to say in the segment and don't duplicate their talking points.

All political and business talk shows practice this protocol, but what was different at Fox News from the other networks I have appeared on was that my producer often asked me to "play ball," meaning to take the side against the liberal, especially when I agreed with the producer's chosen narrative. When I said yes (which was almost always), I got a whole set of new facts and figures from the producer right before the segment was taped that were never shared with the designated liberal for the segment.

The POV protocol at most TV networks is sacrosanct—everyone on the panel assumes they got the same opinions and talking points shared preshow. Not at Fox News—for more than a decade I got new data and talking points from the office printer an hour or less before we taped my show in New York City at 6:00 p.m. Friday night. In fact, I was contractually obligated to be in NYC for 90 percent of my appearances—as what I found out later was the "designated hit man" or the one the producer and host could count on to knock out the normally pathetic libtard.

Why did I play along? Because they were paying me $5,000 a week to be the sure-thing "hit man." The hit man's job is to make sure the segment audience got what they came for: yet another validation of their tribal beliefs and a dramatic exciting-enough victory to get the happy brain drugs automatically flowing.

I was the segment producer's hit man most of the time because, unlike the other paid non-left-wing contributors, I was contractually obligated to be in New York every week for the live and taped shows, and I was available to the segment producers up to the last few minutes. That meant if they were not sure they had choreographed a "famous death" for the always solo liberal on the panel, they needed me to be the designated liberal "hit man" on the segment—again the guy to whom they would give data that was not passed on to the liberal crash dummy. As I mentioned I was also slipped the Ailes/Moody talking point memo when I came into the NYC offices—most times I knew the slant the producer was looking for.

Many times, I was tapped on the shoulder at the last minute and ordered to say what the producers felt was the most convincing case to be made for the right-wing ideology to once again be validated based on some new reporting or late afternoon Friday events.

Key Point: Again, in almost every opinion debate I participated in at Fox News, the token liberal was only a prop. The liberal came in with the talking points that I knew were coming because I had already read and studied them. If the liberal guest deviated much from the line of argument he or she had submitted before appearing, they were left off the producer's call list in the future.

In contrast, my talking points were usually new and refined because they were scripted, and I had been coached by the segment producer and had received my hit-man lines. One of the reasons was our show *Bulls & Bears* was the first show in the 10:00–12:00 "Business Block" and thus the most important show for keeping the audience from the 7:00–10:00 *Fox & Friends* weekend program.

Repeat: At Fox News, there was no such thing as a fair-and-balanced fight on most segments I performed in; almost all were staged debates. The liberal antagonist most often was not aware of my case because, unlike the cases of the other right-wing heroes, it came from the segment producer and had not been shared with anyone else before the show.

So in other words, we not only duped our audience, Fox News also duped the poor left-wing piñatas we invited to our weekly show. They were nothing but ritual sacrifices at the altar of right-wing tribal confirmation-bias performance art. Make no mistake: Fox News is very good at audience duping—it was almost an art form. We told 'em one hundred times a day what we brought to their living room was a "fair and balanced" discussion of the week's most important issues to right-wing partisans. I was there for fourteen years and two thousand episodes of "fair and balanced" opinion debate—I never was in one of the rare times the producers screwed up and we actually had a fair debate.

Blinding Flash of the Obvious: Today, the core Fox News viewer—and its proxy, the Trump base—holds a view of the world and life that is virtually 100 percent different from that held by the top 20 percent of Americans, who live primarily in the thriving knowledge and innovation regions of the country. And, lest we forget, the top 20 percent of American households by income also control 95 percent of the wealth in America and pay 95 percent of the income taxes. They, obviously, are not the target today of FNC's tribal identity and angst programming.

I've come to call the geography containing Fox News's core viewers "America's Desperate Households" to represent the spectrum of dashed and damaged hopes and dreams that this subgroup of America has dealt with for the past thirty years.

Key Point: By far, the most potent and addictive feeling I delivered for too many of the Fox News core middle-class and white working-class elderly audience was not the momentary feeling of tribal victory or vindication. For the Fox News viewers living from day to day in financial distress, the most intense, longer-lasting feeling is the dopamine and serotonin rush they get from personal absolution.

Absolution is defined as "the formal release from guilt, obligation, or punishment." All religions are built from a stone quarry of absolution, and I have found that the devotion for Fox News felt by a majority of financially struggling Fox News addicts is based on the absolution they grant themselves after watching Fox News.

Key Point: Evangelicalism, Fox News viewers' religion of choice, gives many the feeling that they will experience spiritual absolution from their sins in the afterlife. Here on earth, however, Fox News's version of right-wing tribal Evangelicalism gives its viewers profound feelings of personal absolution while they are still breathing. The belief that your lost opportunity and dimmed hopes for prosperity are not your fault is one of the most addicting feelings of all.

Fortuitously for Fox News, that feeling of absolution needs constant reinforcement.

Above all else, Fox News's core middle-class and fallen-middle-class viewers are a prideful and stoic chip off the nineteenth- and early twentieth-century America block. From meeting hundreds of core Fox News viewers in person and via social media, I found deep wounds of lost pride and lost self-esteem have been sewn together with toxic sutures of tribal resentment, crippling anger, and outright despair.

Fox News's continuous tribal blame porn programming is for many a very real communal victimhood that helps mask the pain of living in once proud and vibrant communities that have fallen into disrepair.

Social scientists tell us there is perhaps no emotional force more powerful than gain or loss of self-pride, and Fox News exploits and panders to resentment and fear caused by wounded pride and lost hopes and dreams as a cat plays with a scared mouse.

CHAPTER 13

The Two Superpowers of Fox News

It may be hard for those who don't regularly watch Fox News opinion programming to fathom these facts:

According to Punditfact.com, "78 percent of statements made by FNC and FBN personalities and their right-wing pundit guests check out to be Half True (18 percent), Mostly False (21 percent), 100 percent False (30 percent) and 'Pants on Fire' (wholly made up delusional gibberish: 9 percent).

"Only 10 percent of statements made by on-air FNC/FBN personalities and right-wing pundit guests are 100 percent factual."

FNC and FBN hosts and guests do not burst out laughing as they say and repeat easily disproved propaganda statements over and over again.

Many nonpartisan folks (and any liberal/Progressive) who happen upon a Fox News prime-time opinion segment shake their heads and ask, "How does the audience buy this horse crap? Don't they care that they are being lied to and manipulated?"

The answer—as you know now—is no, they do not.

As you also know now, the Fox News viewers do not tune in to learn about well-documented and proven objective facts and figures. They tune in to get their cultural and political hate on and so they can get the rush from a well-produced tribal-validation feedback loop. Only a small number of independent and non-tribal conservatives are watching Fox News—usually to see how the right wing is spinning the latest political or cultural news event.

That brings us to the psychological construct I've alluded to, what the WWE calls "kayfabe."

Stay with me; this is one of the primary keys to understanding why tribal partisan fear/rage/blame-and-hate-as-entertainment works so well with tribal partisans.

WHAT I BELIEVE IS MUCH MORE IMPORTANT THAN WHAT ACTUALLY HAPPENED

I discovered the concept of kayfabe and the two-way acknowledgment between actor and audience of performance art when I attended a Wrestle-Mania event in DC courtesy of a WWE friend. As I sat watching the wrestlers throw each other off ungodly high stairs and beat the stuffing out of each other with metal chairs, I asked the young female fan next to me, "You know this whole match is set up by the WWE for XYZ to win, right?"

She looked me dead in the eye and told me, "Not to me it isn't."

I pondered that answer and why she said it until Nick Rogers (uniquely a sociologist, lawyer, and pro-wrestling aficionado) explained the concept of kayfabe exceptionally well in a *New York Times* article in April 2017. To paraphrase Mr. Rogers, when Alex Jones (the conspiracy monger who runs the uber-right-wing conspiracy porn outlet InfoWars.com) told the judge in his child custody suit that "his antics are irrelevant to his fitness as a parent, because he is a performance artist whose public behavior is part of his fictional character," some people assumed that Jones's devoted fans would abandon him because he had essentially admitted to being a fraud.

Mr. Rogers's analysis was that they would not, and he was right: Jones's web traffic went up! Remember the backfire effect and what happened when the multiple-week KKK newspaper stories were published in the early 1920s and the KKK gained more than one hundred thousand new members?

According to Rogers, "Alex Jones's audience adores him because of his artifice, not in spite of it. They admire a man who can identify their most primal feelings, validate them, and choreograph their release."

Take that in for a moment. The Fox News contributor/host kayfabe contract with the tribal TV addict audience at home is the very same dynamic. I can't tell you how many times I have been asked by a self-identified "very conservative" Fox News fan in public somewhere about what Bill O'Reilly or Sean Hannity is like in person. When I'd tell them what a sex predator O'Reilly is or what a low-brow Hannity is in person, they always look at me and say, "I don't believe it. I *love* those guys—you're dead wrong!"

Back to Nick. "To understand this, and to understand the political success of other figures like Donald Trump (who not coincidentally is in the WWE Hall of Fame for his many appearances), it is helpful to know a term from the world of professional wrestling: 'kayfabe.' For at least fifty years 'kayfabe' has referred to the unspoken contract between wrestlers and spectators: We'll present you the illusion of something clearly fake under the insistence that it's real, and you will experience genuine emotion. Neither party acknowledges the bargain, or else the magic is ruined."

After reading that explanation, I finally understood not only the core Fox News audience better but also the Trump base voters too. To a wrestling audience (many of whom live in the same 2,626 counties as Fox News fans and Trump voters, so let's assume at least some audience crossover), the fake and the real coexist peacefully. Ignoring the fake is a trade-off for, in the case of pro wrestling, a jolly good and rowdy time rooting for their hero and hissing at their hated villain. In other words, allowing themselves to believe in the fake "cage match" is harmless fun.

For twelve years, I thought FNC's fixed-outcome gladiatorial shows were harmless fun too. Fox News kayfabe is more subtle . . . but there is a very cathartic aspect to it as well. (Cue the "Man I wanted to throw a brick through my TV!" guy in the airport.)

When I asked the young lady next to me at WrestleMania if she realized the match was set up for XYZ to win, I was asking the wrong question. According to Rogers, "If you ask a fan whether a match or backstage brawl was scripted, the question will seem irrelevant. You may as well ask a roller-coaster enthusiast whether he knows he's not really on a runaway mine car. The artifice is not only understood but appreciated: The performer cares enough about the viewer's emotions to want to influence them. Kayfabe isn't about factual verifiability; it's about emotional fidelity." He goes on to point out that "skilled wrestlers captivate because they do what sociologists call 'emotional labor'—the professional management of other people's feelings. Diners expect emotional labor from their servers, WWE fans demand it from their favorite performer, and a whole lot of voters desire it from their leaders."

Key Point: It is the job of the Fox News producers to script the host to do the "emotional labor" and manage the feelings and expectations of core Fox News viewer.

Look, it is no coincidence that Donald Trump is enshrined in the WWE Hall of Fame. Trump performed in the WWE multiple times, most famously in the ring in the *Battle of the Billionaires*. It is also no coincidence that Donald Trump's WWE-like character and his campaign filled with commonly believed Fox News propaganda connected with more than sixty-three million Americans. Donald Trump learned kayfabe from the best: the WWE, Vince McMahon, and Roger Ailes.

When Trump demonizes the media as "enemies of the people," that's a character he is playing and emotional labor he is giving to his tribal liberal-hating believers—in short, it's kayfabe. His summit with the cartoonish WWE-like heel North Korean dictator Kim Jong Un was kayfabe at its best. As conservative columnist Jonah Goldberg accurately points out in an August 2018 column, "Trump's summit with North Korean dictator Kim Jong Un was entirely kayfabe, particularly Trump's ridiculous claim that 'there is no longer a nuclear threat from North Korea.'"

According to Mr. Rogers's cogent analysis:

> Ask an average Trump supporter whether he or she thinks the president actually plans to build a giant wall and have Mexico pay for it, and you might get an answer that boils down to, "I don't think so, but I believe so."
>
> That's kayfabe. Chants of "Build the Wall" aren't about erecting a structure; they're about how cathartic it feels, in the moment, to yell with venom against a common enemy.

Wow. The intellectual clarity of that analysis hit me like a ton of bricks.

Kayfabe isn't merely a suspension of disbelief; it's a philosophy about truth itself.

Kayfabe, like a Fox News opinion panel performance, rests on the assumption that feelings are inherently more important and trustworthy than facts.

After meeting hundreds of the white middle- to lower-middle-class core audience at Fox News (now the "base" of Trumpism), I could never put my finger on why, other than poor economic and history education, they fervently believed what they heard from their Fox News hero (or Trump for that matter) as unambiguous fact. Kayfabe is a big part of the answer: The positive tribal feelings and validation they get from watching FNC (and by extension now a Donald Trump performance) are more valuable to them than the delusional ideas and flawed assumptions presented as objective facts. Besides, they live inside the right-wing media bubble so they actually don't see or hear any contradictory empirical data.

Maybe we have more in common with North Korea than we thought? The point is Fox News's tribal TV opinion panels are most certainly kayfabe-based entertainment. Donald Trump base rallies are a new form of kayfabe entertainment. Why do his followers fall for it? Now you know—because it emotionally feels so good to spend ninety minutes away from their actual lives of downward mobility cathartically yelling, chanting, and throwing their fists in the air. It feels great to dress up in the tribal uniform and put on the MAGA hats and T-shirts and blame faceless others for the economic trauma they feel every day of their lives, or their lost racial and cultural dominance.

Stephen Colbert captured the concept well with his term "truthiness," defined as "the belief or assertion that a particular statement is true based on the intuition or perceptions of some individual or individuals, without regard to evidence, logic, intellectual examination, or facts."

Key Point: We in the media and punditry can fact-check Fox News or Donald Trump and point out glaring lies and made-up "facts," but kayfabe and truthiness render all that effort beside the point. When the media, as Goldberg points out, "breaks the fourth wall" by reporting that almost every claim and statement of fact from Donald Trump or Sean Hannity is not true, they revert to their tribal cognitive instincts and decry that objective evidence as "fake news" and "liberal mainstream media lies" and become even more loyal to Trump. Fact checking merely confirms in their tribal minds the liberal media bias against him and strengthens their support for him as he lashes out at "fake news."

As Nick Rogers so perfectly sums up kayfabe: "Rationalists can and should make the case that empirical data is more reliable than intuition. But if they continue to ignore the human need for things to feel true, they will do so at their political peril."

Kayfabe is indeed about the innate emotional need for things and illusions to feel true. And yes, kayfabe isn't merely a suspension of disbelief; it's a philosophy about truth itself. A Fox News tribal fear opinion panel performance rests on the assumption that feelings are inherently more trustworthy than facts and that only a tribal sovereign or blood brother has the "real facts."

But there is another deeper emotion at play, I think, with the Foxholes who fit the description of some psychologically addicted to their time within the FNC unreality machine—visceral human connection.

FOX NEWS: RETRO AMERICA'S MECHANISM

In the last week of August and first week of September 2018, two Americans that I greatly admire—Senator John McCain and former President of the United States Barack Obama—officially declared war directly against

Donald Trump's political tribalism, and by extension, they attacked Fox News's tribal warfare programming, since they are now both the same tribal identity brand.

The most important lesson I learned from my journey into discovering why the Fox News tribal programming I performed in for fourteen years had morphed into a literal addiction for millions of Americans was this—for most of the hard-core Fox News fans, swearing allegiance to the destruction of "those socialist libtards" is not really an outwardly tribal act.

When you experience a strong rush of emotion—it is a catharsis if you feel better after the rush. If you've been feeling like you need a good cry, you should watch a cathartic movie like *Bambi*—or any film that's sure to make you weep. Things that are cathartic don't always call up tears. Things that makes you scream, like a roller-coaster ride or a boxing match, are also cathartic. Whatever causes you to release a sudden flood of feelings is cathartic. Some therapies ask you to hit a pillow or break dishes because those are cathartic activities.

For most, their daily six-hour pledge-of-allegiance and addiction to Foxism/Trumpism (now one in the same) is actually a more of a psychological coping mechanism to digest and cope with the constant pain of the unresolved emotional and economic traumas in their daily lives.

Now again—I am not a psychotherapist or addiction professional, nor do I play one on TV. But for this book I consulted with many. One that really struck me as the root driver of this Fox News tribal identity pornography came from the recent book *Lost Connections* by addiction expert Johann Hari. He talks about his decades of work in the fields of trauma and addiction and why he believes that the root of almost everything we suffer through in life is trauma that we never figured out how to repair.

Hari tells us that "trauma" is not just a term just reserved for the most severe and unrelenting atrocities one can experience. What struck me as so relevant to the millions of Americans who are quite literally addicted to what addiction experts refer to as a "process or behavioral addiction" and what I have termed white tribal identity activation and validation pornography is Hari's decades of experience with other behavioral addictions.

His analysis of what causes behavioral addiction is also what I have come to understand as one of the core underlying strategies embedded in the Fox News tribal warfare playbook. According to Hari, "Anytime something scares us or enrages us and we do not get over that fear or rage, trauma is created. When we don't believe we have the resources or abilities to cope with a certain problem or stimuli, we create adaptive behaviors to deny or avoid it."

Emotionally speaking, Fox News gets you coming and going—either our tribal activation and validation segment produces the emotional reaction of righteous tribal victory that involuntarily spews happy chemicals into your brain or we produce for you another person or thing to fear or find outrageous so your trauma cycle never ends. Either way, Fox News wins the race to your brain stem and your amygdala (limbic system actually).

Have you ever watched a Fox News opinion show segment with a critical eye? If you do (and after reading this book) you will see Fox News opinion programming for what it really is: a masterful self-contained behavioral addiction and trauma creating feedback loop. Good FNC opinion programming is almost a perfect vicious self-reinforcing circle. Truly every one of the thousands of FNC opinion segments I appeared in or hosted was based on either:

- Creating an unresolved trauma-forgetting event based on a choreographed WWE-like emotional roller-coaster entertainment of fixed outcome righteous victory featuring the viewer's tribal heroes pummeling their viscerally hated tribal enemy (which thanks to your brain stem/limbic system involuntarily spits out the happy dance brain chemicals that temporarily deliver the glorious feelings of intense pleasure).

- Or a viscerally traumatic fear or rage creating event where the segment plants new traumatic images of fearful people, events, and ideas in the viewer's mind (via the 4K high-def display of fearful or anger baiting images and "sound on tape," or SOT in TV speak) which in turn serves to fertilize a new trauma inducing fear or outrage via an overwrought monologue or fixed outcome "debate." After weeks of repeating, an embryo of trauma grows into a new fear or rage (or renews an unresolved existing fear) that then is deeply implanted in the psyche of the Fox News viewer.

Even more fascinating, Hari believes (along with a growing number of addiction specialists) the root cause of addiction is *not* the happy dance brain chemicals themselves. What his research says is happening is those happy making involuntarily released brain chemicals and hormones (dopamine, adrenaline, and heroin-like serotonin) mask (for a while) the real addiction cause—a lack of human connection. Hari points out the work of the well-respected behavioral scientist Richard Cohen who points out that "Human beings have a natural and innate need to bond. And when we're happy and healthy we'll bond and connect with each other."

Here is Dr. Cohen's money shot on Fox News's right-wing tribal identity porn as a coping mechanism for trauma and human disconnection: "But if you can't connect or bond with a likeminded person—because you're traumatized or isolated or beaten down by life or people—you will bond with something that will give you some sense of relief. . . .Now that might be gambling, that might be pornography, that might be cocaine, that might be cannabis, but you will bond and connect with something because that's driving by human nature, that's what we want as human beings—we are psychologically hard wired to want and need to consistently feel the experience of oneness/connection."

Hari defines "connection" or "bond" as "the experience of oneness." Anthropology and social science tell us there is no more powerful bond in the human animal than the experience of oneness with a tribe of like-minded human beings.

Thus watching six hours a day of Fox News tribal identity porn is also a very powerful form of feeling that oneness connection because it's also a tribal connection. When we love a TV show like *Game of Thrones*, we don't viscerally connect at a tribal level—we love the story and the grandeur and it's entertaining and all that, but there is no innate tribal connection.

With Fox News there is a visceral tribal connection—especially for the Retro American viewers who are also living with their own set of other visceral traumas. One of the most profound ironies I discovered in researching this book is the true epidemic we suffer from today is not tribalism but the reverse—it's the lack of tribal connection. Our caveman DNA and instincts drive us to be social, relational, connected tribal beings. When we are emotionally disconnected from too many human beings, it's traumatizing.

Note: If you don't believe Hari or me, take an hour and go visit a senior living facility. Not one of those fancy eight grand a month ones with twenty-five activities per day and an open bar and three gourmet meals and desserts per day. Go to a real one.

We are still animals with brains that are driven to connect—and Hari defines connection as "the feeling of oneness" with other people or tribes. We still need to belong to viscerally nurturing tribes, communal groups, or communities not for personal safety like our ancestors but for our psychological well-being. Hari's decades of work in the fields of trauma and mental health tell him the root of almost everything we suffer through is actually a severed connection or lost oneness we never figured out how to repair.

Fox News tribal activation and validation programming is a very real and visceral way for self-identified conservatives to feel connection and oneness at a cultural and political tribal level. There in fact is no place on earth that a self-identified conservative can have the "experience of oneness" like Fox News, because Hari further defines experiencing oneness as "having shared experiences, relatable feelings, or similar ideas."

Follow me here: If the biggest problem in most people's lives (especially in Retro America) is unresolved trauma, and unresolved trauma is what creates a damaged ability in people to connect with others—that makes Fox News's tribal activation and validation programming by definition a very real kind of psychological connective tissue for self-identified conservatives!

For people who feel like they are a card-carrying member of the right-wing political tribe, Fox News's opinion programming is selling them the experience of digital oneness—and that is a hell of a lot better than none at all.

Boiled down beyond the bleach-blond hair and "Fox News Alert" crawl on the bottom of the screen, for self-identified conservative tribal members, Fox News *is* the experience of oneness Hari tells us we all desperately seek at a very core psychological level. Fox News opinion programming is, of course, 100 percent written, directed, and produced for people who (1) do share similar experiences (especially life in small city/rural America) and (2) have very relatable lives and feelings, and have by definition very similar political, cultural, and economic ideas and worldviews, and very likely share Retro America's ideological religiosity and belief systems.

The other important concept I learned in researching this book is social and humanist psychologists tell us a very significant part of our mental health and well-being comes from the constant replenishment of our social capital. They define social capital as meaningful connections—the experience of oneness that flows from our membership and interactions in small intimate tribes or communities of family, friendships, our worship community, our work colleagues, and those who we connect with via our shared communal passions (hunting or golf buddies, tailgating crew, bridge clubs, or simply pals at our favorite local pub).

When we don't have the true oneness of human connections—an abundance of these nurturing people, relationships, and tribes in our lives that help us overcome our traumas—we are driven by human nature to seek replacements where we can find them.

What is addictive about experiencing tribal oneness on Fox News? Is it the powerful brain chemicals that the righteous tribal victory release which make you feel literally high? Is it the connection of tribal oneness? Both?

Hari's work explained to me like no other that the disease that fuels the addictive power of Fox News's tribal identity and validation pornography—an addiction that is literally poisoning relationships for tens of millions of Americans—is not tribalism. The disease that fuels the attraction and addiction to Fox News tribal identity programming is a toxic mix of corrosive traumas that are unfortunately prevalent and widely shared today in America's twenty-first century:

First, we have the widespread economic trauma incurred by the dysfunction of America's twenty-first-century version of capitalism which no longer works for nearly two-thirds of America's non-college-degreed working-class families as it did in the 1970s and '80s.

Then we have the traumatic contempt for the "elites" who got bailed out of the Great Recession and made out like bandits in the recovery while the working class suffered the stunning economic trauma of foreclosed homes and ruined small businesses (BTW psychologists are united in declaring the emotion of contempt as the most corrosive human emotion, along with jealousy).

Perhaps the most powerful and corrosive trauma in America today is the traumatic disassembly of our social support fabric. These are the nurturing family, friends, and jobs moving away from the regions of America still based on past-their-shelf-life twentieth-century economics that in many ways resemble failed nation economies.

We also have the trauma of premature death of close family and friends that has come to many regions of still-twentieth-century America with declining life expectancy (regions which not coincidently overlap Fox News/Trump TV country).

And for the financially well-off business conservatives I call "country club Republicans," there are the coincident unresolved rage-based traumas of "not recognizing their country anymore" and the conundrum of being repeatedly labeled a morally deficient "racist/homophobe/Islamaphobe/ etc." by their sworn tribal enemy the "socialist liberal idiots" who tells everyone they are the "party of tolerance" but in practice are only tolerant of people who share their social and cultural liberal worldview.

America has a boatload of unresolved fear and outrage based trauma. And *all* of the twenty-first-century traumas listed above collectively result in a true national epidemic of emotional disconnection and vastly depleted stores of mentally and spiritually nourishing social capital for America's working- and middle-class conservatives.

This has driven many Fox News viewers to seek the self-reinforcing digital feedback loop pioneered by Fox News as a working man's digital companion and "virtual connection," replacing personal relationships gone forever.

The evidence of America's running-on-empty social capital depletion phenomenon is unfortunately seen firsthand in Fox News's America today. One clear unambiguous lesson from the elections of 2016 and 2018 is that President Trump and his fellow Republican candidates win in the zip codes where white voters feel they are losing their economic and social status.

Fox News is able to wage its tribalized political civil war on today's nonstop digital battlefield and tap into these corrosive emotions not because tribalized politics or tribal warfare is going to make its one hundred million monthly users' lives any better. Remember, a coping mechanism for dealing with unresolved trauma is just temporary and not a cure. As Senator Ben Sasse so correctly points out in *Them: Why We Hate Each Other—and How to Heal*:

"If only we could vanquish those evil people waving a different banner, this thinking goes, we'd be on the road to national recovery. But nothing that happens in Washington is going to fix what's wrong with America. It's not that our battles over the Supreme Court, over issues like taxes and regulation and immigration don't matter. They matter a lot. The problem is that our ever more ferocious political tribalism and mutual hatred don't originate in politics, so politics isn't going to heal them." Our tribalism, Sasse concludes, "Has a deeper source in the disintegration of communities and loneliness."

Ben Sasse is dead right. Fox News is more than happy to fill right-wing society's void of meaningful connection and to provide faux shared tribal relationships. It's happy to supplement the daily fear and rage fed trauma of dissolving household economics or lost identities. The truth is Foxism and Trumpism are both selling you the same thing: a digital tribal identity badge and a self-esteem building valued "social identity."

The reason that tribal political activation and validation pornography works so incredibly powerfully is because it gives its viewers two things they desperately need: (1) someone to blame for their dissolving lifestyle or livelihood and (2) a way to rebuild some of their lost self-esteem and social capital with a powerful new social identity. And for many for whom "proud conservative" was their proud ID has come a new badge of honor—"proud Deplorable."

Key Point: the awful truth in 2019 is this: for about 66 percent of Americans, traditional tribes and Industrial-Age skillsets that sustained and nurtured them in the past are both in collapse.

In addition, according to a large national survey of adults recently conducted by the health insurer Cigna and the market research firm Ipsos, a majority of Americans are now chronically lonely, based on the industry standard UCLA Loneliness Scale.

So there you have it. In a country with collapsing personal connections, depleting social capital reserves, and widespread unresolved economic trauma, in stepped Fox News with its weaponized brand of tribal identity activation and validation pornography. Fox News's televangelists give right-wing tribalists a much-needed self-esteem booster shot and a welcome rest stop from their unresolved traumas. These tribal heroes viscerally connect with people desperately in need of feeling a part of something bigger than themselves. They provide a heaping side of tribal inclusion and identity superiority.

Psychologically . . . the Fox News Tribal Warfare Playbook is friggin' brilliant. No one in the punditry or media I have read or met has really come to grips with why FNC's hypnotic tribal identity activation is so psychologically powerful.

One answer I learned is FNC's emotionally arousing tribal identity porn is as close to a meaningful "visceral oneness" as tens of millions of largely disconnected Americans running low on connection/high on trauma are going to get today. Senator Sasse gets it close when he says: "None of us wants to be left out. The same isolation we felt at the edge of the cafeteria or as the last kid picked for kickball causes everyone to yearn for a group. . . . Even though political ideology is a thin basis for intimate connections, at least our cable news tribes offer the common shared experience of getting to hate people together. As relational nomads, it's far easier now to be together against something than for something. It's not as fulfilling, but at least we're not totally alone."

At the very least (or unfortunately for many, the very most), what Fox News's fear-and-hate based tribal identity activation and validation opinion programming offers its audience is the appearance or a digital construct of a shared oneness. It's like sitting around a digital campfire of communal victimhood and sharing the ironically healing shared experience of communally hating the 40 percent of Americans who don't belong to your tribe as a team sport (with a special place in traumatic hell for the liberal elites who created your economic trauma).

Too dark? Let me ask you this—do you live in a town or county that is economically failing? Do you live one or two paychecks or one illness/lost job away from moving in with your relatives? Can you write a rent check or car payment from your bank balance? Is your life expectancy 25 percent less than mine? Are your kids in a great school or college? Do you live behind a gate or a triple bolted front door?

I thought so.

Next question: Why so much communal shared hate of the socioeconomic elites/others? Today the answer is simple and has been staring us in the face for thirty years: Beginning in the early 1980s but accelerating in the twenty-first century, America has achieved a unique to the modern world status. We've created the world's first working poverty class, now afflicting over 110 million Americans.

It's only been since June 2018 that macroeconomic nerds like me have had state-by-state research available that confirms what most folks who live in the top 20 percent never see in their day-to-day latte/yoga/Amazon delivery cocoons: 40 million American households white, black, and brown (and over 110 million Americans) live today in "working poverty."

America invented working poverty—we are the only modern economy to have it to this degree. These ALICE Households—Asset Light/Income Constrained/Employed—where total household income is above the poverty line but below the median $61,000, live in constant unresolved fear and rage trauma because they know that they are one car accident, layoff, or illness away from the street or a relative's basement. America's 110 million ALICE household members are economically traumatized on almost a daily or weekly basis.

You want to have an honest discussion about how widespread deeply toxic economic trauma is in America today? Let's start with obvious—the

110 million members of these 40 million households sure could use a big ol' self-esteem boost these days because their twentieth-century skillset in twenty-first-century knowledge-based capitalism is mostly not working for them like it used to.

They are also living 20 percent shorter lives, are much more likely to commit suicide or die of an overdose, and only 30 percent of their kids will make it to college.

Well then voila—for the white working poor enter Fox News's socioeconomic blame and resentment porn content and hourly visual proof of the elite libtard culprits who they blame for causing the massive disintegration of the blue-collar middle class. Socioeconomic background is now the core basis for America's divide in the twenty-first century—and Fox News has weaponized this socioeconomic division in spades.

You would think Fox News invented the term "elite" since it's used a hundred times a day on air in their tribal blame and resentment porn performance art. In fact, it was the Harvard social scientist Robert Putnam who first identified the top third and bottom two-thirds schism of America's new twenty-first-century socioeconomics.

But starting from the 1980s to today, the introduction of a once-a-century economic transition from the post–World War II Industrial Age to the twenty-first century digital powered knowledge and information economy cleaved an even wider divide between the family structure, educational achievement, and economic prospects of this top third of American elites (to me better defined as the 33 percent of Americans over twenty-five with a college degree) and the bottom two-thirds of American households headed by non-college-degreed adults twenty-five and older.

Now I'm sorry to add to this toxic gumbo of traumatic economic events, but recent research by the Brookings Institute about the risk of the already precariously employed losing their blue-collar working-class jobs to automation and artificial intelligence in the *Wall Street Journal* paints an even bleaker near-term future. According to the Brookings Institute, "As technology drives people out of the middle class, economists say, it's pushing them in one of two directions. Those with the right skills or education graduate into a new technological elite. Everyone else falls into the ranks of the "precariat"—the precariously employed, a workforce in low-wage jobs with few benefits or protections, where roles change frequently as technology transforms the nature of work."

In a ghoulish way, more economic trauma (which leads to more familial trauma and less emotionally nourishing connective oneness) is music to the ears of Fox News. It's guaranteed job security for their tribal activation/ righteous validation televangelists too. "The economy has changed radically, but the American social model hasn't," says Mark Muro, an author of the Brookings report. "Coincident with all this automation is the erosion of government benefits that might make the precariousness of some of these positions more tolerable."

Don't shoot the messenger here—it was of course the Fox News fueled Republicans that voted to cut corporate taxes 40 percent and cut Medicaid and ACA benefits to the ALICE cohort that contains more white working-class households than any other ethnic/racial class.

Economic irony is a bitch, ain't it? And the vicious circle of downward economic gravity spirals down. Social scientist Richard Florida of the University of Toronto puts a finer distinction on US socioeconomics today with his three categories of households: the "mobile" and the "rooted" one-third and the "stuck" which represents the bottom two-thirds. The mobile are those who can afford to move to areas with more opportunity; the rooted are those who have the means to move but choose to stay. The stuck are those who lack the resources or education to have these options—and other than winning the lottery they have no realistic choices to make. Guess what, sports fans—the members of the bottom two-thirds of America economically are literally stuck in declining economic regions, with declining life expectancy and declining prospects in general for what the upper one-third would consider the basic essentials of a self-actualizing middle-class lifestyle.

They are the two-thirds of America without a college degree, a valuable twenty-first-century skill, or a stable dual-income household. Odds are overwhelming that they do not reside in the prospering fifteen super urban regions of America that now account for nearly 70 percent of America's $20 trillion annual GDP and 48 percent of its population.

My point? The upshot here is the vast majority of these ALICE households live in the same economically traumatized, at-risk 2,626 counties that voted Trump in 2016. The senior aged ones are the primary target audience for Fox News socioeconomic blame and resentment porn programming.

As mentioned, to understand the power of tribal activation porn, you have to think of people for a second as body comprised of different reservoirs of emotionally sustaining feelings and emotional draining trauma. Social psychologists tell me that for many Americans today, political group identity has become too large a part of their overall identity and self-esteem.

The scientists have various theories how this came about. But I can tell them and you exactly why it happened—because for a majority of American households, they are not suffering just a collapse in their social capital reservoir. There ain't much self-esteem left in their self-esteem tank either. They need a constant self-esteem booster shot from somewhere—and for many of them, hours of watching and reacting to FNC's tribal identity porn is their self-esteem/ego booster shot.

These psychology experts don't read the economic data that I do. They have not visited the regions of American in the bottom 66 percent economically that I have. If they had, they would understand why Fox News's activated and validated tribal political identity has become so important in America to so many. Sadly, for many it's one of the only positive things going on in their lives.

For hours a day, watching and connecting with their tribal brothers and sisters on Fox News is their shared oneness with something bigger and more emotionally nourishing than the working poverty that has engulfed their daily existence.

FOX NEWS: THE DIGITAL NEO-TOTALITARIANISM CHANNEL?

When Fox News morphed from the Obama hate porn channel in 2008 into the sycophantic Trump Television network after the 2016 election, it struck me they had technically become a digital enabler for a new kind of twenty-first-century "digital neo-totalitarianism."

When you read the experts on the ideology of totalitarianism, the general definition is it's just another form of tribal mass movement driven by an ideology that rejects the existing society as corrupt, immoral, and beyond reform.

It projects the illusion of an alternative society in which these wrongs are to be redressed, provides plans and programs for realizing the alternative order, and is founded and developed under a charismatic leader that promises his flock nirvana but demands and gets unflinching loyalty and leeway from his tribal believers on their way to paradise.

Sound like anyone you know?

Philosopher and expert on totalitarianism Hannah Arendt wrote on the core elements that drove the rise of totalitarianism in Germany and Italy in the 1930s and '40s in her seminal 1973 analysis of *The Origins of Totalitarianism*. The similarity to the rise of Fox News's tribal fear and hate porn driven ratings and the mashup of Trumpism and the Deplorables as a political and cultural mass movement are terrifyingly similar.

Sound like anyone you know?

Why? Read a snippet of the recent research on Trumpism and Trumpers titled *How Do We Solve a Problem Like the Donald?* by Julie Novkov, Professor in the Department of Political Science at SUNY Albany, and give it a moment to sink in.

> The Tea Party uprising relied on interest politics to mobilize individuals into action within the Republican Party, but Trumpers are approaching the status of a modern mass in Arendtian terms; a group of disaffected, disengaged, cynical, isolated and atomized individuals who come together and derive a sense of their place in the world through association with a movement. . . .
>
> Bereft of a positive political identity, they can be organized around principles of resentment or revenge, and require only the repetition of key simple ideas. Distrustful and cynical, they are ready to embrace any simple system that makes sense of their world and validates their resentments. Masses are particularly inclined to embrace propaganda. As Arendt explains, "They do not believe in anything visible, in the reality of their own experience; they do not trust their eyes and ears but only their imaginations, which may be caught by anything that is at once universal and consistent in itself. What convinces masses are not facts, and not even invented facts, but only the consistency of the system of which they are presumably part."

Roger Berkowitz, the founder and academic director of the Hannah Arendt Center for Politics and Humanities (and associate professor at Bard College) captures the essence of what I have come to call Fox News enabled Digital Totalitarianism in in-depth review of Arendt's works:

> The astonishing statement Donald Trump made at a January 2016 campaign rally in Iowa seems like the essential moment in his unexpected rise to power: "I could stand in the middle of

Fifth Avenue and shoot somebody," he said, "and I wouldn't lose voters." In saying that he could kill in broad daylight and remain popular, Trump did more than draw a logical conclusion from polls showing that his supporters demonstrated unprecedented loyalty. He understood that he was not running a political campaign but was the leader of a mass movement. Most importantly, he understood something that his critics still fail to understand: the essential nature of loyalty in tribal mass movements.

That description of mass movements sounds just like the raison d'être of Fox News as envisioned by Roger Ailes in 1974 doesn't it?

Key Point: one of the key parts of totalitarianism in the 1930s and '40s was the totalitarians built and paid for the establishment of their own in-house tribal identity and validation networks. The totalitarians controlled the newspapers, the movie production, and the radio networks. These propaganda machines were expensive to build and run but they were crucial to the goals of delegitimizing enemies, critics, and journalists.

In contrast, for the tribal right wing in America, Fox News paid over $1 billion to build their tribal identity and validation programming machine and spends over $2 billion a year to run it. Trumpism and the Deplorables didn't spend a dime to benefit from the world's most sophisticated and powerful tribal identity and validation programming network ever seen.

The French philosopher and political activist Simone Weil wrote that "to be rooted is perhaps the most important and least recognized need of the human soul." The modern condition of rootlessness is a foundational experience of totalitarianism; totalitarian movements succeed when they offer rootless people what they most crave: an ideologically consistent world aiming at grand narratives that give meaning to their lives. By consistently repeating a few key ideas, a manipulative leader provides a sense of rootedness grounded upon a coherent fiction that is "consistent, comprehensible, and predictable."

George Lakoff, former distinguished professor of cognitive science and linguistics at the University of California at Berkeley, writes, "That's why authoritarian leaders always attack the press. They seek to deny and distract from the truth, and this requires undermining those who tell it. . . . Corrupt regimes always seek to replace truth with lies that increase and preserve their power. The Digital Age makes this easier than ever."

Yes, it does, Mr. Lakoff. Especially if one hundred million Americans are engaged within a self-reinforcing tribal activation and validation feedback loop and 35 percent of voters do not interact with mainstream news media. Professor Lakoff writes on his blog: "Yet we live in an age of weaponized information, where nefarious memes and false narratives of dubious origin can also travel far. These can become dangerous when repeated millions of times. . . . They wrongly believe that bare facts and logic alone win the moral debates. A recent study of the strategies used by Russian and terrorist trolls online found that they have a strong grasp of basic brain science."

According to cyberwarfare expert Haroon Ullah: "Recent research into both the Russians' and the Islamic State's models of propaganda, as well as interviews with defectors, unveil that: 1) people tend to believe something when it is repeated, 2) Russia and Islamic State fanboys gain the advantage when they get to make the first impression, and 3) subsequent rebuttals actually work to reinforce the original misinformation, rather than dissipate it."

Sound familiar????

Roger Ailes, in his dream of a Republican television network, most certainly understood the essential nature of mass movements and tribal psychology. He also knew Donald Trump for decades. But I still bet he had no idea that Trump would morph from swashbuckling reality show host and self-centered C-level celebrity clown to become the messianic leader of a mass movement of white working-class Americans.

Think of it this way: It cost Rupert Murdoch $1 billion or more to build a weaponized right-wing tribal activation and validation entertainment channel. It cost Facebook, YouTube, and Twitter tens of billions to build the digital infrastructure to distribute Fox News tribal hate porn content to one hundred million Americans every month. It didn't cost Donald Trump a dime to build the mass movement of Trumpism.

Key Point: Can you imagine what a real Fascist totalitarian regime could achieve with a nonstop tribal activation and identity validation feedback loop? As long as Trump sucks the oxygen out of the twenty-four-hour news cycle, he can only grow more powerful unless the reality-based world starts to see the Trumpian kayfabe for what it really is.

As conservative commentator Jonah Goldberg reminds us, Donald Trump's demonization of the media as the "enemy of the people" is mostly kayfabe.

Now you know that the term kayfabe means presenting staged events as if they're real. Pro wrestling is theater, not sport. But it thrives on the illusion that it is the latter, not the former. And so, of course, is Fox News theater, not news. Goldberg implores us to "see Trump's kayfabe for what it is. Don't overreact, and don't fall for the performance."

Yet as Nazi propaganda genius Joseph Goebbels told the world:

"It would not be impossible to prove that with sufficient repetition and a psychological understanding of the people concerned that a square is in fact a circle. They are mere words, and words can be molded until they clothe ideas and disguise."

"The most brilliant propagandist technique will yield no success unless one fundamental principle is borne in mind constantly—it must confine itself to a few points and repeat them over and over."

"Man is and remains an animal. Here a beast of prey, there a house pet, but always an animal."

My take: If you have gotten this far in my book, and you are not yet irreparably lost down the Fox News/Trumpian kayfabe rabbit hole, you are now well armed to never fall for the Fox News/Donald Trump kayfabe performances.

CHAPTER 14

How Fox News Became a Significant Branch of the 94-Million-Strong Evangelical Church

So who is Fox News's real competition for the attention of their core elderly small city and rural right-wing audience? By now you know it's not MSNBC or CNN.

Listen to Jordan Riley, a Christian pop singer in Seattle who works with Daystar, the largest televangelist network in America. Despite the fact that Daystar describes itself as a church, if you watch Daystar programming, you will find that it does not resemble a church in any traditional sense. "Church to me is when I'm gathered with other believers," Riley says. "I don't consider [Daystar] an electronic church—it's just church."

Take that concept in for a moment.

Fact: the combined revenues (read: nontaxable donations) and viewer ratings of the top thirty "TV ministries" dwarf those of Fox News and every other news and broadcast network combined. The Evangelical and Fundamentalist Christian televangelism racket puts FNC's white tribal activation and identity porn business to shame.

Ed Stetzer, executive director of Nashville-based LifeWay Research, recently released data on Christian television viewership that would stun most Americans—especially secular Americans. "Most people would be surprised that one in three of their neighbors is watching Christian TV. Do one in three adult Americans watch the nightly news? I don't think so. It's an overlooked segment of society that is larger than most people think," he said.

Much of the market for right-wing partisan television overlaps the sixty-five million viewers of Christian TV. Roger Ailes did not overlook televangelism as his real competition; he purposely programmed against it with his own televangelists that Fox euphemistically labels "political talk show hosts."

Christian TV is selling everlasting life and forgiveness of sin. Roger knew that to get right-wing cultural conservatives to Fox News, FNC's programming had to be a lot more fun and much more addictive than Christian programming.

It worked better than anyone ever imagined.

For many Fox News viewers, their radicalized partisan conservatism might as well be a religion or cult, with Fox News as the televised "church" service. As you know now, that's by design. Many of the Americans who self-identify as political and social conservatives and fundamentalist or Evangelical Christians (more than ninety-four million) learn their tribal rules, belief systems, and ideology today not just from the pulpits of their churches.

Today, Evangelical leaders report that a lot of their Evangelical liturgy and belief system comes from their nightly five-hour visit at the pulpit of the Church of Fox News. As Kaitlyn Schiess from the Evangelical Dallas Theological Seminary recently told Molly Worthen, a professor of history at UNC Chapel Hill and a *New York Times* columnist, "A new ritual has superseded Sunday worship and weeknight Bible studies: a profane devotional practice, with immense power to shape Evangelicals' beliefs. This 'liturgy' is the nightly consumption of Fox News."

Ms. Worthen points out, "Liberals love to complain about conservatives' steady diet of misinformation through partisan media, but Ms. Schiess's complaint is more profound: She sees Sean Hannity and Tucker Carlson aren't just purveyors of distorted news, but high priests of a false religion."

In other words, Evangelical Christianity is losing out to the major Evangelical TV channel of Fox News. "The reason Fox News is so formative is that it's this repetitive, almost ritualistic thing that people do every night," Ms. Schiess says. "It forms in them particular fears and desires, an idea of America. This is convincing on a less than logical level, and the church is not communicating to them in that same way."

Sound familiar?

So yes, sports fans, Sean Hannity, Tucker Carlson, Laura Ingraham, Jeanine Pirro, and good old Lou Dobbs at FBN really are high priests of the partisan conservative tribal religion, making up their tribal liturgy and writing new scripture every night like any good televangelist. Hmm—that is just like I was taught to do as a Fox News host by a big time Fox News EVP—coincidence?

One of my favorite conservative columnists, Rod Dreher, writing in *The American Conservative* magazine, puts a fine point on how the rise of

American political partisan tribalism has exploded under Fox News and now Trumpism:

> The world isn't being destroyed by Democrats or Republicans, red or blue, liberal or conservative, religious or atheist—the world is being destroyed by one side believing the other side is destroying the world.
> The world is being hurt and damaged by one group of people believing they're truly better people than the others who think differently. The world officially ends when we let our beliefs conquer love. We must not let this happen.

How did we get to the point that America is being destroyed by one political and cultural tribe believing the other tribe is destroying the world? At least partly it's because that tribal identity message conflated with a fundamentalist Armageddon message has been preached to Fox News viewers and users at least one billion times since 1995.

When Fox News reached just 50,000 or 500,000 people a month with little digital footprint or social media redistribution, this message did not matter. When Fox News started reaching more than one hundred million Americans via TV, streaming video, and social media, the daily drumbeat of this message became perhaps the most powerful and destructive media force in America.

Reality: The $10 billion-a-year industry of creating and broadcasting toxic political tribalism is growing every day. The collateral damage of its emotional toxicity is multi-dimensional. That damage includes getting one side believing the other side is destroying the world just like Richard Hofstadter amazingly foresaw in 1964.

Fox News: Turning the conservative tribe into virtual jihadists and building a religious schism brick by brick against the liberal tribe is just what we do.

PS: Ever wonder why the Fox News/Intolerables/Fundamentalist Christian "Believers" don't care about Trump's 7.8 lies every day on Fox News?

Neuroscientist Bobby Azarian from George Mason University writes that one reason Trump supporters believe his lies comes from a basic fact about the brain: it simply takes more mental effort to reject an idea as false than to accept it as true. In other words, it's easier to believe than to not believe. This fact answers a lot about the surreal situation we find ourselves in today with a pathological liar POTUS whose lies are repeated as gospel truth by the Trump TV network and believed by theoretically sin-averse fundamentalist Christians.

This insight is based on a landmark study published in the journal *PLOS One* in 2009, which asked the simple question, how is the brain activated differently during a state of belief compared to a state of disbelief?

What these findings show is that the mental process of believing is simply less work for the brain and therefore often favored. Azarian the neuroscientist tells us "the default state of the human brain is to accept what we are told, because doubt takes effort. Belief, on the other hand, comes easily."

Hey that's just great, isn't it?

For Fox News-watching Christian fundamentalists (many Fox News viewers self-identify as fundamentalist Evangelicals and belong to fundamentalist denominations), Azarian claims that being taught to suppress critical thinking begins at a very early age. "It is the combination of the brain's vulnerability to believing unsupported facts and aggressive indoctrination that create the perfect storm for gullibility. Due to the brain's neuroplasticity, or ability to be sculpted by lived experiences, Evangelicals literally become hardwired to believe farfetched statements."

When you think about it, this sort of makes sense. This hardwiring begins when they are kids and taught to accept Biblical stories not as metaphors for living life practically, purposefully, and morally, but as objective truth. Mystical explanations for natural events train young minds to not demand evidence for beliefs. As a result, Azarian claims, "The neural pathways that promote healthy skepticism and rational thought are not properly developed. This inevitably leads to a greater susceptibility to lying and gaslighting by manipulative politicians and greater suggestibility in general."

The punchline? Azarian makes the point that we all must understand that when it comes to our human mind, believing is more of a reflex than a careful and methodical action.

After meeting thousands of Foxhole addicts, you will get no argument from me on this.

CHAPTER 15

The Facts About Fox News TV Addiction

According to Nielsen Media Research, Inc., in 2018 the average American watched TV for 4 hours 32 minutes every day. As you know now, Americans over age 65 watch 7.2 hours a day.

The time people have spent in front of the TV, in spite of the warnings about obesity and other harmful effects, strongly suggests that America had a severe addiction to TV before Fox News. In fact, a *Scientific American* study and multiple other longitudinal studies have found that yes, TV acts on the brain like any addictive drug.

THE DIFFERENCE BETWEEN ADDICTION TO TV AND ADDICTION TO FOX NEWS'S TRIBAL IDENTITY PORN IS THE KEY

The question on TV addiction is, "How many different channels do you watch?" According to the latest Nielsen report, the average household receives about 190 channels—up 45 percent from 2008. Over the past six years, however, the number of channels consumers watch has remained consistently around 17.

What we have found is that the one key marker of Fox News addiction is that the Fox News addict watches primarily only one Pay TV channel (other than sports coverage): Fox News.

What differentiates the regular TV addict from the Foxhole addict is the sheer amount of time spent on just the Fox News channel. Back-of-the-napkin math says the Fox News addict may consume up to more than 7,900 hours of its potent brand of tribal hate pornography per year.

When we asked the spouses, children, relatives, and friends of Fox News addicts, "How often is the main TV in the home tuned to Fox News?" the overwhelming majority answered, "All day. Their main TV is always on Fox News. They never turn it off!"

Major Point: Addiction to television to zone out, kill time, or stop boredom is one thing. Binge-watching three or more hours of Fox News tribal identity hate porn every day is a whole other thing.

Vegging out to TV shows and visiting imaginary TV friends is a form of estrangement, without question. But the critical difference between the everyday TV addict and the Fox News addict I have found is that the everyday TV addict is not:

- proactively poisoning family and friend relationships.

- pushing people away with radicalized tribal partisanship and dogma.

- developing degenerative and emotionally corrosive feelings of hate and fear toward (or conspiracy theories about) people of color or people of other political perspectives.

- desocialized to the point of becoming estranged from spouses, children, relatives, and friends.

There is clearly a spectrum of desocialization related to TV addiction. That spectrum begins with "benign desocialization" (so much TV watching the addict does not have time or interest in much social behavior) and ends with "radicalized partisan desocialization" (tribal political/cultural behavior and opinions of the addict are so intense and socially obnoxious that family and friends are pushed away, resulting in chronic loneliness for the addict).

FOX NEWS ALERT: IF YOU HAVE A FOXAHOLIC IN YOUR FAMILY OR CIRCLE OF FRIENDS, YOU CAN TELL THEM ODDS ARE THEIR FOX NEWS ADDICTION IS KILLING THEM

New public health data shows up to 60 percent higher risk of premature death in desocialized and estranged Americans aged sixty and over. Dr. Juli-anne Holt-Lunstad, professor of psychology at Brigham Young University, reports, "There is robust evidence that desocialized isolation and loneliness significantly increase risk for premature mortality, and the magnitude of the risk exceeds that of many leading health indicators including obesity, alcoholism, and smoking. With an increasingly aging population, the effect on public health is only anticipated to increase."

Guess what? Many Foxholes age sixty and older are by definition desocialized via their social derangement disorder, and many are estranged from family and friends because of their radical hyperpartisan behavior.

The most controversial research I am presenting in this book is the connection between Foxaholism and up to 60 percent higher rates of premature death from the chronic loneliness that results from the Foxaholic's family and friend estrangement.

According to polling from my firm Transformity Research and published public health data, desocialized addiction to Fox News that results in close family and friend estrangement is more lethal to senior Americans than obesity or smoking fifteen cigarettes a day.

How can that be?

The 2017 report out of Brigham Young University on the chronic loneliness epidemic in seniors shows that chronic loneliness is deadlier than either obesity and smoking and should be considered a significant public health hazard in America. In this review, BYU researchers looked at 218 separate studies of the health effects of social isolation and loneliness involving nearly four million people over age forty. They discovered that chronically lonely people have a 50 percent increased risk of early death compared to those with good social connections. Similar studies show 60 percent higher rates of premature death in this group. In contrast, obesity raises the chance of dying before the age of seventy by around 30 percent. As Julianne Holt-Lunstad puts it, "we are facing a 'loneliness epidemic.' The challenge we face now is what can be done about it."

Here is Dr. Dean Ornish, the founder of the Preventive Medicine Research Institute, on the effects of chronic loneliness: "I am not aware of any other factor—not diet, not smoking, not exercise, not stress, not genetics, not drugs, not surgery—that has a greater impact on our incidence of illness, and [chance of] premature death than chronic loneliness."

NOW WE KNOW *WHY* AND *HOW* CHRONIC LONELINESS PREMATURELY KILLS SENIORS

Chronic loneliness has been linked to everything from heart disease to Alzheimer's disease for decades. It is no secret to anyone who cares for or lives with seniors that depression is common among the lonely. Oncology research shows that cancers tear through their bodies more rapidly, and viruses hit them harder and more frequently than socially engaged seniors. But a new long-term research study out of UCLA's biologic psychology department suggests why this is. It turns out the pain of chronic loneliness activates the primordial caveman response of—wait for it—our amygdala triggered fight-or-flight response!

Now hmmm, let's see—which kind of people have been proven by neuroscientists to be genetically more sensitive to fight-or-flight fear? You got it—self-identified conservatives! When I first read this study on why chronic loneliness raises the risk of prematurely killing seniors I was blown away.

Yes—this is the same involuntary amygdala response that comes from frightful images and sounds being flashed on viewers' screens. It turns out that our caveman logic tells our brain that being lonely is imminently dangerous. Our caveman logic sees loneliness as the equivalent of being literally forced out of our tribe and back in the fearful food chain of nasty predators. To your still primordial brain, feeling lonely is a signal to prepare your body for being at high risk of being attacked.

Once again, let's follow another self-reinforcing negative outcome feedback loop for intense radicalized Fox News tribal identity hyperpartisans. This time, the end result is not just tribal activation and validation—this outcome is deadly:

1. If you are a self-identified conservative, neuroscience has proven you are significantly more sensitive and reactive to fearful images and sounds than self-identified liberals or politically unaffiliated people.

2. As such, you are much easier to emotionally manipulate into tribal mode using fear-based TV images, sound, and copy sent into the safety of your home.

3. When you viscerally react to fearful images, your brain involuntarily kicks into fight-or-flight mode and you are emotionally and physiologically engaged.

4. When you are emotionally engaged, you are much easier to manipulate with the carefully orchestrated cascade of tribal activation and validation opinion segment triggers.

5. The pleasure chemicals released to a tribal viewer from feeling the visceral Fox News emotional dump then air punching righteous victory segments are highly addictive.

6. If you become an addicted and desocialized Foxhole watching thousands of hours of Fox News's tribal activation and validation pornography,

7. You are at high risk of becoming desocialized and estranged from family members and long-time friends by your political and cultural intensity which ultimately pushes them away.

8. Which in turn results in you becoming chronically lonely.

The net result of this degenerative self-reinforcing feedback loop is simple: Self-identified conservatives who watch many hours a week of Fox News's tribal identity pornography are more at risk of becoming hyper-tribalized Foxholes and chronically lonely than normally socialized Fox News watchers—which raises their risk of premature death up to 60 percent over normally socialized non-hyperpartisan senior Americans.

Period.

According to a recent NPR article on this new research by Angus Chen:

> For decades, researchers have been seeing signs that the immune systems of lonely people are working differently. Lonely people's white blood cells seem to be more active in a way that increases inflammation, a natural immune response to wounding and bacterial infection.
>
> On top of that, they seem to have lower levels of antiviral compounds known as interferons. That seemed to provide a link to a lot of the poor health outcomes associated with loneliness, since chronic inflammation has been linked to everything from cancer to depression. The human body isn't built to hold a high level of inflammation for years.

Loneliness in essence "hits the switch" on the defense plan our bodies initiate in the face of mortal danger, Cole thinks, if isolation is somehow truly lethal. "At this point, my best guess was that loneliness really is one of the most threatening experiences we can have," he says.

Where does this hardwired human instinct come from? You guessed it—back to our innate primordial caveman logic. Go back to your tribal psychology. Our ancient forebears banded together for food and for protection. More important—"to be ostracized from your tribe was a death sentence,' says Charles Raison, a psychiatrist at the University of Wisconsin, Madison. . . . 'In that case, the stressful response to loneliness would simply be the body's way of trying to survive exile.'"

So now we know the physiology and pathology related to chronic loneliness resulting from family and social estrangement. Now let's home in on the part that Fox News brain plays with hyper-intense tribal partisan behavior.

WE ALSO KNOW THE MAIN CAUSE OF ELDER ESTRANGEMENT

Granted fewer Americans aged sixty and older today are married and have as many children as seniors a generation ago. Many retired Americans move to Florida or elsewhere in the Sun Belt and away from regional family and friends. Yet in a massive UC San Francisco research project, the No. 1 cause of family estrangement from elders was not geography or divorce; it was "pushing away loved ones" as in desocialized seniors pushing family and longtime friends away with their intense hyperpartisan behavior.

Twenty years into the age of Fox News, one of the most common ways that the elderly push away family members is by becoming that radicalized, hyperpartisan obnoxious nut job whom no other family member wants to be around.

As author Edwin Lyngar shares in his book *How I Lost My Father to Fox News*:

> How did I lose my Dad? He consumes a daily diet of nothing except Fox News. He has for a decade or more. He has no email account and doesn't watch sports. He refuses to so much as touch a keyboard and has never been on the Internet, ever. He thinks higher education destroys people, not only because of Fox News but also because I drifted left during and after graduate school.

SO WHAT, WHO CARES, AND WHY DOES THIS MATTER?

I'm sure at this point you are asking how much of this epidemic in geriatric estrangement and increased risk of premature death of estranged seniors is a direct result of Fox News brain and Foxhole social derangement syndrome.

I will be using part of the proceeds of this book to commission a research study on that very question, but the early evidence suggests that the answer to the question is "massive."

I have more than enough evidence from e-polling and from reading thousands of stories from people estranged from Foxaholic family and friends to estimate that Foxaholism affects hundreds of thousands of American families and millions of American relationships.

Key Point: At this point, Foxhole social derangement disorder is undeniably correlated to the epidemic of increased premature geriatric death in many parts of America.

As I've shared with you, because of the latest biological and social psychology and neuroscience research, a few things have become crystal clear to me with regard to Fox News's powerful brand of tribal activation, validation, and arousal pornography:

Tribally hardwired human beings in general are not psychologically evolved or prepared to continually binge-watch tens of thousands of hours of viscerally emotional and tribally arousing video pornography without sustaining damage.

Because of their sensitivity to fear images and sound stimuli, self-identified conservatives are especially psychologically unsuited to binge-watching tens of thousands of hours of this material.

The most vulnerable people on the planet to Fox News's political and cultural tribal identity and activation pornography are the more than one hundred million Americans living in ALICE households whose everyday personal trauma is so profound and self-esteem so depleted that the best source of positive self-esteem in many cases comes from what they see on Fox News.

The First Amendment has become weaponized and algorithmicized to enlarge and inflame America's political and cultural divisions to pre-Civil War levels solely for the profit of commercial tribal identity media and entertainment enterprises.

Part of the bad news here is social science psychologists tell us "loneliness is contagious." Older adults who feel lonely are more prone to behave in ways that may cause other people to not want to be around them—like becoming a Foxhole.

Psychologists from the University of Chicago who analyzed data from the Framingham Heart Study, a long-term ongoing cardiovascular study, found that solitary seniors tend to further isolate themselves by pushing people away and not making efforts to engage with others.

Let's not forget the backfire effect embedded in our hardwired tribal cognitive bias: Social psychologists tell us that with the radicalized self-identified right-wing tribe member, any perceived slight against their tribe from anyone feels emotionally traumatizing to them. Psychologists also report that after enough rejections and being made to feel like an outcast, a tribalized Foxhole begins to believe that people—even their family members and friends—are cruel and will never "get" the moral and political superiority of his tribe and ultimately are not worth the effort to stay connected with.

Social scientists say that because these tribal hyperpartisans begin to perceive people as threats to their sworn allegiance, they disengage from those threats, family member or not.

Just what we all needed, right? The final phase of the self-reinforcing tribal activation and validation digital feedback loop is the addict's disengagement from the only people who give them unconditional love. Still think massive doses of tribal hate pornography are just harmless fun?

CHAPTER 16

What Then *Is* the Only Logical Conclusion About the Power, Intent, and Pathologies of Fox News's Tribal Warfare Playbook in 2019?

All my inside Fox News stories, my producer conversations, my social and evolutionary psychological research, my meeting thousands of Fox News fans, and my meeting and reading the words of hundreds of Foxholes up-close and personal brings me to this dangerous conclusion: that allowing the unchecked growth of emotionally toxic, nuclear-grade, digital, white tribal activation, validation, and amplification video porn content is ultimately a national and inter-family relationships suicide pact.

Said more simply: When big tech's predatory technology exploits our innate primal weaknesses with Fox News' video content, it's Fox News that gains control of your psyche and your brain stem—*not* the technology. The $100 billion-plus digital surveillance and content redistribution industry is simply the delivery vehicle. Without tribal fear and hate-based media content, big tech has nothing with which to exploit mankind's numerous, easily hackable, psychological flaws, in general, and the hackable flaws of *proud* self-identified political and cultural conservatives (and liberals), specifically.

We're all proud of what we consider our virtues, but something is way messed up when a person feels virtuous when hating on thirty to forty percent of their fellow citizens. Especially if you consider these "others" as your existential, cultural, or political enemy, whom you actively despise, loathe, and hold toxic contempt for during most waking hours of your life.

Big tech's information and digital-communication technology and platforms do indeed spread nuclear-grade right and left wing tribal fear and hate activation content to over 200 million Americans every day. But unlike the lack-of-recognition that addiction to watching three-plus daily hours of Fox News's white tribal identity porn is profoundly unhealthy for many Americans (yet we acknowledge the emotional toxicity of sex porn?), addiction to big tech applications for hours per day is now considered by all experts to be mentally unhealthy.

We have identified and are researching an epidemic of anxiety in young people due to their living online for many hours per day, but we don't recognize the serious emotional toxicity issues directly related to binge-watching hours upon hours of Fox News's extremely powerful white tribal identity porn.

It's a conundrum. Tech ethics advocate, Time Well Spent co-creator, and ex-Googler Tristan Harris notes that the unstoppable growth and reach of big tech digital apps and platforms may very well be like the slow-but-oncoming march of climate change. However, he fails to point out that without the unlimited amounts of white tribal fear and hate video content—most prominently from Fox News—our social media feeds would be largely full of cute animal porn, smiling babies, sports, and funny memes instead of tribal fear and hate based white tribal identity porn.

But that didn't happen. Why?

The answer is simple—it's the money, stupid. There is not nearly the profit to be made in producing emotion activating content that makes people kinder, more loving, and more egalitarian as there is in producing white tribal activation content.

For instance, while News Corp. did own the National Geographic cable channel (until it was sold to Disney), the Fox News Channel is worth twenty times more value with just five times Nat G's cable audience.

Message received: there is big media money to be made today sowing and harvesting tribal identity activation and hate amplification—forget the collateral damage.

There is also unimaginable political power that comes to ethnic nationalists and populists from producing binge-watchable fear and hate distributed on Facebook, YouTube, and other digital media platforms. In just one example, Brazil's YouTube-watching obsession catapulted a little-known populist named Jair Bolsonaro from obscurity to the Brazilian presidency in less than twelve months. Mr. Bolsonaro ran no traditional political TV ads, he just produced hundreds of hours of fear-and-hate-based YouTube video porn.

Closer to home, the most recent data says the zip codes targeted via Facebook by Russia's Internet Agency with white tribal fear and hate porn within key counties had significant influence, helping to convert 77,000 votes from Obama in 2012 to Trump in 2016. Those are the same votes that caused Michigan, Wisconsin, and Pennsylvania's Electoral College votes to go to another better-known tribal fear and hate populist who, with zero minutes of his life elected to anything, was sent to the most powerful office in the world.

Moreover, there's no tribal happy dance or victory lap for the cute-animal viewer, and thus they get none of the most pleasurable and powerful brain juice released (serotonin) that white tribal identity porn addicts get watching Fox News. No happy dance of tribal superiority and victory over one's tribal enemy also means no neurochemical release or behavioral addiction to the video content.

It's a fact: no one gets an ego gratifying shot of self-esteem built from watching a baby deer and puppy play together. It makes you feel all warm and fuzzy and say, "Ahh how cute," but in order to feed your ravenous self-esteem with the chemical booster shot it constantly seeks via tribal hate-based gratification, you must make the tribally identified person see and hear new scorching self-congratulatory evidence as to why they should hate and *feel* righteously superior to their tribal enemy.

In his recent presentation to tech nobility, Tristan Harris notes that problems such as "tech addiction, polarization, outrage-ification of culture, the rise in vanities [and] micro-celebrity culture" are all, in fact, symptoms of a larger disease. He called it: "The race to capture human attention by tech giants."

His main point: in the race to own the bottom of our brain stem, the fear and hate based content that big tech retargets and delivers to billions of people worldwide is indeed making all of us "dumber, meaner, and more alienated from one another."

Addiction to tribal hate and fear content is also symptomatic of a larger disease in America—the decaying of our social capital and poisoning of our meaningful and vitally important social and personal connections. Yet the data today also proves that in order to win the race to the brain stem of those conservative Americans, you need the type of content that most rapidly and powerfully activates their brain stem. So what is the video content they are most sensitive and reactive to? I know—it's shocking: fear, hate, and victimized blame-shifting videos.

Ergo, that is exactly the content that the Fox Hate Channel produces and publishes. It's not a bug in their system—it's the primary feature. The business of making as many politically and culturally right-wing Americans as possible hate as many politically and culturally left-wing Americans as possible IS the business strategy that Fox News monetizes at $3 billion a year and growing. And tribalized video content from the liberal media is now slowly catching up to Fox News's nuclear-grade white tribal identity porn, too (oh joy).

So yes, the math about the Fox Hate Channel is as simple as it is stunning: the more Fox News's white tribal activation and the Foxhole spiral can get right wing Americans to hate their tribal Other, the more profit Fox News makes for the Murdoch family.

From reaching hundreds of thousands of Americans in the late '90s with new glorious and virtue-signaling reasons to hating the left wing liberal apostates, Fox News's right wing ego gratification content today now reaches at least 100 million Americans monthly via all kinds of digital devices and platforms. From losing nearly a billion dollars building their Liberal Death Star machine, the Murdoch family now earns a billion dollars or more per year from the Fox News Channel sowing white tribal identity fears and hatreds.

Tristan Harris captures one part of this very real crisis perfectly, I think, when he concludes on an episode of *Recode Decode* with Kara Swisher: "It's sort of a civilizational moment when an intelligent species, us, we produce a technology where that technology can simulate the weaknesses of the creator. It's almost like the puppet that we've created can actually simulate a version of its creator and know exactly what puppet strings to pull on the creator, so we're all outraged."

And then he adds: "Technology is holding the pen of history right now. Every major election, and the culture of a new generation, is being written by whom?"

I can tell you something you must understand now, too—we know who is writing the history for America's white tribal identity clan—it's the American Foxocracy. And all that tribal fear, hate, and blame porn is still produced exactly according to Fox News's playbook of tribal warfare that I've shared with you in this book.

Mr. Harris is right, but I think there's one major flaw—all that digital information technology doesn't *create* the content that the big tech video distribution system vomits up twenty-four hours a day to exploit and profit from human nature's most exploitable psychological weaknesses. It's the American Foxocracy ecosystem, the $10 billion business of the white tribal identity activation, and the amplification content industry that knows exactly how to write, produce, and perform the emotional content that pull the primal and involuntary "puppet strings" of tribal fear, hate, resentment, and contempt for the tribal Other.

All that the big tech platform companies really understand is exactly how to digitally surveil, identify, target, and algorithmically exploit human emotion at enormous scale on their digital platforms. They execute this predation with content their user has voluntarily shown themselves to be the most likely to emotionally react to and consume. In the case of Fox News and the people who demonstrate via their views, likes, shares, and comments that they are the most vulnerable to having their attention hacked with white tribal identity content—the predation challenge is done. It's game over. Big tech simply retargets and sends as much white tribal identity porn as humanly possible at unimaginable scale to as many of the people they know with one-hundred-percent certainty are the most vulnerable and easiest to emotionally manipulate on their digital platforms. Hard stop. It's the easiest money they make every day.

Big tech *is* indeed leveraging and activating our innate tribal instincts— but without killer white tribal identity activation content or better said "tribal fear and identity activation digital bullets" manufactured and published by the American Foxocracy, they can't "aim their digital trance gun" and exploit the hackable weaknesses embedded in innate human psychology of proud conservatives.

Stated another way, big tech is the digital gun aimed right at your brain stem, but like gun enthusiasts always like to say, "It's the bullets and the person pulling the trigger that kill people, not the gun." Fox News people produce and broadcast the most powerful white tribal identity bullets in the world. Those emotionally lethal bullets allow the big tech platforms to, in turn, fire them into the brain stem of self-identified proud cultural and political conservatives in order to capture and monetize as much of their attention as possible.

But make no mistake—Fox News's predatory white tribal activation and amplification porn content was already doing its predatory attention and monetization job very well, even before big tech's surveillance capitalism was unleashed on the world in the early twenty-first century. Today, as the result of connecting two to three billion people around the world who all carry the same innate but latent tribal behavior virus, by injecting them with plutonium-grade, tribal-identity activation and validation pornography via their favorite digital device, the Fox News audience reach has been enlarged by thirty times in America since the early 2000s.

And let's be clear—no matter your culture or country, where there is a Fox News wannabe aping the Fox News white tribal warfare playbook, there is YouTube, Facebook's various apps and other digital platforms there to propagate and monetize tribal fear and hate—especially when it comes to ethnic nationalism.

Where does this madness end? Are we powerless to stop or at least slow down this emotional health plague? You may remember that as a society we used to run ads with doctors and celebrities smoking and looking gleeful and attractive. However, when the public data proved that smoking cigarettes was the leading cause of lung cancer and cardio vascular disease we did not ban cigarettes, but we banned the advertising on TV. We educated a generation on the health risk of smoking cigarettes.

And the anti-smoking campaign eventually worked. Why? Because the data also proved that the audiovisual power of TV was the single most powerful media when it came to making smoking cool and attractive outside the movie theater.

Well, my new friends, the data now proves without a doubt that there are very real and extensive mental and physical health risks that primarily come to older Americans who allow themselves to be sucked down into the rabbit hole of Fox News addiction and "Foxholeism." In other words, there are very real negative consequences that come to a nation full of Foxholes. Many of them, after years in the degenerative digital tribal fear-and-hate Foxhole spiral, wind up so desocialized and estranged from their kids, their close family and important friends that they can no longer hold a civil and civilized agree-to-disagree conversation. They cannot participate in a discussion about their cultural beliefs and political ideology with someone who does not exactly share their world view.

So who is the "snowflake" now?

And of course, according to the right-wing polling Guru Frank Luntz, we now have 80 million or more Americans who report they are estranged from at least one close family or friend over politics. Help me here: if 80 million Americans are estranged from at least one person over politics, doesn't that mean there are 80 million *other* Americans who are estranged from that first group?

All of which begs the questions:

1. What choices are we, as a society, going to make with regard to the easily proven corrosive pathologies attached to Fox News's white tribal identity activation and radicalization content?

2. Where does Fox News's disinformation and white tribal identity porn content fit in the deadly online spectrum of radicalized white tribal identity and far-right white nationalist extremism?

3. Is Fox News indeed a gateway drug that brings some of the most disaffected and insignificant-feeling men in their digital audience to seek more extreme online right-wing content (e.g. white nationalist radicalization content on 8Chan and Gab.com) so that they eventually feel even *more* extreme feelings of white tribal identity? Already on Fox News every night, the highest rated Fox News white tribal televangelists like Sean Hannity, Tucker Carlson, and Laura Ingraham mainstream the core white nationalist ideology of "white replacement theory" and "immigrants are invading the country that we know and love."

And, of course, while Fox News tribal fear and hate televangelists' use and normalize all the extreme white nationalist terms, and warn their largely white male audience that "the liberals' goal is to turn the United States you know and love into one big liberal California socialist nation" etc. It's the bully pulpit of the President of the United States that now out foxes Fox News when it comes to speaking and tweeting white nationalist propaganda.

If this book does nothing more than at least remove the shroud of denial or pretense that "Fox New is just infotainment for old white folks," then perhaps we can at least start *that* important and needed conversation. That conversation, like the one we had about smoking long ago and the negative impact from out-of-control big tech that we are having today, is long overdue.

We all must learn and appreciate that falling down the proverbial rabbit hole of white tribal identity is a very long continuum. Clearly, in America today there are horrific outcomes for those in society who fall too deep down that white nationalist rabbit hole and reach the extreme bitter end where white tribal identity morphs into a white supremacy spiral.

We have a choice. We can let Fox News' playbook of tribal warfare continue to tear apart the core fabric of American life in many millions of American families, or we can fight back.

If you want to fight back, come to www.StopTheFoxocracy.com and join the fight.

If you are a Foxhole that is estranged from the person(s) who gave you this book, come to www.FoxNewsRehab.com and learn how to re-engage with your loved ones. If you are the victim of estrangement to one or more Foxholes, come to www.FoxNewsRehab.com and learn how to begin the healing process.

But please—do something.

AFTERWORD

America is Better than This: It's Time for the Fox News Reckoning to Fight Back Against Commercial Tribalized Partisanship

Always take sides. Neutrality helps the oppressor, never the victim. Silence encourages the tormentor, never the tormented.
—ELIE WIESEL

■

I imagine one of the reasons people cling so stubbornly to their hates is because they sense once hate is gone, they will be forced to deal with the pain.
—JAMES BALDWIN

■

Tribalism was an urge our Founding Fathers assumed we could overcome. And so it has become our greatest vulnerability.
—ANDREW SULLIVAN

Whew! I really hope you feel you've gained a new level of awareness about the untold secrets inside Fox News. I hope you now understand the immensely negative psychological impact that the commercial televised/streamed tribal identity pornography industry has on over two hundred million Americans every day.

If nothing else, you now know that you hold the power to inoculate yourself from the seduction and addiction to tribal-hate porn from Fox News or from any source. You also now know if you choose to go down the tribal fear and hate rabbit hole, my research and data say that voyage, without a very real intervention, will have very negative social and health consequences.

The conclusion I've come to after a year of research and after fourteen years of working within the Fox News tribal-hate-porn empire is thus pretty simple:

The production and digital redistribution of Fox News's predatory, seductive, and addictive brand of right-wing tribal identity hate-and-resentment pornography to more than one hundred million Americans monthly serves only one purpose: to fertilize and monetize America's already enormous toxic levels of tribal hate, polarization, and cultural warfare to harvest billions of dollars in profit.

Under the pretense and cover of its news division, the real business of Fox News is a morally and ethically incendiary conspiracy that weaponizes America against itself.

This leads me to the real question: Is Fox News tribal fear and hate pornography the kind of business you want to support? Do we as a country want to support a commercial enterprise that preys on and manipulates the personal anguish and resentments of the most emotionally vulnerable citizens in America just to monetize tribal hate, economic misery, and chronic loneliness?

When do we address America's massive tribal-hate-porn industry and stop this insanity? I know one thing for sure: We can't solve a problem if we don't first acknowledge that it exists. For that reason alone, I hope that you now understand the outsized and highly toxic role played by the fast-growing, out-of-control, weaponized white tribal-identity-porn industry (led by Fox News) in America's ever-increasing levels of tribal TV driven political and cultural estrangement.

The recent removal of Alex Jones's InfoWars conspiracy pornography from digital platforms is a start in the fight against tribal hate porn. YouTube's and Apple's addition of a meter to show users how many hours a day they are watching their algorithmically selected video content is another positive step in the right direction.

We were guilty of ignorance pre-2008—nobody imagined or foresaw how algorithmically engaging and addictive massively pervasive social media digital platforms would create self-reinforcing negative feedback loops available on any device with Wi-Fi access.

But we have no excuse to ignore the powerful dark side of the American Foxocracy at this point.

The digital and self-reinforcing tribal-hate-validation feedback loop has enormous psychological and behavioral power over our entire society. In the least worst-case scenario, this self-reinforcing digital feedback loop is emotionally degenerative. In the worst-case scenario, this digital feedback loop empowers a twenty-first-century version of digital totalitarianism where a mass movement of disaffected, disengaged, cynical, and emotionally and isolated people come together through their association with an anti-democratic and illiberal mass movement.

IT'S TIME TO CALL OUT FOX NEWS FOR WHAT IT REALLY IS: THE FOX HATE CHANNEL

As the 2020 run for the presidency ramps up, America's Foxocracy (Fox News plus the Trump Reality Presidency TV Show) and their white tribal identity porn programming strategy have both morphed into Fox News 4.0—the Foxocracy as white ethno-nationalist ego gratification channel.

By July 2019, Fox News and Donald J. Trump quit pretending to be the voice of forgotten working-class Americans—there is a much bigger mission afoot. Donald Trump has always been a very effective race warrior. Now, the Foxocracy has tacked its toxic playbook even harder right to join him in a new effort to activate, validate, and radicalize the new American white nationalist movement.

The Foxocracy's tribalized white identity audience is no longer the disrespected and downtrodden forgotten Intolerables brand—they are now being rebranded by Fox News and Donald Trump as the proud white nationalist "Inevitables."

It is undeniable that in the first nine-hundred-plus days of his presidency, Mr. Trump never made one iota of effort to expand his base. Fox News has added a few token new Democrats to its contributor lineup, but then it doubled down on the tone and tenor of its white nationalist identity porn programming in prime time.

Today, Fox News and Trumpism's white tribal identity and white-grievance politics programming strategy has shifted: It is now to inflame, radicalize, and weaponize Trump's base into an even more toxic race warrior cycle of "Us vs. Them" existential white tribal ethno-nationalism. The promise: victory over the immigrant Others is inevitable if you rally behind Trump for four more years.

Fox News now mainstreams this hate-filled white nationalist ideology twenty-four hours a day with impunity to its deadly consequences. Elizabeth Warren had it right when she was asked earlier this year if she would ever attend a Fox News Town Hall, and she slammed Fox News as a "hate-for-profit machine" and vowed never to accept an invitation. In the wake of the two mass shootings over the first weekend in August 2019 that left thirty dead and fifty-three injured, Warren doubled down on her stance, tweeting,

"We need to call it out: Fox News is a hate-for-profit machine that gives a megaphone to racists and conspirators."

Leah Greenberg, co-founder of the Indivisible Project, gets it just right in his tweet: "Let's be really clear on this—The shooting in El Paso was a terrorist attack targeting Latinx people. It was spurred by the same white nationalist ideology that is promoted by the President of the United States and mainstreamed by Fox News."

The new Foxocracy white nationalist membership drive strategy had already become crystal clear in Greenville, North Carolina, on July 17, with the mob-like chants of the assembled Trumpian crowd induced by their leader to scream "Send Her Back, Send Her Back."

The crowd of MAGA hat- and uniform-wearing Trumpists was referring of course to POTUS Trump's overtly racist tweets regarding the newly elected Somali immigrant Congresswoman Ilhan Omar and three other new congresswomen of color from the 2018 election—Alexandria Ocasio-Cortez (D-N.Y.), Ayanna Pressley (D-Mass.), and Rashida Tlaib (D-Mich.). In his tweets he suggested that if they have complaints about America, they should "go back" to their own countries.

After the show, the President of the United States of America tweeted: "Just returned to the White House from the Great State of North Carolina. What a crowd, and what great people. The enthusiasm blows away our rivals on the Radical Left. #2020 will be a big year for the Republican Party!"

Most history-challenged American adults might not know that telling people of color to "go back to where they came from" is almost literally the foundational white nationalist insult in America. America's nativist streak has run through the anti-Catholic riots of 1844, the Chinese Exclusion Act of 1882, and the internment of Japanese-Americans in 1942.

But when nine black teenagers integrated a school in Little Rock, Arkansas, in 1957, a televised mob of a thousand-plus white people heckled them with screams of "Go back to Africa." And my guess is that that image and sound must have struck a chord within the mind of one ten-year-old future POTUS living in Queens, New York.

Donald J. Trump has undoubtedly become the Foxocracy voice of the permanently enraged and perennially victimized white Americans in search of revenge against their elite oppressors and America's heterogeneous invaders. Fox News is now the very willing digital content creator and broadcast network of the instant gratification tweets and musings of demagogic Trumpism. Both Trump and Fox News together instinctively understand that their committed white tribal identity believers need ever-stronger doses of the hate-based, self-congratulatory, self-esteem-building video content. Today that tribalized white conservative ego-gratification can only come from their leader, and their white tribal identity glorification cable TV network of choice, Fox News.

Thus, America's symbiotic and symbolic Foxocracy reigns supreme in 2020: Trump speaks and tweets overt messages of white nationalism and nativism only slightly less overtly racistly toned than Alabama governor and candidate for president George Wallace.

Then Fox News prime-time programming produces and scripts monologues and B-roll video proof of white tribal apostasies perpetrated by the socialist left. Finally, all this white tribal fear and hate porn is edited and cut into three-minute algorithmically hyper-targeted white tribal identity porn videos.

But as I hope this book made clear, what follows in the wake of this white identity video porn content explosion is a tsunami of digital fear and hate content delivery and retargeting. What follows next no one ever imagined would happen in the liberal Western culture: every minute of every day, social media platforms will pour billions of these emotionally smoldering white identity porn segments into the digital information cocoons of self-identified aggrieved white social media users.

The most powerful 24/7 white nationalist digital moral panic spiral and tribal superiority validation feedback loop in history is being created.

Scared? I am too. No one knows what happens to a country when 40% of its voters entertain themselves by hating on each other's tribal cultural enemies—but I can tell you this: I don't want us to find out.

For your information, historians tell us that at its height, the Nazi Party in Germany was joined by only 6.5 million, or about 9 percent, of Germany's citizens. So yes, self-reinforcing authoritarian and Fascist tribal feedback loops constantly using the infamous "Big Lie" tactics have been proven by history to be extremely powerful and dangerous to free democracies when fewer than 10 percent of their citizens swear allegiance to a disruptive tribal banner.

WHEN WILL THIS CYCLE OF TRIBAL BLAME-AND-HATE PORN "ENTERTAINMENT" END?

The answer is simple: When we as a nation and a society rise up against it and tell the advertisers who finance this plague on our lives, families, and country that we are done—enough is enough. Advertiser boycotts have been the most effective weapon against the producers and distributors of weaponized tribal identity porn.

Data shows that Fox News advertisers benefit and Fox News suffers from consumer-driven boycotts. As Michael Hiltzik points out in a *Los Angeles Times* column, "Advertisers of consumer products fear controversy more than anything—especially political controversy." In June 2018, Fox News's most tribally hateful and polarizing prime-time shows (Hannity and Ingraham) reported 20 percent lower ad revenues. That's a good start!

In short, white tribal identity porn needs its own #MeToo moment. The #StopTheFoxocracy hashtag is a start.

Organizations like Media Matters and Think Progress are leading the charge against Fox News's commercial right-wing identity porn. I started www.StopTheFoxocracy.com to build awareness about the tragic effect that addiction to tribal identity porn is bringing to millions of American families and to our "agree-to-disagree" adversarial form of democratic self-government.

HOW CAN YOU START FIGHTING BACK?

You can start by sharing this book, then posting on social media about your experiences with tribal hate porn. Just sharing the link to www.Stop-TheFoxocracy.com or sharing social media comments on what you have learned from this book will make a difference to many of the people you socialize with on Facebook or Twitter.

And by all means, visit and join, like, share, or tweet our StopTheFoxocracy Facebook page (https://www.facebook.com/StopTheFoxocracy.com).

Let's make no mistake here: Staying with the status quo of the American tribal identity activation and validation industry is the moral equivalent of driving down a freeway where you see a pile-up of crashed cars on fire.

Would you consider it to be ethical and moral for you to stop your car, pour gasoline on those car fires, and then post the video to YouTube to earn money from the pre-roll advertising attached to your video?

Is that the country we want to be? Is this the country that our forefathers fought and died to protect from tyranny and to promote "our better angels?" I can't help but remember the marvelous thoughts and words from Presidents

Obama and Bush at my friend Senator John McCain's memorial at the National Cathedral in DC.

"So much of our politics can seem small and mean and petty. Trafficking in bombast and insult, phony controversies and manufactured outrage. It's a politics that pretends to be brave and tough, but is instead born of fear. John called on us to be bigger than that, to be better than that," Obama said. "Today is only one day in all the days that will ever be, but what will happen in all the other days will depend on what you do today. What better way to honor John McCain than follow his example."

President Bush added, "if, as a nation, we forget who we are, John's voice will always come as a whisper over our shoulder: 'We're better than this, America is better than this.'"

Senator Joe Lieberman, who became an Independent in 2006, also took aim at the current political climate, saying McCain's death has "reminded the American people that these values are what make us a great nation, not the tribal partisanship and personal-attack politics that have recently characterized our life."

Our country and leaders allowed the First Amendment to become weaponized. Unlike the dawn of the TV age in 1948–49, where Congress carefully set nonpartisan ground rules for televised political commentary and opinion programming, today's political and cultural identity porn industry is allowed to flourish unchecked while it addicts and monetizes our most vulnerable citizens.

How do we fight back against Fox News and overcome tribal identity pornography?

We must take personal responsibility for ourselves and our family members *first*.

Now that you understand the strategy, tactics, and adverse outcomes that power the tribal-identity-porn industry, we have to convert your newly minted awareness of these techniques into something good for ourselves, our families, and our country.

Ultimately, it is the responsibility of adults, parents, teachers, business leaders, and elected officials to not ignore the personal and social ramifications of the oncoming tsunami of new televised and streamed tribal fear and hate TV coming in 2020.

At the end of the day, the consumer is responsible for the management of her own personal tribal partisan hate-porn diet. As Ev Williams, the co-founder of Twitter, suggests, "Ultimately it will be up to users to choose, and stick to, their own information diets. There's a huge buffet. If you eat whatever's put in front of you, you're not necessarily going to be making the best choices."

Look—we stood up to cigarette addiction, sugar water addiction, and junk food addiction. Now it's time to stand up against weaponized white tribal identity porn and white nationalism. Think of it as digital junk food. If you don't manage your diet of right- or left-wing tribal hate porn, you will become susceptible to the next big thing in tribal partisan pornography. I can't tell you today what that is, but I can tell you with certainty that it is coming.

BIG BOLD DISCLAIMERS MUST BE PLACED ON THE TV SCREEN BEFORE ANY TRIBAL HATE PORN SHOW ON ANY NETWORK EVEN STARTS

This technique is sorely needed and is easy to implement. We have long detailed disclaimers on infomercials, for crying out loud. We have disclaimers on addictive slot machines and video games. We used to have disclaimers on editorial TV content that clearly stated, "The following opinions are not from the news department, and we do not, in fact, check or endorse any opinions discussed on this program." Even that disclaimer at the beginning of the Fox News tribal-identity-opinion-porn programs would be a good first strike at the tribal identity pornographers.

Yes, it will take a return of a Democratic majority in Congress and the White House to get a twenty-first-century Digital Media Fairness and Disclosure Doctrine. But a simple disclosure like this attached to any tribal partisan identity porn from any producer or distributor would go a long way to raising awareness of the mission and manipulation the industry:

> The following program and opinions are not from the Fox News Channel news department and should be considered entertainment programming and not news programming. Research has proven consumption of more than a few hours per day of political or cultural entertainment programming can be addictive for many viewers. Fox News does not fact-check any opinions discussed on this program. The host of this program is an entertainer and not a journalist. There has been no effort in the production of this program by Fox News to provide a fair and balanced presentation of the issues discussed in this broadcast.

The paid contributors appearing on this program are paid by Fox News and should be considered to be explicitly and exclusively partisan in the views they perform on this entertainment-not-news program.

Why don't we do this kind of forced disclaimer for explicitly partisan FNC or MSNBC opinion/entertainment programming now? The only answer I can come up with is that we as a society are in massive denial about what cultural and political warfare as entertainment has done (and continues to do) to our nation.

WE ALL NEED TO RAISE AWARENESS OF WHITE TRIBAL IDENTITY PORN

Our Founding Fathers, from Madison to Lincoln, recognized that the default behavioral wiring of human beings was not to seek our "better angels" but to seek safety and inclusion within ideological tribes. A big part of the original idea of America was to become no longer subservient to our innate human wiring for tribalism and tribal behavior.

Call me old-fashioned and out of touch, but apparently, this reality seems to be lost among a broad cross-section of America. Our schools have failed to teach advanced democracy for decades; this mistake has caught up and bit our culture in the rear. A big part of making democracy work is to be educated so we can't be manipulated by tribal identity pornographers.

Key Point: America was created mainly to be the antidote to kings, aristocracy, and tribalism. We swear allegiance to an idea, not a king or tribe; we swear allegiance to the idea that all men and women are created equal, that everyone who becomes a citizen of America signs up to pursue a mutually shared vision of citizenship with responsibilities conferred therein. In exchange, everyone gets a shot to pursue their ambition and dreams with (mostly) unlimited opportunity.

In short, our Founding Fathers fought and died for the right to not be subservient to the old tribal ways of living and of defining themselves by the enemies they hate.

What happened to us?

I hope you now understand that the inescapable short answer is that many of us have allowed our innate tribal nature to retake control of our lives and impulses.

ACTIONS YOU CAN TAKE RIGHT NOW TO STOP THE TRIBAL-VALIDATION FEEDBACK LOOP

Visit www.StopTheFoxocracy.com and join the movement. It's free, and I promise we will keep you in the fight against Fox News's tribal identity pornography.

Email/text/social media post and spread the word and mission of this book and of StopTheFoxocracy.com to your social media followers repeatedly!

Join the petitions to boycott Fox News advertisers. As the Hannity and Laura Ingraham ad boycotts proved, attacking the sponsors of tribal identity pornography is the most effective tool we have in fighting back against Fox News.

Share your story! If your family is suffering estrangement from a loved one with a severe case of Foxhole disorder, tell the world. Email me at MyFoxNewsStory@StopTheFoxocracy.com

Support BetterAngels.org who are sponsoring and running group depolarization workshops in schools, churches, and synagogues.

Support HearYourselfThink.org. They have taken the lead in advocacy and training against tribal hate pornography. As they say on their website, quoting Benjamin Franklin: "We the People are—and will remain—the world's oldest constitutional republic. If we can keep it."

America is better than this. I hear John McCain's voice whisper over our shoulders. We can do better. We have to do better.

Each journey starts with a first step. By reading and thinking about this book, you have taken not just a step but also a leap!

Spread your knowledge of the dangers of weaponized tribal identity pornography with those you love!

At the very least, we all must acknowledge that the American democracy is under attack by purveyors of white nationalist moral panic spirals who are in business to profit by weaponizing and monetizing our tribal fears and hatred of the Other. Eugene Robinson writes in the *Washington Post*, "History teaches us that the way to deal with hateful demagoguery is not to ignore it, not to downplay it, not to hope it somehow exhausts itself, but to confront it. Trump's fomenting of hate has to be called out. It has to be denounced. It has to be resisted."

That goes for Fox News too. The 2020 election must be a referendum on both Trump's weaponized racism and all Fox News predatory business practices. The Associated Press reports that Trump and his campaign believe that placing "racial polarization at the center of his call to voters" carries "far more benefits than risks." That of course means Fox News will follow Trump's lead.

A lot is at stake here. As Vox's Sean Illing notes, the sight of Trump "leading a white mob in a chant" about sending a black Congresswoman "home" will be "featured in history books for decades to come."

The world and history are indeed watching. The time to stop the Foxocracy from metastasizing into an even larger and more powerful fascist monster is now—you have taken the first step. Take another and make the effort to reclaim a relationship poisoned by Fox News addiction.

History will indeed rightfully judge us if we knowingly let this self-inflicted plague of fear and hate consume the liberal democracy which we inherited from our forefathers but left weaker and more divided on our watch.

—Tobin Smith, October 8, 2019

INDEX

ABOUT THE AUTHOR

Tobin Smith appeared in more than two thousand opinion panel segments on Fox News during his fourteen-year tenure as a paid FNC Contributor and Guest Anchor. Contractually obligated to be at Fox News's New York City studios at least forty-eight weeks a year to tape the weekend talk show *Bulls & Bears* on Fridays, he was the only full-time right-wing panelist always in the NYC studios, constantly asked by segment producers to play the role of the "hit man" or the panel member counted on to make the final right-wing argument for the right-wing audience at home. He also guest hosted sixty-plus episodes of Fox News and Fox Business Network programming from 2000–2013. While working with producers inside Fox News NYC and socializing with Fox News staff at favorite watering holes after work, he learned never-before revealed strategies Fox News production staff used to rig the outcomes of FNC opinion debate segments. Smith is also a *New York Times* bestselling author whose books include *Change-Wave Investing 2.0* and *Billion Dollar Green*.